Entrepreneurial Opportunity

Successfully starting a new business venture depends upon more than having a brilliant idea, getting funding and getting the product or service to market. Entrepreneurs must also learn to read the market and understand the environments in which they must operate. *Entrepreneurial Opportunity* places the emphasis on reading and making the most of things that may be beyond the entrepreneur's control, from defaulting contractors to the opening and closing of business niches. It also considers previously under-considered options, such as "the political entrepreneur." This long overdue text provides a far more realistic view of entrepreneurial opportunity and the importance of the business environment.

Yet despite its realist stance, the book is decidedly optimistic, showing readers how markets evolve over time and present opportunities through that evolution. As Clydesdale states, "it's not always fair out there," but this book captures the excitement of the market and its role in delivering opportunities.

Drawing on a broad range of academic research, *Entrepreneurial Opportunity* is written in a manner that is accessible for students and practitioners, with examples and mini-cases from a variety of industries, including high technology, hospitality and motion pictures.

Greg Clydesdale lectures in the Department of Management and International Business at Massey University, Auckland, New Zealand.

Entrepreneurial Opportunity

The Right Place at the Right Time

Greg Clydesdale

Routledge
Taylor & Francis Group

NEW YORK AND LONDON

First published 2010
by Routledge
270 Madison Ave, New York, NY 10016

Simultaneously published in the UK
by Routledge
2 Park Square, Milton Park, Abingdon, Oxon OX14 4RN

Routledge is an imprint of the Taylor & Francis Group, an informa business

© 2010 Greg Clydesdale

Typeset in Times by
Integra Software Services Pvt. Ltd, Pondicherry, India
Printed and bound in the United States of America on acid-free paper by
Walsworth Publishing Company, Marceline, MO

Library of Congress Cataloging-in-Publication Data
Clydesdale, Greg.
Entrepreneurial opportunity : the right place at the right time / Greg Clydesdale.
p. cm.
Includes bibliographical references and index.
1. New business enterprises—Management. 2. Entrepreneurship. I. Title.
HD62.5.C597 2009
658.1′1—dc22
2009007096

ISBN10 (hbk): 0–415–99709–7
ISBN10 (pbk): 0–415–99710–0
ISBN10 (ebk): 0–203–87246–0

ISBN13 (hbk): 978–0–415–99709–6
ISBN13 (pbk): 978–0–415–99710–2
ISBN13 (ebk): 978–0–203–87246–8

Contents

List of Figures

List of Tables

Chapter 1

If You're Such a Genius, Why Aren't You Rich?

An expanding economy is ripe territory for motivational experts. It is a time when you can follow your hunches, research what looks like a market opening, raise a loan and launch your product. Before long, you sell 50,000 products and your business survives a critical period. The local newspapers hail you as an entrepreneur with great foresight. You can look back upon your achievement with pride.

In a declining economy, you can do exactly the same things: follow a hunch, get a loan and launch a new product. But you only sell 45,000 products, not enough to survive those crucial early years. Your business goes bankrupt and you experience the shame and self-doubt of failure. Although you acted exactly the same, the results were very different. It is very hard for a small entrepreneur to estimate market demand for a new product. A difference of 10% is not great, but it can be crucial. Perhaps you should have paid greater attention to the changing economic conditions, but there is so much to do when you launch a product. And what happens if circumstances turn midstream?

Many entrepreneurs have succeeded not because they were particularly bright but because they rode a wave, while many intelligent entrepreneurs have failed because the tide turned. Often circumstances are more important than any thing done by business leaders. However, pointing this out is not always a rewarding task. Those who note that failure was beyond the power of any one person are "apologists," while those who credit success to fortunate circumstances are likely to be considered "small minded" or "petty."[1]

This book suggests that not enough attention is given to the role the environment plays in determining whether an entrepreneur succeeds. Many fortunes have been made because entrepreneurs have caught a wave of environmental change. An entrepreneur needs to be able to read market dynamics and the signals they give to achieve sustainable success. Drawing on research on entrepreneurship and industrial development, this book examines environmental and industrial forces that open up windows of opportunity. With greater knowledge on market dynamics, I hope you will be empowered to catch the wave that provides the many opportunities that will exist in the future.

* * *

The football game had finished and the conversation turned to more serious
topics. "What you need is a new idea." He lowered his glass to the bar.
"Something no one has ever thought of before."
"Why does it have to be a new idea?" I asked.
"Because if it wasn't, someone else would have already taken it."
"But maybe," I suggested, "there's another reason someone hasn't delivered on
the idea. Maybe no one has found a way of making it work. Think about the
scooter. A couple of years ago, someone made a mint selling scooters to kids.
There was nothing new in that."
He thought about it. "You're right. But it has to be a good idea."

The preceding conversation is common enough. The words might change, but the
theme is always the same. People recognize that entrepreneurial success is built
around an idea. However, an idea by itself is not sufficient. Millions of people possess ideas that never turn into the golden egg. Getting a business started involves a
lot more than just having an idea. It involves a whole range of activities from hiring employees, buying machinery and plants, renting facilities, marketing, raising
finance, forming relationships with suppliers, and so on. Chiasson and Saunders suggest that, when entrepreneurs act, they follow "scripts" or recipes that they borrow,
follow and modify to get things done.[2] To keep the language in this book consistent
with that used by the business world, I will replace the term "script" with the term
"business model." Many entrepreneurs, when starting a business, simply imitate the
models of the businesses they see around them. The business model might require
some modification. On the other hand, entrepreneurs may come up with something
new, in which case they will still look for guidance from the businesses around them.

When entrepreneurs consider starting a business, they need to put together a number of ingredients and make a number of connections to create a business that works.
It is such a daunting process that it is not surprising that many budding entrepreneurs
never get started. Entrepreneurs are often left with the question "where do I start?"
People who have experience in their industry have the advantage in that they can look
at how their previous employers operated. Their old employers provide the model to
follow. It is no surprise that entrepreneurs generally do better in businesses in which
they have experience. But what if you have no experience in that industry? Or what
if you are introducing a new product?

How can you get financiers and suppliers committed to you if your model has
not been seen before? The success of your business is highly dependent on the perception of others. But these people can also be a source of valuable information on
how to fine-tune your model for success. Various customers, venders, government
agencies and other stakeholders communicate positive and negative feedback to the
entrepreneur about the use and structure of a business model. But given your reliance
on these people for capital and resources, Chiasson and Saunders state that a business model will only work if it these stakeholders consider it morally and practically
acceptable, if it provides the entrepreneur with control over the necessary resources,

and if they allow the user to act quickly to achieve results. With this in mind, the business model is very dependent on the environment in which it operates. For example, a business model for a restaurant in 1970s Japan may not produce the same results if used for a New York restaurant in 2004. Consequently, the business environment plays a large role in determining which businesses will succeed and which will fail.

For success, entrepreneurs need to be aware of the need to modify their business model to the environment in which they operate. Entrepreneurs need to be sensitive to the differences in various environments and develop an ability to read the environment. In this light, opportunity identification can be redefined as the selection and modification of business models for the environment in which entrepreneurs operate. However, once you have established a business model, it is not set in stone. You will continually need to modify the model as the environment changes and you learn more about the environment in which you act. Business is a process of ongoing modification and response to environmental signals.

The problem all entrepreneurs face when building their businesses is that, because of the time involved in putting it all together, they are effectively building for a situation that occurs some time in the future. Markets exist in time and space, and time and space evolve and transform. This means it is not sufficient to be able to read the environment in its current state. Entrepreneurs must anticipate what the environment will be when their business is up and running. However, the future is uncertain, and attempts to predict it open up a large range of possibilities. Will the economy go up or down? Will new competitors arrive? Will terrorist actions affect the market for my product? People's predictions are based on their own personal experiences, the information they have access to and how they interpret that information. Given this uncertainty and the subjective nature of thinking, it is no surprise that people with different knowledge have vastly different views of the prospects of a business. When trying to gain support for their projects, entrepreneurs often have to deal with people who don't share their optimism.

Individuals interpret their past experiences differently from others and then build on these interpretations to construct their own subjective view of the future. Because their knowledge differs, their expectations of the future diverge from those around them. And when the future does arrive, entrepreneurs will be faced with new flows of information that will cause them to revise their plans and modify their models.[3] It is no surprise, then, that what some consider an opportunity to start a business others consider "pie in the sky." Each person's view of the future and business potential is unique. Consequently, Sarason, Dean and Dillard state that opportunities "do not exist as singular phenomenon but are idiosyncratic to the individual."[4] The sad thing is some of those projections will be wrong, and even the most accurate will still be in need of modification to account for unforeseen circumstances and new information flows. Some of the new situations that occur in the environment may in fact be a result of the entrepreneur's own actions. In that way, the business and environment interact and co-evolve. But even this evolution will be idiosyncratic as entrepreneurs are exposed to new personal experiences that cause them to reflect and interpret the new information that their own actions have generated.

One of the things that all entrepreneurs dread is waking up one morning to find they have mis-anticipated the readiness of the environment for their business. Often the success of a business is constrained by features of the environment that are needed to support its feasibility. These include favorable demand conditions and technological advance. For example, my home town is close to a mountain on which an excellent ski field could be built. There is nothing new in the idea of making the field and it is well known to all. However, no one has launched this business because of insufficient demand. In time, as airfares fall and tourism increases, the feasibility of the project will change. But that demand threshold needs to be crossed first.

Of course, through a well-planned and resourced marketing campaign, you can help to raise demand levels to a necessary threshold. However, the small entrepreneur lacks the marketing resources of large companies. We are more dependent on capturing the trends in the environment or, at least, moving with them. A small business will struggle if it tries to swim against the tide. On the other hand, if it catches a wave, it can ride a path to prosperity.

The difference between an idea and an opportunity is its feasibility, and feasibility is strongly determined by features of the environment.[5] When an environmental threshold is passed, the idea becomes possible and an opportunity opens. Thresholds are not opened only when markets shift. They are also created when technological thresholds are passed. With new technologies, ideas that once were not feasible become opportunities for entrepreneurs to seize. Each new technology creates an opening, but when technological frontiers are reached, those windows close.

The business environment constantly changes, creating thresholds that open opportunities. Entrepreneurs who are in the right place at the right time when those thresholds are reached are the ones who often succeed. For the individuals concerned, luck can play an important role. However, preparation and foresight help people to become lucky.

The effect of the environment is not just limited to determining success. Directly or indirectly, the environment is the source of all business ideas. For an obvious example, a ski field could not be developed if there was not a suitable mountain in the environment. The environment also has a more subtle impact. It determines what information is available. Employers and education facilities determine what skills we obtain, and financial institutions determine what venture capital possibilities are available. All these factors in the environment determine what we think about and the ideas we construct. However, in stressing the environment, we do not mean to downplay the role of creativity, for the available knowledge and information still needs to be synthesized. This is where creative entrepreneurs stand out from their peers who have access to the same information and resources.

Given the widespread recognition of the importance of the business environment for venture creation, there is a paucity of research on the subject. Most entrepreneurship research has focused on business planning, raising capital, and the motivation and personality of entrepreneurs. They give little attention to the environmental forces that create business opportunities. This book attempts to address this deficiency and to throw light on some of the factors that determine entrepreneurial success or failure. Hopefully, it will stimulate more work in the area. There is some similarity to marketing books that stress the need to identify trends; however, this book is different in that its focus is on the entrepreneur and it draws on research from industrial economics.

What To Do: Trade, Make or Speculate?

"Value for money" is an old and simple phrase, but in the world of entrepreneurship, it explains so much. Business is about the exchange of value. If you want my money, give me something of value in return. If you can't give me something I value, the only alternative way of getting my money is deceit or theft. Value exchange is at the core of all three paths of entrepreneurship: arbitrage, speculation and production.

Arbitrage occurs when an entrepreneur finds that a product is sold in one market for a cheaper price than it is in another. For example, you might find that pineapples are cheaper in Hawaii than in New York. In this case, your logical response would be to export pineapples from Hawaii to New York.

Arbitrage was the most common form of entrepreneurship in pre-industrial days, as people traded goods that were readily available in their local environment for exotic luxuries. Spices were exchanged for ceramics from China or silver from South America. This type of entrepreneur was normally called a merchant or trader. To be successful in this line of business, a number of capabilities are needed. First, one needs knowledge of the selling market. A trader has to make judgments as to what sort of volumes the market could take and what is a suitable selling price. Mechanisms that facilitate a smooth flow of goods and reduce the costs and dangers of trade need to be in place. This includes reliable distribution mechanisms with appropriate inventory levels. Knowledge of shipping, storing and marketing are also required, as are skills in negotiating supply. The sorts of people who succeed at arbitrage are those who have knowledge of two different markets or, alternatively, have contacts in different markets. Immigrants often do well in this as they have knowledge of the markets in their old home and their new home.

The form of arbitrage mentioned above occurs when two markets are separated geographically, but arbitrage can also be done in different markets in the same town. For example, a secondhand dealer can buy furniture at an auction for a low price and then resell it at a secondhand store. But even here an intimate knowledge of the market is required. A secondhand book dealer once told me how difficult it was to succeed in his business:

> Anyone can get a loan, go to an auction and buy a pile of secondhand books. But they invariably buy the wrong books. They'll buy children's books that their children enjoyed, or university textbooks that are no longer used. They might buy old English cookbooks when the trend is for Italian. This market changes all the time. It's subtle, and if you are not in touch with what the consumer is buying, you fail. The number of times I've seen new shops loaded with stock they can't sell . . . I can't tell you. And these guys have loans to pay off. They soon go down.

A second common form of entrepreneurship is speculation. This involves buying something with the belief that its value will go up in the future. In which case, you can sell it at a later date and make what is hopefully a comfortable profit. Common targets for speculation include property, shares, gold and, in Japan, golf-course membership.

All forms of entrepreneurship involve some degree of crystal-ball gazing, but with speculation the ability to read the future is the sole basis of action. If we could be projected five years into the future and read the business papers, then be sent back in time, we would be highly successful at speculation. Without a time machine, we need to have knowledge of the factors that affect the long-term supply and demand of the commodity in question, as it is this that determines its final price.

The biggest danger with speculation occurs when speculative bubbles are created. This occurs when the market becomes dominated by speculators wanting to make a future profit. With so many buyers in the market, the price is pushed higher so that it no longer reflects its intrinsic value. We saw this with the recent dot-com bubble. Investors bought shares with little regard for their potential to pay dividends. While people were prepared to buy, the price went higher, and this only encouraged more people to speculate. As is always the case, such bubbles invariably burst.

In times of bubbles, investors hope to make a quick profit buying low and selling before the bubble bursts. But how do you know when the bubble is about to burst? If you sell too early and the share price begins to rise, you become poorer compared with those around you. The idea is to hang out until the market peaks. Of course, by then it's too late. Joe Kennedy claimed that "only a fool holds out for top dollar." Kennedy was lucky. He had shares in RCA, which was subject to a takeover in 1929. He sold his shares just before the Wall Street Crash. While those around him lost fortunes, he became the 12th richest man in the United States with the resources to later fund his son's presidential campaign.

A dangerous but not uncommon practice during share bubbles is borrowing money to buy shares. Many did this in the 1920s and, when the bubble burst and the share price fell, many were left holding valueless shares and big debt. It was a disaster for many that illustrates the folly of borrowing to speculate. Prices can come down. On the other hand, many people have made small fortunes from speculation. The simple rules are spend only what you can afford to lose and don't be greedy.

The last common pathway for entrepreneurs is to produce a product or service valued by customers. This includes those in mining who provide resources for industrial customers, farmers engaged in agricultural production, manufacturers from Henry Ford to Bill Gates and service providers from gardeners to taxation services.

Value for Money and New Ideas

The economist Joseph Schumpeter stressed that a key function of entrepreneurs is innovation.[6] According to Schumpeter, it is innovation that defines an entrepreneur. Schumpeter claimed that entrepreneurs innovate by introducing new goods and production methods, opening new markets, conquering new sources of materials, and creating new types of industrial organization. This view shows that entrepreneurs are not victims of environment, but it is the environment that is changed by the entrepreneur. Which view is correct?

It also leads to the question "Do all entrepreneurs have to innovate?" It depends on your definition, but in this book we say no. Entrepreneurship is about mobilizing resources, taking risks and capturing a market. This can be done in established industries with tried-and-true techniques. For example, people who open restaurants can be highly entrepreneurial even if they use established methods of operation and marketing.

Nevertheless, innovation lies at the core of most business strategies, but innovation for innovation's sake is not going to lead to success. For example, new types of industrial organization are only of use if they somehow make the business operate more efficiently, perhaps by reducing costs through improved coordination. The changes identified by Schumpeter are only of use if they help us to provide more value for money to more customers. Seen from this angle, a new idea or innovation can lead to success if it does one of four things:

Creating New Forms of Value

One way an entrepreneur can stamp his or her mark is by giving greater value for money by **creating new forms of value**. By that we mean creating new products or services that people value. However, coming up with new ideas for products sounds easier than it is. A good rule of thumb is that, if you have a problem, someone else is also likely to have that same problem. If you solve that problem, you have a marketable product. Take Peter Alexander. He had a problem. He couldn't find a decent pair of pajamas for his sister's birthday. The products in the shops just were not suitable. "You had the two extremes: *Little House on the Prairie* and red, lace sex kitten. I wanted something that had those memories of childhood: that made you feel safe and secure. It's that old idea: you're home, you've had a bath, your hair is parted and brushed to the side."[7]

So Peter did what any good entrepreneur should do. He solved the problem himself. He had 20 pairs made up, kept one for his sister and sold most of the others to a department store. So he made some more and continued to sell them to the department store, until one day, the store cancelled a huge order, leaving him with 2,000 pairs of pajamas sitting in his mother's garage. "It was a disaster. I'd paid for the stock, and I had Mum's house mortgaged for the business." The outlook was grim. "Eventually I thought, 'Look, I'll have to take this chance.' So I took out an ad in a magazine: one page with a photo of the pajamas and a line saying to call this number if you'd like to buy a pair."

Within the first three weeks, he had received 4,000 phone calls. The response was substantially beyond what he had expected, and he had to return $100,000 in checks. But he kept the addresses of all the respondents, and a mail-order business was born. Peter had no idea of the consumer-behavior forces that underlay his success, but as he now realizes, pajamas are an ideal product for mail-order. Pajamas do not need to have a snug fit, so consumers do not need to try them on in shops. Color and style is more important, and here Peter excelled. Before long Kylie Minogue, Tom Cruise, Nicole Kidman and Linda Evangelista were all sporting his bedtime apparel. He entered the U.S. market with the slogan "Have you ever slept with an Australian?" Peter became famous, appearing on local TV shows and signing autographs. His business was making $10 million and growing at 20% a year.

In many ways, this experience goes beyond conventional wisdom. Peter did not have an idea. He reacted, got carried along on a wave, and ended up in a situation he had never dreamed of. He explains that "I never wanted to be a big businessman.... I felt like I was a surfer and I was on this wave that was just getting out of control." Peter eventually sold his business to Just Jeans but remained as general manager.

Adding Value

A second innovative path for entrepreneurs is giving greater value for money by **adding value** to existing products. An example of this can be seen in the Razor Scooter. Scooters have been around for years, but in 1993, a Taiwanese bicycle-parts designer added value to them and created a new market. The designer's name was Gino Tsai. He initially transformed the scooter for his own use. Having short legs, he moved around the factory slowly, so he invented the Razor Scooter to solve his own problem. He upgraded the old scooter with new materials: airplane-grade aluminum, polyurethane wheels, and a patented rear-wheel brake. A collapsible handle meant the whole scooter could be carried and stored in small places when not in use. Gino doubted that he was the only business professional who would enjoy the benefits of this value-added scooter. He released the product, aimed at an adult market. Fortunately, the Razor Scooter caught a wave, but it wasn't in the adult market. The scooter became a fashionable item among children. The scooter became "childhood chic" in the same way the yo-yo was when I was a child. This is one of the most rewarding market waves to ride because, once tapped, the market has a life of its own. Kids want one because their friends have one. There is only one problem with such fashion-driven markets: They are short lived.

Reducing Costs

A third pathway for entrepreneurs is giving greater value for money to customers by **reducing costs**. Entrepreneurs who find a way of producing a good or service cheaper than anyone else can increase their market share through cheaper prices and by freeing up resources for other activities like marketing. There are 1001 different ways of reducing costs, from more efficient organization to more efficient production technologies. Cost reductions were one of the strategies pursued by John D. Rockefeller, who dominated the world oil market at the end of the nineteenth century. His formula was based on very large production facilities that delivered significant economies of scale. His refineries produced 6,500 barrels a day at a cost of

0.452 cents a gallon, one-third the cost of other refineries. There was nothing secret in this. Low costs based on economies of scale and large production facilities were the basis of American success throughout the twentieth century.

Developing Markets

The fourth option involves giving greater value to more people by **developing markets**. This can be done in a number of ways. It may involve opening a shop where one doesn't exist. It includes entering new markets, perhaps by exporting to new regions or by more intensely approaching existing markets. Peter Alexander's success mentioned above was based on a new distribution technique that opened up a previously untapped market. The Internet has revolutionized this strategy, with companies' web pages open 24 hours a day, allowing customers to make purchase decisions in the comfort of their own homes.

*   *   *

Although I have listed these strategies separately, most of them occur together in some combination. For example, the Razor Scooter was not just a value-added product. The intention was to develop a new market as well. There is constant overlapping between these strategies. In fact, pursuing a number of these pathways at the same time is more likely to engender success, for the result is more value, for less cost, to more customers. Behind all these strategies is the reminder that business is about the exchange of value. Each involves providing people with value in return for their money.

Economics has been described as "common sense made difficult." Much of what appears in this book can be described as basic economics, maybe even basic common sense. I make no apologies for that. Entrepreneurship is not brain surgery. Many people have made it rich on ideas that, in hindsight, appear to be common sense. Everyone was aware of the business idea, but few people responded to the opportunity. This book does not contain "secrets of success." Its goal is to bring entrepreneurial awareness to the forefront of your thinking, so that when an opportunity occurs, you can seize it with speed, not in hindsight.

*   *   *

The period from the end of the nineteenth century until the 1920s was a great age of entrepreneurship in the United States. It produced people like Henry Ford, Carnegie and Rockefeller. The end of the twentieth century was another great age of entrepreneurship associated with people like Bill Gates and Steve Jobs. Why were there so few entrepreneurial stars in the period in between? In 1967, the esteemed economist J. K. Galbraith wrote that the American entrepreneur was a "diminishing figure," replaced by "technocrats," organizational men and women.[8] America appeared to be losing its industrial dynamism. Did something happen to the American psyche in between? Did Americans lose their desire to make money? Did Americans lose their creativity? Did they lose their desire to increase prosperity and create jobs for their fellow citizens? The 1960s might be seen as the age of free love, but it is an insufficient explanation to explain the little activity by businessmen and -women.

If the explanation cannot be found in the American psyche, maybe it is the environment. Perhaps the success of American entrepreneurs reflects the environment in which they were working. Although there has been little study of how the environment creates opportunities, there has been substantial academic research on the relationship between firms and the environment. The school of thought that places most emphasis on the environment is "population ecology." This school says that environmental shifts open up niches that allow firms to set up and exploit those opportunities. Firms that succeed in that niche are those best suited to the environment—a commercial survival of the fittest. On the other hand, if the environment changes and becomes less supportive, businesses in that niche will suffer. This school has been criticized for placing too much emphasis on the environment. It says that businesses are pawns to their environment with little ability to determine their own outcomes. In that way, it is almost anti-American in that it takes our destiny out of our own hands, saying our business fortunes are the result of forces we cannot influence.

Is population ecology totally unrealistic? Consider oil companies that have risen to success on the backs of automobile use and the internal combustion engine—can they really determine the size of the market through their advertising, or is their advertising a battle for market share with other companies? Let's put it another way: Beyond price changes, do you think an oil company can affect how much gasoline you buy? The gas you use is determined by how much you drive, so let's phrase it another way: Can oil companies affect how much you drive through their marketing efforts? And what would happen to oil companies if an efficient solar-energy car was produced? Surely these companies, which are among the world's most powerful, are largely vulnerable to technological forces over which they have no control.

Other programs studying the relationship between organizations and the environment include neo-institutional theory, which focuses on institutional change in the environment such as professional activists, market forces and demographic change, and adaptation theory, which is based on the punctuated equilibrium model, which says that major environmental change destroys inertial forces in established companies and creates opportunities for new firms. Economists studying regional economics, industrial districts and clustering of industries also stress the importance of a favorable environment.

More recently, Chiles, Meyer and Hench (2004) have drawn on complexity theory to show the emergence of new firms in Branson, Missouri.[9] They reveal entrepreneurship not as a simple supply-and-demand formula but as a systemic evolution with feedback loops that amplify and reinforce commercial fluctuations. This book is indebted to these schools of thought and draws on all of them. But it diverges by asking what this means for the entrepreneur looking for opportunities. How can this research help the entrepreneur looking for a business opportunity?

Entrepreneurial opportunities are found in two places: the environment and the mind of the entrepreneur. These two places interact to construct business models. The following chapter examines the psychology and processes that create ideas and turn them into nascent businesses. Chapter 3 provides an introduction to the more commonly known environmental forces supporting entrepreneurship: supply, demand and government. Chapter 4 examines the relationships among technology, new products and the success of pioneers. This chapter is probably of more interest to those with a technological bent, but later chapters show how opportunities for others open as markets age. Chapter 5 explores the evolution of a product and how opportunities emerge throughout its life cycle. Chapter 6 takes this idea further, exploring how emerging niches in markets create opportunities and how large companies may leave these opportunities open for the small player.

Chapter 7 takes a broader perspective, no longer just looking at products but analyzing with an industry perspective. It reveals that as industries grow they form forward and backward linkages that open up opportunities for entrepreneurs. Then, using a historical example from the movie industry, this chapter illustrates how industries can change over time in their product offerings opportunities up and down the industrial links. Chapter 8 explores entrepreneurship in two very different environments, one of constraint and one of opportunity abundance. Building on the work of Perez and Freeman and a punctuated equilibrium perspective, this chapter shows how such shifts have opened opportunities for entrepreneurs. The recent Internet wave and the dot-com bubble are explored and analyzed with the theory in this book.

In contrast to previous books that suggest control is in the hands of the entrepreneur, Chapter 9 argues that it's not always fair out there, providing a case study of a successful entrepreneur who ran close to failing before finally pulling through. The importance of relying on other businesses through contracts is discussed with an eye to reducing your vulnerability. The importance of caution continues through Chapter 10, which looks at barriers that prevent people from exploiting an opportunity. It reminds us that turning a business model into a successful entity is a skill in itself.

Given that many aspects of the environment are beyond the control of the individual, Chapter 11 considers what governments can do to promote a more conducive environment. In light of the previously mentioned patterns of entrepreneurship, this chapter surveys the literature on government policy toward new business development.

A question all people wanting to be entrepreneurs ask themselves is "What sort of entrepreneur should I be?" Drawing on the patterns illustrated thus far, Chapter 12 provides a typology of entrepreneurs, depicting the type of opportunity and how it can be seized. This typology is valuable to people wanting to establish and position their own entrepreneurial ventures. Success is often a matter of being in the right place at the right time, being there when the opportunity happened. The last chapter summarizes the book and stresses the importance of being prepared for that opportunity, knowing the industry and setting yourself up for catching the wave.

Entrepreneurs are like drops of water; they get carried along in waves, and in so doing they contribute to the force of that wave. So do entrepreneurs ride or make the waves? The answer is they do both.

Chapter 2

Creativity and Opportunity Recognition

PLAYBOY: How do you define smart?

BILL GATES: (Rolls his eyes) Oh, come on. It's an elusive concept. There's a certain sharpness, an ability to absorb new facts. To walk into a situation, have something explained to you and immediately say, "Well, what about this?" To ask an insightful question. To absorb it in real time. A capacity to remember. To relate to domains that may not seem connected at first. A certain creativity that allows people to be effective.

PLAYBOY: . . . Are you smart?

BILL GATES: By my own little definition, I'm probably above average.

(Source: "The Bill Gates Interview," *Playboy* magazine 1994)

Why is it that some people always seem to have good ideas? And why is it that some people always seem to be in the right place at the right time? It's as if they have a "nose" for the market, an intuition that can't be explained. This chapter sets out to explain that market intuition. It examines the idea of creativity and discovery, who discovers new ideas and who creates them.

Sometimes, entrepreneurial ideas come about out of pure chance.[1] For example, in 1905 Frank Epperson stumbled on a successful product at the age of 11, purely by accident. A popular drink at the time could be made at home by mixing soda-water powder together with water. However, on one occasion, young Frank left the mixture out overnight with the stirring stick still in it. The following morning his drink was frozen solid. Eighteen years later, at the age of 29, Frank began commercializing the product as the "Epsicle ice pop." His children persuaded him to change the name to "popsicle." Today 3 million popsicles are sold each year in the United States.

Another example of an unexpected hit comes from Garnet Carter, who was keen to attract visitors to his Tennessee hotel. He came up with the idea of attaching a miniature golf course to the hotel, which he called Tom Thumb golf. His success was well beyond his expectations. Not only did it boost business at the hotel but it became his main line of business. Carter patented the game and the vegetable fiber surface on which it was played. Within three years, he employed 200 staff and served 25 million customers. He retired a wealthy man.

These last two enterprises stem from very little research and a lot of luck. Such stories do happen, but they are few and far between. More common are the stories of a creative entrepreneur in action or the discovery of change in the marketplace. In fact, according to the economist Kirzner, the discovery of opportunities is the core of entrepreneurship.[2] Entrepreneurs find and exploit opportunities by recognizing things that others do not. Yet who is most likely to find these opportunities? How can some people spot an opportunity and seemingly create something from nothing?

One of the oldest explanations of creativity involves the idea of making a connection between two ideas or elements that have previously not been connected. This view of creativity is supported by this book, for example as we see new combinations of technology or components of a business plan. However other explanations exist. The psychologist Herbert Simon has done much to explain who the creative people are who come up with new ideas.[3] According to Simon, creativity requires the same processes as other intelligent acts. Creativity is thinking, and that means processing information in our heads. It is by processing information that people come up with novel, creative ideas. The more information we have in our heads, the more material we have to work with. Although we may think of the creative genius as someone who can create something from nothing, in reality, those creative sparks are the result of a buildup of knowledge and information over time. For example, Henry Ford would not have been able to create a car and capture the growing market if he had not possessed engineering knowledge.

The creative process is the same whether in business, the arts or science. The people who are most likely to innovate are those with the necessary information and know-how to use it. In the words of Louis Pasteur, "chance favors the prepared mind." For example, Mozart showed remarkable creativity, but his mind had been prepared from a very early age. At the age of four, he was writing music, although his original compositions were not that great. But over time, he learned to understand sound and the use of instruments. With this growing knowledge, he was able to write innovative music.

To create business ideas, Simon talks about building up knowledge over time. Knowledge and information are the building blocks with which we construct ideas. Entrepreneurs construct profit opportunities in their minds from their knowledge of the business world.[4] This entails making new connections between different types of knowledge.[5] The more knowledge we have, the more options we have when it comes to piecing together new ideas. In this light, making ideas is not the creation of something from nothing. It involves taking existing notions, technologies and capabilities and putting them together in new ways.[6] In other words, if you want to be creative, become an expert in the industry you want to enter.

Not only is being an expert the prerequisite to creativity, it also helps to make the types of discoveries that seem accidental. Many famous discoveries, like the discovery of radioactivity or bacteria, could have been made by scientists other than the ones who first observed them. However, these discoveries could not have been made by just anyone. It had to be someone with scientific training. A person without the necessary training would not have observed and understood what was happening or its implications. This also applies to business ideas. People with the necessary knowledge have a strong advantage when something out of the ordinary happens. They will find it much easier to identify a shift in the marketplace and the implications of that shift. They will recognize the opening of a niche and other unique situations as if they have a nose for the market. They will respond almost by intuition.

One explanation why some people are quick to seize opportunities is because they are the first to have access to important information. The quality of any investment decision is dependent on the quality of information on which it is based. But not everybody has access to the same information. Consequently, Mark Casson believes an entrepreneur has better or more relevant information than others. Potential entrepreneurs gain much from being in the right place at right time. Of course the potential entrepreneur has to make use of that information. The entrepreneur has to piece it together with other information on the industry, like "the pieces of a jigsaw that have to be fitted together to get an overall picture."[7] Information on market shifts need to be analyzed in regard to information on costs of design, production and distribution. The first to synthesize that information gains an advantage.

This suggests that people in a good position to discover opportunities are those whose work puts them in positions of early detection. Someone in retail or marketing is more likely to discover a change in the market than someone in production. He or she is most likely to observe changes in customer needs, unfulfilled needs and problems. Similarly, someone in production or R&D would be most likely to identify opportunities opened up by technological change.

Entrepreneurs succeed by providing customers with businesses and services they value. This requires knowledge of what people value and how to provide those goods and services. It is hard to succeed without that knowledge. The person who observes a change in consumption patterns will not necessarily realize its importance unless he or she is familiar with the product or industry. Business people draw on their knowledge acquired from experience to make more accurate assessments of areas of possible demand. Part of this involves getting into the heads of the consumers to see how they perceive products in relation to their needs. In so doing, you need to be aware of changes in lifestyles of consumers and their product needs. With this knowledge, you can create a product that connects with the changing lifestyles of the potential market. Firms that put together new combinations of technologies and build products that fit into buyers' thought systems should have greater potential for survival than those that do not.[8]

Not surprisingly, most business opportunities are seized by people already in that industry. Studies of entrepreneurship reveal that many entrepreneurial ideas are born out of experiences at work. For example, two separate studies done in 1972 found that approximately 85% of new firms started with products or services that drew on the founders' previous technical experience.[9] More than 90% of the founders of the new companies had previously worked in the same industry.[10] The person who knows the market can understand the importance of a change and respond to situations in a way that seems intuitive.

With this in mind, it is no surprise that many highly creative people are workaholics. It brings to mind the saying "the harder I work, the luckier I become." This recognizes the importance of motivation. Creative people are generally motivated to work hard and be open to changes. In business, science and the arts, these motivations are the same: the satisfaction from accomplishment (or solving a problem), material rewards, recognition, the esteem in which others hold us, and power.

This suggests that, if you want to succeed, you should start building industry knowledge, but the process of building knowledge is not without problems. Our knowledge can sometimes make us blind to new opportunities. Thomas Kuhn was the first to notice this, although his focus was on science. Kuhn noticed that, outside of chance happenings, innovators can only solve problems within their intellectual and educational outlook.[11] Education provides the scientific community with a particular way of viewing the world and practicing science in it. That education determines how discoveries are interpreted and results in an emphasis on finding scientific discoveries that support what is already known. We find it hard to recognize opportunities that go against what we have preciously learned. In effect, our existing knowledge determines how knowledge advances in the future. Commitment to the old paradigm is so strong that scientists can not merely give up their old way of viewing the world. There is a resistance to new modes of thinking.

Kuhn's approach was first applied to business by Peter Earl.[12] Sometimes business people are entrapped in their old view of the world, and this restricts their perception of change. This makes it difficult for them to recognize appropriate strategic changes and can throw a company on the corporate rocks. But this can be good news for entrepreneurs. When existing companies are entrapped by their old view of the world, this can open up opportunities for new players. An interesting question to ask is "How well do existing companies know their market?" Are their thought patterns and strategies outdated or based on limited information? If the answer to these questions is yes, there may exist an opportunity to start a successful business in an established industry.

When people are entrapped by a paradigm, discoveries are most likely to come from people who think outside the box. This suggests that experts can sometimes miss out on discoveries, but Herbert Simon denies this. He says that the discoveries are still likely to be made by experts—but experts in another field. Consequently, we see that many of the major discoveries of modern molecular biology were made by biochemists or even physicists, rather than by traditionally trained biologists.[13] These people possess high-level knowledge, but it is knowledge that is different to those entrapped by the paradigm. However, we don't know what we are about to discover and therefore do not know what is the right field in which to possess knowledge for these discoveries. It is sometimes just a case of gambler's luck.

Another reason why some people are quick to spot opportunities is that they actively search for them. One study compared 51 entrepreneurs who founded their own companies with 36 executives working in a large company.[14] The study found that entrepreneurs spent more time searching for information in their off hours than the managers. It appears not only are successful entrepreneurs keen to learn about business opportunities, but they actively search for information on opportunities. They make a habit of scanning their environments for information and make use of different types of information that may lead to new business opportunities.[15] This includes feedback from customers, employees, suppliers and professional acquaintances, patent filings, technical literature, libraries, distributors, consultants, and investors.

Successful entrepreneurs see themselves as being alert to entrepreneurial opportunities.[16] They describe themselves as being opportunistic and enjoy casually thinking about new opportunities. They also see themselves as creative, and a large number set aside a few minutes each day or week to be creative. Sometimes, entrepreneurs engage in what is called "passive search," a state in which they are not actively looking for opportunities, but they are in a state that makes them receptive to an idea when they hear of one.

Factors that help the identification of market opportunities include social networks. If entrepreneurs have mentors or are part of informal industry networks or professional forums, they are more likely to receive information alerting them to the possibility of an opportunity. Some personal factors have been identified as affecting the possibility of finding an opportunity. For example optimistic people are more likely to see an opportunity where others do not, and much research has been done on the personality traits of entrepreneurs. However, there is some question over their findings. Founders of the coffee chain Coffee Republic believe there is no entrepreneurial type. They did not see themselves as entrepreneurial types:

> Entrepreneurship wasn't in our genes. We don't come from a family of entrepreneurs. . . . We were in no way exceptional. Neither of us were overachievers or underachievers at school or in our hobbies. . . . Creative is something we were not.[17]

In their book, titled *Anyone can do it,* Sahar and Bobby Hashami detail how they built the coffee chain. Sahar first noticed the deficiency in the London market for a decent coffee shop after a trip to the United States, where she fell in love with the New York espresso bars. She complained to her brother "I really miss the skinny cappuccinos and fat-free muffins from those New York espresso bars. I can't believe there is nothing like them in London." Her brother responded, "you know that is a great business idea."[18]

Although Sahar, a lawyer, recognized the deficit in the market, she did not see it as a business idea. It was her brother who recognized what the market gap meant. He was the one with business training and had previously assessed a prospectus for a coffee chain when he worked for Lehman Brothers.

While it is true that no specific personality type is necessary to create a business, the Hashamis take their argument too far when claiming you don't need skills or experience. While it is true that they did not have experience in the food and drink industry, her brother's experience assessing the coffee chain at Lehman's clearly aided opportunity recognition. Furthermore, he had been looking for a business idea and this, no doubt, primed him to the importance of what his sister was saying. At the same time, Sahar could be described as a "sophisticated consumer." Her time in the U.S. coffee market heightened her awareness of market deficiencies. By themselves, they did not have the required expertise, but together they had what it took to find the opportunity. Often it requires a team to recognize or create a business opportunity. It requires a blend of knowledge that one person by him- or herself does not possess.

To make their business succeed, Sahar and Bobby immersed themselves "in the world of coffee and became *experts* in that field as quickly as we possibly could" (emphasis added). They visited existing outlets for coffee and found that there was large demand as evidenced through the long customer lines, but existing product was poor because the sandwich bars and kiosks that sold them concentrated on the food they sold. Coffee was a secondary product. Sahar and Bobby drank, read about and talked about coffee wherever they could. In the library, they read market reports, directories and any other available information. They talked to supplier after supplier and, in the process, built their expertise and knowledge on how this industry works.

This illustrates that you should not be put off by the word "expert." You can build expertise. Second, we need to clarify what we mean by the word expert. By that we don't mean having a PhD. On the contrary, often the most highly educated people are out of touch with market and production activity. In which case, it is people involved in the industry on a daily basis who have the greatest expertise. Expertise can be gained through a number of ways: through life experience, job function, or simply having a unique combination of experiences. Some consumers gain significant expertise in an industry. They become sophisticated consumers, highly attuned to the nuances of consumer demand, and this helps them to identify market potential.

Warren Buffett, whose business reputation stands on the fact that he was the world's richest man, stresses the importance of restricting yourself to those areas where you have expertise. He calls it your "circle of competence":

> Knowing what you do understand and don't understand—that is the key. It's defining what I call your circle of competence, and everybody's got a different circle of competence. The important thing is not how big the circle is. The important thing is staying inside the circle.[19]

Buffett describes how his investments succeed because he sticks to what he knows, and those people who venture outside their expertise are inviting danger. In academic circles, we speak of a similar concept we call a "knowledge corridor." This concept stresses that your prior knowledge helps you to recognize successful business ideas. Your knowledge helps you to identify opportunities where others wouldn't, but it also stops you from seeing opportunities that others with different experiences might notice. In other words, your ability to spot an opportunity is determined by what you have done in the past. So, for example, although Sahar knew there was deficiency in the coffee market, her prior knowledge did not help her recognize it as a business idea. Everybody has his or her own individual "knowledge corridor" because everyone has his or her own unique combination of life experiences.

Scott Shane, who has written much on this subject, states that the type of prior knowledge that helps identify opportunities includes knowledge of markets, knowledge of ways to serve markets, and knowledge of customer problems. To move to the next stage and turn that idea into a business requires knowledge and experience in general business, relevant industry experience, and functional experience in marketing, product development, or management. Finally, you are more likely to succeed if you have had previous experience starting up a business.

Coming up with the idea is just one part of the entrepreneurship process, which involves many levels of creativity. At the second level is creating the actual business. This is a far more absorbing level of creativity. It involves renting or buying premises, raising finance, hiring and training staff, buying equipment, ordering supplies and performing numerous other activities. When creating a business, creativity works at yet another level: creating the components of that business. This can include creating the business plan, the product and the strategy.

Finally, in the process of doing all these things, an entrepreneur may create a business model. It may not be the goal of an entrepreneur to create a business model. It is merely something you do while trying to build a successful business. However, as you encounter problems and solve them, you may create new ways of doing business— new combinations of production and marketing. It is not always necessary to create a new business model; there is nothing wrong with imitating someone else's model if it is successful. This can be seen in the efforts of Howard Schultz, who transformed another coffee chain into a global empire.[21] Starbucks was originally started in 1971 by three friends who had a passion for coffee. However, their shop was nothing like the coffee shops we know today. It focused on fresh coffee beans and the equipment used in brewing and roasting. This business model was successful, and by 1980 the company had six retail outlets.

In 1982, Howard Schultz was hired to help the company with marketing. Not long after, he went to Italy on a business trip, where he had the chance to observe the Italian coffee culture. In Italy, the cafes sold a variety of coffees. More important, he observed customers chatting and enjoying themselves in cafes with elegant surroundings. He soon realized that it was not just about the coffee. The cafes were centers for social gathering where people could linger and relax. Through imitation, Schultz soon developed a new business model to take back to the United States.

Back in Seattle, he presented his idea to the business owners, and a trial was performed, but the owners were more interested in the bean and roasting side of the business. They were not interested in selling cups of coffee, so Schultz created his own coffee lounge called Il Giornale (the daily). To refine his business model, Schultz made another trip to Italy to research the idea in depth. He visited hundreds of espresso and coffee bars and, in the process, developed a business model based on a "social coffee experience." Selling cups of coffee was only part of the offering to customers. His business model added consumer value through the choice of equipment, service, operations, information systems, store layout, design and ambience. Back in the United States, he further fine-tuned his model through experimentation.

Shultz then bought Starbucks from the original owners who preferred to focus on coffee beans and equipment. Schultz then repeated his business model in town after town, building an entrepreneurial empire.

The Environment as a Source of New Business Possibilities

> Our research shows that neither entrepreneurship nor invention is random. . . . What looks like chance is actually the result of differences in national environments. The particular firm or individual that will do the innovating is less predictable, though, than the nation or nations in which they are likely to be located.
>
> (Michael Porter, *The Competitive Advantage of Nations*)

The world is awash with motivational books telling us we can get out there and do it. So many of them say the biggest barrier to success is ourselves, that it is hard to believe that there are many factors beyond our control. This tendency to focus on the individual is encouraged by biographies of successful entrepreneurs that stress their skills, motivation and foresight, but sometimes we have to take a step back and look at the bigger picture. The truth is the fate of many commercial ventures is determined by the environment. Learning how to understand the environment and maneuver in it are some of the most important qualities to acquire if you are to have success.

When looking at succesful entrepreneurs, we need to ask what was happening in the environment at the time their businesses took off. Instead of asking what personal qualities made Henry Ford so succesful, we need to recognize what was happening in the U.S. market at the time that allowed him to achieve his success. Why is it that so many of the great American entrepreneurs succeeded around the same time? Carnegie, Ford and Edison appeared around the same time as they all rode the same wave. Theirs was a time of rapidly growing demand in the U.S. economy, which allowed the adoption of efficient mass production techniques. No other country at the time offered the same environment for entrepreneurs.

It has long been recognized that business creation is concentrated in particular periods of time and space. As early as 1911, Joseph Schumpeter wrote that "entrepreneurs appear periodically in swarms."[22] Again, in 1965, Stinchcombe observed that "an examination of the history of almost any type of organization shows that there are great spurts of foundation of the type followed by periods of relatively slower growth."[23] Periods of growing market and spreading productive techniques offer a great environment for entrepreneurs. Entrepreneurship occurs at this nexus between the individual and the opportunity.

Our conventional view of creativity focuses on and depicts a talented individual puzzling over problems and generating creative ideas and insights. The environment plays a small role. However, Yale professor Jonathan Feinstein disputes this. In his book, *The Nature of Creative Development,* Feinstein argues that creativity flows from the individual's enagement with the world.[24] Creativity is born from the experiences and elements people encounter in the environment. This view seems to parallel the business research. Michael Porter's book, *The Competitive Advantage of Nation,* was a landmark in studies of internationally competitive industries.[25] It showed that the environment plays a crucial role in determining which businesses are created. For example, the United States has many characteristics that make it an excellent environment for commercializing medical innovations. In fact, so positive is the environment for these businesses that many foreign entrepreneurs have come to the United States to start their medical product companies.

Of course, chance can play a role. Sometimes an entrepreneur will get an idea through serendipity, but this is more likely to be at the inventive stage. When it comes to commercializing that invention, the environment is pivotal. The development of a business requires a number of characteristics such as sufficient demand to support the product. The following section briefly discusses characteristics of the environment that help determine creativity and innovation.

Demand Characteristics

The first and most obvious environmental force is demand. The nature of potential customers has a strong bearing on what businesses sprout, for they are the ones who will buy the product and support the business. And, as we have already seen, customers are often the source of business ideas.

An obvious desirable characteristic is a fast growth in demand. If a population is growing or becoming richer, it will provide an incentive for entrepreneurs to invest in new plants and innovative products. However, it is not just the wealth of local consumers that is important. Other characteristics of demand play a role. The problems that customers face can open business opportunities. An example of this can be seen in the development of businesses making air conditioning equipment. The first successful enterprises were in the eastern United States in the early 1900s, and, yes, the prosperity of Americans was a key factor as they could afford the luxury of air conditioning. But equally important was the desire of people to escape the heat and humidity. The environment determines what people value and what products they buy.

Another characteristic is the size of home demand. Large markets are good environments for producers to find market niches. It is a reminder of Adam Smith's 200-year-old observation that the level of specialization in an economy is determined by the size of the market. A large market allows producers to specialize and create businesses serving specialized niches. This is one of the beauties of America's big cities. They are so large that shops can prosper selling just one product like ties or specialist foods. In towns with smaller markets, businesses need a wider product range in order to survive. Often people in smaller markets will make specialized products, but the market will not support them.

A smaller market might provide the same benefits if it has a larger number of customers as a proportion of its population who want a certain product. For example, New Zealand has a large number of farms compared with other nations, and this means it has a more obvious demand for fences to control the movement of animals. Consequently, the first electric fence businesses were born there. The local environment gave greater need for the product than other lcations, but once produced, it could be exported to the world.

In line with the concept that businesses are often born to solve problems, entrepreneurs are more likely to arise in a country where a problem first occurs. For example, the mountains in Switzerland created transportation problems for the people living there. This problem gave birth to pioneers in drilling equipment that could build tunnels. These enterprises now sell their products and expertise on the world market.

Innovation and new business ideas are helped if the customers in a country are sophisticated and demanding in what they expect from a product. We have already stated that customer requests often generate good business ideas. This is no new phenomenon. One of the earliest industries in the world, Chinese creamics, advanced because the Chinese court demanded quality ceramics, which stretched Chinese ceramics producers to innovate. In this way, it was the customers who made the Chinese producers so good.

Related and Supporting Industries

Given that many entrepreneurs get their ideas from work, it should be no surprise that the birth of new business is determined by the industries that already exist in a country. For example, one of the factors that led to the creation of the Italian ski boot industry was the existance of a local industry producing climbing and hiking shoes. Northern Italy already possesed a skilled pool of footwear producers, and many of these soon entered ski boot production after the second World War as many people began enjoying the opportunity to go skiing. Demand grew further in 1956 when the Winter Olympics were held in the local resort Cortina.

There is no end to the number of examples where companies have been born from others in the region. Often entrepreneurs leave existing companies to start their own business. They may be driven by ambition or the desire to be their own boss. They may be fustrated that the company refuses to develop good ideas, so they set up their own companies to do what their employer wouldn't. They start a company and commercialize those ideas. Often the new entrepreneur targets market segments that the old company was not interested in, or maybe they had an idea for a new product. Whatever the case, it leads to a new bout of economic development. Spin-off companies like these are very healthy for the economy, as they unlock new product and process innovations that were stifled by bureacratic inertia or the strategies of the old firm.

Often the spin-off company is located in the same region as the old one. This may be because it is the home town of the entrepreneur, but it also has economic advantages. If you set up shop in an area with similar businesses, you can tap into networks and knowledge in the area. You will have access to trained staff, supplies and other facilities in the area. Supplier industries in the area can provide access to machinery and other inputs; however, their most significant benefit is the flow of information and communication. Businesses in the same area will discuss new methods and opportunities to apply new technology. They may discuss joint problems and share R&D, leading to fast, efficient solutions. Through their discussions, they may develop technologies that benefit all parties.

The importance of local links should not be underestimated. Research indicates that entrepreneurs spend nearly half of their time during their start-up phase in making contacts and building networks. These networks provide support and motivation; examples and role models; expert opinion and counseling; and access to opportunities, resources and information.[26] Often the success of a coworker who spins-off a new company encourages others to do the same. The result is a cluster of businesses in related industries that generate prosperity for their local town.

Factor Endowment

Another aspect of the business environment that leads to the development of new businesses is the local factor endowment. This is an extension of the old "factors of production" you learned about in economics (i.e., natural resources, labor and capital. The factors of production, particularly natural resources, have always been recognized as being an important determiner of which businesses are built. For example, the Gujarat textile industry was born out of local geographical conditions that favored growing cotton. The Swedish steel industry grew because it had local deposits of low phospherous iron ore. It is the local availability of natural resources that often provides the initial impetus for a new business.

Many of today's businesses are based less on natural resources and more on human technology and knowledge, as it is through knowledge and technology that we have the greatest capacity to add and create value. Not surprising, many new companies are born from ideas developed during academic training or university research. Educational institutions are also important for providing skills needed for entrepreneurship and business.[27] Universities and educational institutions also play an important role in training the staff that young enterprises employ. Consequently, environments with a strong endowment of scientific and educational institutions are more likely to produce entrepreneurs in advanced industries.

Another important factor for the establishment of a new business is availability of capital. People attempting to build a new business require financial assistance for several purposes: for start-up capital, to diversify or spread risk, and to finance growth and expansion.[28] The wide range of sources of venture capital in the United States is yet another reason why it is such a favorable environment for entrepreneurs. Compared with many nations, there is a great deal of capital available, and financial markets have been created to get this capital to entrepreneurs. This situation contrasts strongly with many developing countries and emerging market economies, where only a few venture capital companies and commercial banks exist, and alternative sources of finance are almost nonexistent.

The ability of an entrepreneur to operate is also determined by the quality of the local business infrastructure. Products must be transported. Suppliers and customers must be contacted. Production needs energy. All of these things require an environment with reliable energy, communication and transportation facilities.

Social Conditions

It has already been stressed how important motivation is in developing a business. Consequently, how society views entrepreneurship can have a big impact on the birth of businesses. If a society has successful entrepreneurs, these people serve as role models and send a message to potential entrepreneurs that business is an attractive career option. Similarly, if a society values entrepreneurs, more people will feel inclined to give it a go. On the other hand, a nation that puts less value on commercial values, perhaps with a preference for spiritual-religious values, may not be so supportive, although this is not always the case.

Government

Governments play an important role in shaping the commercial environment, and there are a number of ways that policies can affect the birth of young businesses. First, governments can have a negative impact on new business creation if they are overly repressive. If an economy is characterized by too many rules and procedural requirements, potential entrepreneurs may be discouraged from risking their time, savings and energies. This suggests that governments should keep barriers to entering an industry at a minimum and ease any requirements for registration and licensing. Rules and regulations governing entrepreneurial activties should be easy to adhere to and not overly bureaucratic. A more detailed range of policy options will be covered in Chapter 11.

Rivalry

One last word on the enviroment is the level of competiton. Michael Porter stresses that a high degree of competition among local firms forces a company to upgrade and become internationally competitive. However, studies reveal that entrepreneurs entering industries with high levels of competition are more likely to fail.[29] These studies suggest that too much competition can hasten a company's demise. On the other hand, rivalry can have the positive effect of forcing a company to improve its competitiveness and achieve its potential.

How Do Entrepreneurs Come Across Opportunities?

A number of studies have been conducted to reveal where successful entrepreneurs get their ideas,[30] two of which are presented in Table 2.1. What stands out about these results is that the sources of the vast majority of ideas could be explained. There were very few examples of inspirations that just popped out of the blue. Studies have shown that successful business ideas come from a number of common sources. These include the following:

Previous Work

A number of studies confirm that the largest source of ideas is the workplace. Findings vary depending on the survey, but somewhere between 43% and 61% of entrepreneurs find their business ideas at work. This is consistent with Simon's idea that people are most likely to have creative ideas if they are knowledgeable on the subject.

Hobbies

A common source of ideas is hobbies, with 16% to 18% of ideas coming in this way. This also supports Simon's idea that expertise is a prerequisite to creativity. People can build up great levels of knowledge about their respective hobbies. Many computer-based enterprises have been born in this way. Perhaps the most famous example is Steve Jobs and Steve Wozniak, the founders of Apple Computers, whose interest started in their preteen years. By the time they started their business in their 20s, they had built up significant knowledge about the technology and its applications.[31]

Solving Problems

A number of venture ideas are born from problems that required a solution. Many businesses have been created by entrepreneurs who needed a product or service but could not find a supplier who could meet their needs. So they developed a solution. Eventually, they realized that their needs were also felt by a large number of people, and the solution they developed could form the basis of a business. For example, one entrepreneur described the following:

> I couldn't find anyone I had enough faith in to repair violins I was playing, so I started repairing myself, and the word got around that I would do that. So I started doing that. After a while, it got to be a burden doing it for free, and I started charging people for it.[32]

For others, the problem was brought to them, and they developed a solution.[33] For example, one doctor had trouble taking certain types of measurements. No instruments existed that could do the job. The doctor mentioned the problem to a friend who did work in electronics research. The friend took up the challenge to build such an instrument. He succeeded, and the resulting product became the basis of a multimillion-dollar business. It is a reminder of the old maxim that if you have a problem, someone else is likely to have that same problem. If you solve that problem, you have a marketable product. Even if only 1% of the population shares your problem, this could still represent a sizable market. This is a particularly encouraging source of opportunity as society is turning out new problems every day as technology changes, solving some problems and creating new ones. However, it was noted that in order to solve those problems a profound technological knowledge is needed.

Table 2.1 Source of Ideas

Sources of Venture Ideas in 2994 Firms (Data Source: Cooper et al 1990)	
Source	Percentage
Prior job	47%
Hobby/personal interest	16
Chance event	8
Education/courses	7
Activities of friends/relatives	7
Family business	6
Someone suggested it	6
Other	3
	100

Source Importance for Identifying New Business Ideas (Data Source: Hills and Shrader 1998)	
Item	Percent who thought item very important
Customer/clients	75%
Employees	59
Suppliers	47
Professional acquaintances	41
Trade publications	40
Family	32
Magazines/newspapers	26
Prior employment	25
Distributors	18
Technical literature	18
Consultants	16
Personal friends	14
Investors	14
Hobby	10
Libraries	8
Other	21

Market Shift

Another fundamental source of opportunity arose from market change and customers:

> Typically ... the idea for a fast growing business appears in a ... pedestrian fashion. The structure of a marketplace shifts, maybe ever so slightly. A new niche opens up. And all at once, people ... who may have never expected to become entrepreneurs are out on their own and amazed by their own success.[34]

A large number of entrepreneurs stated that their own business was derived from a market-driven idea. To find ideas, prospective entrepreneurs should focus their attention on markets and customers, as this increases the probability of recognizing entrepreneurial opportunities. With this in mind, it is no surprise that 84% to 91% of the successful entrepreneurs in one survey stated that they listen "extremely well to what customers say" as a way of identifying opportunities.[35] This had the added advantage of helping to identify future customers. In fact, a large proportion knew who their customers would be before introducing their first product or service.

Other People's Ideas

Sometimes people don't just bring the problem; they also bring the solution. A number of entrepreneurs have indicated that other people commonly bring new venture ideas to them.

Technology

Although technology is widely recognized as a driver of new business opportunities, it was not as common a source as might be expected. Research indicates that, although technological change can be critically important for many opportunities, overall it is far less important than markets.[36] However, this obviously depends on the state of the industry. It will also vary depending on the traits of individual entrepreneurs. Someone with a strong technological background is more likely to find and pursue technological opportunities.

Accidents

As mentioned earlier, accidents can be a source of ideas, and a number of successful people reported that "the idea behind their business just seemed to suddenly appear." However, it was only a small number that identified this as the cause, and a larger number "made a deliberate effort to search for an idea to start a business."[37]

Imitation

A number of people got their ideas by looking at other people's businesses. They saw someone else at work and felt that they could do it better. Around 15% of the ideas were obtained in this way.

Improve Existing Products

Entrepreneurial activity is frequently linked with the introduction of improved products. This improvement may come about as a result of discoveries in science and technology, or alternatively from greater knowledge of consumer demands. In Chapter 4, we take a look at the lighting industry, which reveals a close relationship between science and products and also the way that products build in value for money. The product that contains the most value for money superseded the one before it.

You do not necessarily need to be a technician to improve on a product. Even the most basic product can be improved on. For example, Nor' West clothespins developed an improvement on the basic clothespins. Recognizing that the old clothespin became brittle and lost its shape and color in the sun, the company created a clothespin made from a form of polyurethane that kept its shape and color. It also redesigned the clothespin, which made it easy to open, a huge benefit for those suffering from arthritis.

One useful approach is to think of a product that has a problem. Think about how you can improve on it. In any single day, you use thousands of products: the couch you are sitting on, the spoon you stir your coffee with, the light you are using to help you read. It is hard to think that one of them could not be improved upon. Normally when a product lets us down, the first thing we do is complain. But the old maxim "a problem is an opportunity in disguise" rings true. It is up to you to turn that problem into opportunity by defining the problem and finding a way of solving it.

I would suggest you take time out and pick up any product within your reach and think about the times it has let you down. It may also be helpful to think about products that have not had any improvements in years. Many of the products we use, from pencils to clothespins, are based on very old technologies.

Be warned that your first attempts to do this will likely render no result and will be very frustrating. In fact you may have to do this with many products before you come up with an idea. But in the process, you will start to think about products in a new way. Don't just use them. Question their ability to do their job and their potential to do more. Once you are used to thinking in this way, some ideas will jump out and hit you in the face.

Re-Evaluating Rationale for Design

When a product is designed, it embodies the technology and customer needs at that time. However, customer needs and technologies change, but product designs do not always change with the time. This lag provides an opportunity for new players to analyze the product and think about its changing requirements.

One way to do this is to list all the assumptions we make about the product. You might research the history of the product and see why design decisions were made at the time. Another good way of questioning underlying assumptions is through word association. Approach your friends and ask them to list the first five things that come into their heads when you mention a product. This will tell you a lot about how people perceive a product. Then, go over that list and question whether any of these assumptions could be changed to create a better product or service more relevant to today's market.

Combining Industries and Technologies

Many ideas are born by taking something from one industry and applying it to another. John Dyson built a very successful business in this way. He was dissatisfied with one product in his life, the vacuum cleaner. Annoyed at its limited suction power, he investigated further and discovered that the pores of the bags inside the cleaners quickly became clogged. This reduced air circulation and the sucking power of the machine. His solution came from a totally different industry: sawmilling. He noted that, at sawmills, excess dust was extracted from the atmosphere by a large conical funnel that generated a vortex of high speed air to spin the dust to the edges where they fell into a collection bag. Dyson decided to apply the same technology to vacuum cleaners. His new product was released in 1993 and within two years had become the United Kingdom's top-selling upright cleaner, selling more than established companies like Hoover and Electrolux.[38]

Sometimes the secondary applications of the technology are more successful than the original. When Edison introduced the phonograph, he produced a list of 10 possible uses to which it could be put. The main purposes for which he thought it would be used were "taking dictation without the aid of a stenographer, talking books for the blind and teaching public speaking." Despite being hailed as a technological marvel, the phonograph languished in the market for 20 years. It was not until the 1890s that the recording industry made the technology commercial. Edison had considered recording music, but it was only fourth on his list.[39]

Finding Ideas Is a Process

Probably the most important finding is that the vast majority of entrepreneurs believe that "identifying opportunities is really several learning steps over time, rather than a one-time occurrence." The more times you go through the process of identifying and evaluating opportunities, the more you learn what to look for. You build up knowledge about what makes a good idea and what doesn't. With experience also comes greater confidence and greater alertness to business opportunities. Furthermore, the process of looking at one idea often leads to other opportunities. As you investigate one idea, other ideas or insights may be generated that can be applied in a different setting.

*   *   *

When we look at the various sources of ideas, what stands out is the importance of environmental factors such as market shift, technology, or customer needs and ideas. An expert or an entrepreneur who actively searches for ideas may be the first to spot an opportunity, but, directly or indirectly, the source for all ideas is the environment.

Also, we should not over-emphasize the importance of new ideas. Sometimes business opportunities stem not from new ideas or changes in the market but from old ideas. For example, everyone knows that a great idea for a product is a car battery that never dies. The idea is old, but how do you make such a product? When the problem is eventually solved, it will probably be a result of an environmental shift (i.e., a development in science that makes a solution possible). Alternatively, it may be a result of someone piecing together existing knowledge in a way that no one has done before. Perhaps that person will experience something unique that will allow him or her to see something that others have not. This person could take this unique knowledge and apply it to the problem. Whichever way it comes about, this product may be made by piecing together knowledge in different combinations than that in existing car batteries.

Perhaps the most important finding is that successful entrepreneurs believe you should not overrate the idea. Many believe that "new ideas are a dime a dozen. Evaluation is the key." It is a reminder that a good idea does not necessarily mean it will be commercially successful. To proceed with the idea without evaluating it could be fatal, wasting your time, energy, emotion and money. After coming up with an idea and evaluating it, the next task is putting the business together. More than half of the entrepreneurs agreed that putting capital and other resources together was more important than the actual idea. It is yet another reminder that "a good idea is nothing more than a tool in the hands of an entrepreneur."[40] Recognizing venture ideas by themselves is just one step in the entrepreneurial process.

The research provides key lessons for people wanting to be entrepreneurs. The first is to restrict yourself to areas in which you have expertise or, alternatively, to do substantial work to develop your expertise. I encourage my students to have a "hobby industry," an industry that they hope one day to get into. They are told to build news logs on that industry; read trade magazines; and acquire knowledge on that industry's production, marketing and other aspects. If done properly, that industry becomes part of their "knowledge corridor" and "circle of competence."

The second lesson is that entrepreneurship is not a one-off event. Entrepreneurship is a learning process, done over time. The more ideas that you consider and examine, the better you will be at making judgments. You will learn to get a better idea of the costs involved in setting up and operating a business. You will also gain more awareness of the vagaries of the market.

The importance of customer feedback was stressed by the successful entrepreneurs. This suggests that focusing on markets and customers increases the possibility of recognizing entrepreneurial opportunities. It also suggests that you should become immersed in the market to obtain that sensitivity necessary to spot openings. When it comes to identifying ideas, immersion in an industry is far superior to formal market research. Besides, by the time the information appears in formal surveys, it is normally well known by those on the shop floor.

Being in the right place at the right time is not just a matter of circumstances. It is also a matter of fit with those circumstances. Someone without the necessary expertise may not recognize an opportunity when it comes or be capable of exploiting it. By being immersed in a particular industry or market, you are in a good position to pick up the pieces of information that signal an opportunity. With this in mind, it is no surprise that intuitive judgment, or "gut feel," is considered an extremely important part of judging market potential. That gut feeling that an idea will be successful helps generate belief in the idea, and this motivates entrepreneurs once they begin to piece the business together.

Chapter 3

Environmental Change and Windows of Opportunity

Ability is of little account without opportunity.

(Napoleon Bonaparte)

It used to be a common practice in Britain for record companies to force shops to sell their records at a set price. This system was called retail price maintenance. Retailers could not sell the product at a reduced price, and this ensured the record companies got a healthy return. It also meant customers had to pay higher prices. Such restrictions on market activity are now recognized as being against the interests of the consumer and the market, so in 1964 the British government made the practice illegal. This meant that people could sell records for whatever price they liked, opening the opportunity for price competition.

This change in the law created a window of opportunity for an entrepreneur to enter the industry and sell records at a price lower than that of established retailers, but for five years the window stayed open. No entrepreneur seized the opportunity. Perhaps they did not want to become involved in a price war, or perhaps there were problems getting supplies of records. Or maybe they did not want to offend the record companies that supplied them.

In the meantime, a young British entrepreneur named Richard Branson had been trying to establish a student magazine without much success.[1] In the late 1960s he decided to spread his interests and take advantage of the new legal situation. He obtained records from shops who had been trying to unload excess stock, but instead of selling the records through a shop, he set up a mail-order business. People would see his advertisements, write to him saying what they wanted and enclose a check or money order. The standard price for records at the time was 39 shillings and 11 pence. Branson advertised his records at 37 and 6 pence. His business took off.

The environment can open up opportunities, and it can close them again. In the early 1970s, a major threat was looming. In particular, a two-month strike by postal workers threatened to scuttle Branson's business. He needed another way of getting his records to the public. Branson responded by opening his first Virgin record store. The venture was a success and set Branson on the road to entrepreneurial superstardom.

It is widely recognized that there are more opportunities for entrepreneurs in times of environmental change.[2] Something in the environment changes, like the legal change described previously, and this opens up a window of opportunity. This view is held particularly by economists of the Austrian school.[3] They see markets as being in a state of equilibrium, but a change can shift the market into a state of disequilibrium, where what people demand is not in alignment with what can be supplied. It is entrepreneurs who seize the initiative, open new businesses and bring the market to a new equilibrium.

Evidence from history seems to suggest that change opens opportunities for entrepreneurs. The greater the changes occuring in an industry, the greater the opportunities. Successful entrepreneurs recognize these opportunities and act on them. However, not everyone is aware of these opportunities. People living in different places at different times will have access to different information. Opportunities are situational, stressing the importance of being in the right place at the right time.

In the same way that people with knowledge of these changes have an advantage, people who can anticipate changes before they happen have an even greater advantage. This explains the importance of searching for information, which so many entrepreneurs do. Information is a strategic asset. It allows business people to get a head start and exploit the opportunity before others do. Time advantages are very important. It takes time to work out whether an opportunity is worth pursuing and then to pull together resources to achieve it. The window of opportunity is not going to be open forever. It will close the minute someone seizes the opportunity or when another environmental change occurs.

Demand-Driven Opportunities

According to Fortune magazine, Henry Ford was "the businessman of the twentieth century." This is the man who made the motor vehicle available to the everyday person and revolutionized life in the process. Prior to Ford, motor cars were an expensive product for the elite. Henry Ford recognized that there could be a demand for the car among America's growing middle class. At the time, America was enjoying a growing wave of demand. Through population growth and immigration, the United States was building a middle-class market larger than in any other nation in the world. If Henry Ford could find a way of tapping this market, he could ride the wave of growing demand. His goal was explicit: "I will build a motor car for the multitude so low in price that the man of moderate means may own one."[4]

Ford found a way when he introduced the cheap, reliable, mass-produced Model T. The market response to the car was phenomenal, and it was in response to this demand that the assembly line was introduced to speed up production. The key to Ford's initial success was the size of the U.S. middle-class market, which allowed him to pursue his strategy of mass production. No other country in the world offered this opportunity. Like many other successful entrepreneurs in the United States at this time, Ford was a wave-rider, surfing America's growing demand.

Changes in demand are a key aspect of entrepreneurial opportunity. After all, it is customer demand that generates the revenue on which a business exists. Research has shown there is a strong correlation between the rate of growth in demand and growth in the number of new businesses.[5] It is a time when new players can enter the industry without reducing profit.

Unlike large companies, entrepreneurs do not have significant resources to influence demand through large marketing campaigns. They have a greater chance if they swim with the tide. Sometimes this happens out of luck. Many successful entrepreneurs have been fortunate enough to be in the right place at the right time. They have invested in an industry just as the market is about to take off. Others, like Henry Ford, saw the changes happening and acted to exploit them. It is better not to leave your future to fate but to understand the forces at work. There are several possible causes why demand may grow, such as changes in the demographic nature of the population, rising wealth, growing population or just a change in the patterns of consumers.

Population growth and changing demographics have provided opportunities for many entrepreneurs, including some of America's most successful. Those who rode waves of demand fuelled by population growth include the Vanderbilts, who provided transportation for New Yorkers during the nineteenth century. This was a time of rapidly growing immigration to New York, providing Vanderbilt with a growing wave of demand he was well positioned to milk.

Possibly the most obvious example of entrepreneurs who ride waves fuelled by immigration are the real estate and construction fields. Rising immigration increases the demand for housing, and this creates ideal conditions for real-estate and property developers. Of course, growing populations can also increase the market for other products, but the unique thing about property is, unlike other products, it can be very hard to increase supply. We can build taller buildings, but producing land is a far tougher assignment. Consequently, an increase in demand can have a significant impact on the price, and landowners can do very well from immigration.

Populations grow for three reasons: increased birth rates, decreased mortality rates and immigration. The economics of demographics are well known, so we'll deal with them only briefly. The impact of birth rate is best illustrated by the impact of the baby boomers. In the years immediately following the second World War, there was an increase in the number of births. As these babies grew older, they invigorated a number of markets. As babies in the 1950s, they fuelled the market for baby products. In the 1960s, they boosted the market for toys. In the 1970s and 1980s they boosted the housing market as they began to settle down.

Another cause of population growth is declining mortality rates. These have had an obvious impact on health care and retirement markets. This is particularly relevant in the United States and other Western nations, as people who live longer are fuelling the demand for retirement villages.

Many population forces are regionalized. For example, immigration may be higher in Hawaii and Washington state than in Idaho. There are also changes within populations that cause some niche markets to grow and some to decline. This is best illustrated by the growing Latino market in the United States, which reflects the large proportion of immigrants from the South.

Opportunities also arise when there is a change in consumer tastes and preferences. Once the shift is noticed, an entrepreneur must provide the product to satisfy the new tastes. Steve Pateman was one who succeeded in this way. He was the owner of a family shoe-making business in Northamptonshire, England. His business came under pressure from cheap imports. He couldn't compete. Realizing his investment in leather-making skills and machinery could be used in another niche, he adapted his machines to build boots and leather gear for the fetish market.[6] To help boost sales, he even shaved his legs to personally demonstrate his goods at erotica shows. In so doing, he discovered a growing trend that helped his business survive cheap shoe imports (his story is dramatized in the movie *Kinky Boots*).

Even though an industry might not be growing, changes in what people want may create openings for entrepreneurs. Markets are in a constant state of flux as consumers change their tastes and preferences. People create fashions, and they respond to fashions that are thrust upon them. New niches open and close, each demanding different product characteristics. Cultural fads represent opportunities as they embody new beliefs about what products represent and how they should be consumed. The transitory nature of fads is perhaps the most explicit example of the limited life of niches and the need to be aware of their eventual death (and with it the opportunity for your business). But if your firm's productive technologies can be applied to the next fad, your business will represent a process of continual evolution.

The more the characteristics of demand change, the more opportunities are created for entrepreneurs who can respond rapidly to the changes. Research has shown that the greater the sales dynamics of industry niches, the greater the formation of new ventures.[7] The task is to be close to the market and to see the changes coming.

Demand can also be influenced by our expectation of the future, particularly for speculative goods. If people expect share prices will go up in the future, this will increase the demand for shares now. They will buy the shares with the intention of selling them at a higher price in the future. If enough people expect prices to go up, it could become a self-fulfilling prophecy, as those people buying shares do in fact push up demand. Playing on expectations is a common strategy of real-estate agents who "talk up the market" and encourage people to buy before the price goes up. Expectations can also affect non-speculative markets, but as in other areas of entrepreneurship, having early knowledge of trends and timing requires knowledge of the market. The distant investor who follows the herd is most likely to be hurt.

Opportunities can also be found by observing the price and changing consumption of complementary goods. Complementary goods are products that are used in conjunction with other products. This implies that you should look for products that complement others that have experienced price decreases (assuming the price decrease is not caused by a fall in demand). For example, cheaper airfares have meant more people are travelling, and this has expanded the market for accommodation, luggage, car rentals, insurance, tourist attractions and facilities.

The most obvious force that can increase the demand for a product is an increase in wealth. Generally speaking, a nation's wealth is determined by its ability to produce things that people want to buy. As a nation develops its productive capability and builds new markets, its wealth grows. Key factors behind this are technological advances and the rate of investment, as these raise a nation's productive capability. The most spectacular example of this over the past few decades has been in East Asia. With export success, more Asians were employed and earned more money, which created a growing domestic market for local entrepreneurs to exploit. They became wave riders on the growing demand.

Projections of future economic growth are easily obtainable from any bank but, because they are so freely available, gaining this information is unlikely to provide any great strategic advantage over your competitors. What is more important is information on which industries and niches are growing.

One feature of demand that can have a dramatic effect on the success of a business is the cyclical changes in demand. Business cycles can have a great impact on the prosperity of new businesses, because they raise the level of spending and potential demand. The term "cycle" implies that these variations are regular occurrences; however, they are far from regular. In fact "fluctuations" may be a better description. There is a great deal of variation in the length and intensity of these economic episodes. For example, the depression of the 1930s lasted for an entire decade and resulted in severe economic decline. Since then, the declines have been minor in comparison.

A number of factors can cause these fluctuations. In the long term, fluctuations are driven by the development of a country's productive capabilities, innovation and entrapment. For example, China is currently experiencing rapid growth in wealth as it acquires new production technologies. However, there are much shorter cycles than these. Some cycles have been linked to random effects such as sunspots, which affect our climate. Sunspots could have a major impact in the days when economies were predominantly agricultural. A change in climate could have a dramatic effect on agricultural output and prosperity.

Another event that affects economic output is war, but the impact of war depends on the nature of the economy and the nature of the war. In the days when economies were predominantly agricultural, a war would destroy crops, kill labor and disrupt trade, with a negative effect on economic growth. Wars in places like Africa still have this impact. However, wars can lead to a huge demand for military equipment and supplies that can boost production. This is particularly relevant in modern days when weaponry is sophisticated and requires much industrial activity to produce. Consequently, World War II resulted in a dramatic increase in economic activity. However, the danger with such artificial outbursts is that they are followed by a period of decline when the war ends.

Some business cycles have been linked to advances in technology. For example, the introduction of railways in the early 1800s provided a great spur to economic activity making trade and communication easier, while production of the railways themselves mobilized significant resources into higher value activity. In the following century, similar business cycles were stimulated by the arrival of the car and synthetic fibers. Some economists link business cycles to changes in the money supply. If the government puts too much money into the economy, it can stimulate the economy, albeit at the risk of causing inflation. On the other hand, if the government reduces the amount of money in the economy, the economy will enter a period of declining output and unemployment. In this way, the government's handling of monetary policy can have important implications for business opportunities.

A common feature of all these theories is the key role of investment. There is virtually universal agreement among economists that instability of investment is one of the main sources of economic fluctuations.[8] Whether the initial cause is an increase in money supply or a new product, it leads to an increase in the level of investment as people channel funds into production.

During the upswing of a typical cycle, businesses invest in plants and factories and employ more staff. These new workers will spend their income on other products, and this increases demand again, amplifying the initial burst into other parts of the economy. Other businesses enjoy this rise of custom and they too will increase their investment and hire more staff. This is an exciting period with an air of optimism pervading the business community. Some entrepreneurs may feel the time is right to launch business ideas they have been thinking about for some time, and many new technologies are commercialized during such upswings. They raise money for investment from banks and the share market, which typically enjoys a bull run.

If businesses think the economy is going to grow, they are more likely to invest in new business opportunities and take advantage of the growing market. That means buying capital items like equipment and plants. On the other hand, during a downswing few people are likely to invest in large-scale capital items like new factories if the outlook is bad. It is not surprising that the industries most vulnerable to business swings are those producing capital goods. For example, in the Great Depression of the 1930s, gross national product (GNP) in the United States fell by 30%, but output of producers of durable equipment fell by 75%. Businesspeople were not prepared to invest in plants during these trying economic conditions.

Clearly, people are more likely to invest in new production facilities during the upswing of a cycle; however, not all investments are productive. Historical experience has shown that business upswings are often associated with speculative frenzies. This happens when people invest not on the basis that their investment will lead to increased productivity but because they expect the value of their investment to increase. This happened in the United States in the 1920s as investors bought shares in the hope that the value of the shares would increase.

During speculative bouts it is often hard to distinguish between a safe and secure investment. The normal gauges involve comparing earnings from your investment with earnings from other forms of investment. For example, if your investment is paying a poor rate of return compared with the interest you could earn putting your money in a bank, it suggests that investment is being driven by speculation and the hope that your capital value will grow. On the stock exchange, "earnings per share" normally provides a healthy guide; however, many young companies don't pay in their early years, so there can be some confusion. However, over time, as these frenzies become more developed, it becomes more obvious which investments are based on sound business sense and which are merely milking the speculative investor. But this might not stop the hysteria simply because so much money can be made.

In the end, common sense can only be ignored for so long, and eventually these bubbles burst. People who thought they were great entrepreneurs during the bull run begin to discover the true depth of their entrepreneurial strategy. The sad thing is these burst bubbles have a negative impact on demand and, in so doing, bring an end to speculative investment and a reduction in productive investment.

Other factors, outside anyone's control, can also bring a positive run to an end, such as shocks in the international economy. Downturns can also result from too much investment as large numbers of investors jump on the bandwagon. We end up with too many producers seeking too few customers. Ian Richardson, an economist, pointed out that one problem investors have is they don't always know what other investors are doing.[9] This is a problem for many entrepreneurs who do their research and have a good product but have no way of knowing that other people are also eyeing their market. If they could coordinate their investment, we would be able to avoid these crises caused by overinvestment.

Fortunately, our ability to manage cycles has improved. Economists have learned a lot since the Great Depression, and a number of policy options exist to reduce the extremes of cyclical fluctuations (namely fiscal and monetary policy). To get economies out of troughs, governments can embark on expansionary fiscal policies whereby they increase spending to stimulate the economy. Alternatively, governments can revert to monetary policy options, which include tightening up on the money supply to stop an economy from getting overheated during the upswing (and carried away with speculative investment). During downswings, the government loosens up on the money supply to make it easier to invest. These options are widely known for their effectiveness, and it's amazing that many American entrepreneurs were surprised when the Federal Reserve raised interest rates at the peak of the dot-com boom.

* * *

Clearly, there are a number of things you must be aware of as a business cycle progresses. When the economy is expanding, it is a good time to start a business, but you must be open to several possibilities. First, other people who you are not aware of may be investing in the industry. This could lead to a situation of over-supply. Second, the Federal Reserve may respond with a rapid increase in interest rates to quell overheating in the economy. Third, the growth in demand will not go on forever, and there may be a sharp downturn. This can throw you into somewhat of a quandary—during the upturn, do you expand slowly and cautiously, keeping debt low so that you are ready for the shift in circumstances? Or do you go for all-out expansion and seek strength from a dominant market position?

Too many entrepreneurs start businesses with ambitious goals that they created during the cycle's upswing. They assume the good times will last forever. This is a particularly easy trap to fall into if the upswing has been particularly long. Good times become the norm, and it becomes hard to imagine just how painful a downturn can be. There may even be good logic behind expansive investment. For example, later in this book we talk about the importance of expanding output quickly to gain economies of scale and reduce costs. This places the entrepreneur in a bind over whether to batten down the hatches and reduce debt or do the opposite and finance expansion. It places an emphasis on reading long-range economic forecasts.

The answer to these strategy options will depend on a number of factors. Principally, what is driving the growth? For example, if the boom is being fuelled by a number of new products, how long will it be before the markets are saturated, bringing an end to the growth? This leads to the second factor: the age of the cycle. If the upswing is relatively new, it would suggest that the downturn is some way off, allowing time to stake out a market share. However, as the cycle ages and the downturn appears nearer, it might be wise to be more cautious. Of course, other factors will affect your eventual decision, including the state of the industry at the time, its outlook, and the quality of information you have about the industry.

When cycles are associated with speculative bubbles, a good gauge of how much to invest can be found in the value of those items that speculators are investing in. For example, if people are speculating in land because its value is spiralling, it is wise to look at the returns from land in terms of rental and compare that to the returns gained by putting money in the bank. If the rental returns are very low compared with bank returns, it tells you that the value of property does not reflect underlying fundamentals. A market correction can be expected—it is just a matter of when—and when that correction comes, it could hurt you even though you are not in the property market, as many Americans are learning following the subprime mortgage collapse.

The cycle is important, as it affects the income flow, but if you have sufficient capital to ride out periods with low income, downturns can offer great possibilities. It is a period in which many businesses, land and capital are available at low cost. The problem is estimating how long the trough will last and therefore how much capital you need to endure it.

One key characteristic of economic cycles is that, although there are always rises and falls, the overall trend is one of rising economic activity. The peaks and troughs are always higher than the ones before it. In the long term, modern economies have a tendency to grow, as do the markets that make them up. If your market shares this tendency, the key is to survive the temporary downturns by limiting exposure. If a downturn is imminent, reduce your debt, forget those high-risk deals, and pay closer attention to the credit worthiness of your customers. They may go down and take you with them.

Supply-Driven Opportunities

> The successful man is the one who had the chance and took it.
> Roger Babson, founder Babson United, Inc.

In the 1850s, the thought of using steamships for transoceanic trade was nothing new, but few people could make it work. The first movers met a bad end, including the pioneering Great Western Steamship Company, which ceased operations in 1852. It was an idea but not yet an opportunity. The problem was fuel. The engines at the time consumed huge amounts of coal and were not economical. Until someone designed more efficient engines, no one was going to make it rich from ocean-going steamships.

Compounding was one possible solution. The process of compounding expands the steam twice, therefore getting more use from the coal and reducing coal requirements (and costs). But to make engines strong enough to handle the pressure, stronger steel was needed. In other words, there was little opportunity to create a steamship business due to the poor supply of engines, and these engines in turn were handicapped by the supplies of poor steel.

It required a change in the environment to turn the idea into an opportunity, in particular improvements in technology and related industries. Eventually, advances in the making of steel (with the converter patented by Henry Bessemer and the refinement of the open-hearth process by Siemens, Martin and Gilchrist Thomas) meant that stronger steel boilers could be made to withstand higher pressures. This opened a window of opportunity as engine makers could now supply economical steam engines to entrepreneurs who could build and manage steamship companies. In 1874, the first deep-sea commercial steamer fitted with a triple-expansion engine was built, and a new wave of entrepreneurship was launched in which many people made their fortunes.

In this example, a change in supplies turned an idea into an opportunity. All businesses are dependent on the goods with which they are supplied, and a change in these can open opportunity. In particular, if the cost of supplies is coming down, it can open up markets that previously could not afford a product. If you can find an industry with declining costs and customers who are price sensitive, a good opportunity might be opening.

There are a number of forces that affect supply of a good in the market. These include resources and other producers that use them. However, opportunities can come not just from the initial change in supply but from a second wave of opportunities that the initial change spawns. This spawning of opportunities can be seen in the activities of John D. Rockefeller, who at one time was the richest man in the world. When oil supplies were being discovered in the United States, Rockefeller did not invest in the first wave of opportunities, oil wells, for he saw too many "wildcat" oil men drilling for oil and pushing down the price. Instead, he invested in oil refineries, where he could take advantage of the cheap oil the wildcats supplied him with. Sometimes we need to look beyond the first range of opportunities and see what supplies are needed and what industries it supplies.

In basic economics we are taught that the supply of a product is affected by the changing price of the resources used in its production. In the steamship example, the price of steel affected the viability of the engine and steamship industry. It was also affected by other industries that used steel. But the relationship is not always straightforward; for example, in some cases, if other industries also used steel, this could have pushed up the price of steel for shipbuilders. On the other hand, these other users may have encouraged steel producers to invest further into cost-reduction technologies and exploited economies of scale. This would have reduced the price of steel for shipbuilders and made their businesses more profitable.

The price of a resource affects the industries that use it, and some entrepreneurial opportunities might be found by observing industries that use similar resources. For example, sheep farming and forestry are unrelated industries except that they both use land. A reduction in the price of wool will reduce the price of agricultural land. As land becomes cheaper, it makes it easier for entrepreneurs to use it for other business ideas, whether they be forestry, tourism or other agricultural uses.

Paul Sykes built a business venture that utilized resources made available after an industry declined, specifically the UK steel industry, whose demise freed up land in Sheffield's Don Valley. With that industry's decline, the price of land fell, and this made it possible for Sykes's idea to become a reality. Sykes believed the trend for out-of-town developments prevalent in the United States at the time would eventually spread to the United Kingdom. Consequently, the land gave him the resources to pursue an imitative strategy. In a partnership with property developer Eddie Healey, the center was built. The center was sold in 1999 for £1.2 billion, at which time Sykes had a 40% shareholding.[10]

Another factor that you must keep an eye on is the number of sellers in a market. It is basic economics that if there are many sellers in a market, competition will push the price down and reduce profit. Research has shown that industries with a higher rate of competition had a higher rate of business failure.[11]

Rockefeller's strategies were guided by the principle that competition reduces profit. It was the large number of competitors that put him off entering the drilling business and led him to invest in refineries where the competition was less intense. But even in the refinery business, Rockefeller was driven by this simple principle. He spent substantial effort to reduce the number of oil refineries in the business to the point where his company, Standard Oil, ended up in a near monopoly situation.

The number of competitors reflects how easy it is to enter an industry. Some industries are easier to enter because they need low skill levels or capital or perhaps they involve simple technologies. If you enter an industry with few barriers of entry, you may soon be faced with large numbers of competitors, which can reduce the price of the product and your profit.

Because of this relationship, it is generally believed that if there are only a few businesses in an industry, there must be barriers to entry, but this is not always the case, as Richard Branson discovered. In 1985, AIDS was becoming a serious health issue in Britain, but very little money was being spent advertising condoms. One of the main reasons was the structure of the industry. One company, London International Group, dominated the industry. Its product Durex accounted for 9 out of 10 condoms sold. The company had grown fat and was happy to charge high prices and milk the market. Richard Branson's interest in this industry was not profit but preventing the spread of disease. He wanted more people to use condoms to help stem the spread of AIDS.

Branson decided to set up a new company, aggressively advertise and lower the price of condoms so they would be more readily available. To manage the task, he employed John Jackson, who had broad experience with health care products, and he contracted Ansell, an American company, to make the product. This done, they then inserted 18,000 vending machines in pubs and gas stations around Britain. Even though the price was 60% less than that charged by Durex, the company made a £1 million profit in its first year of operation. The lesson is obvious: some industries with few suppliers may be easy to enter and generate exceptional profit, because existing companies have gotten fat.[12]

Another factor that affects supply is the expectations of those in the market. We have already mentioned how expectations affect demand. They also affect supply. For example, if we believe that prices for a product we sell may go up in the future, we may hold onto it to gain a higher price in the future. In Chapter 8, we will see this strategy used by Sri Lankan entrepreneurs who stored their rice until the harvest glut was over and then released their product on a higher market. To be able to follow this strategy requires knowledge of how markets change over time and an ability to store products over time. It would not work with perishable goods like bananas or products that can rapidly become out of date.

Perhaps the biggest force that affects supply is technology. When considering the effect of technology on supply, economists normally think in terms of cost-reducing technologies that shift the supply curve to the right. But, as we will read in the following chapters, technology can also play a major role in creating new products, adding value to existing products and developing markets.

Sometimes technologies provide opportunities for new players, simply because established companies don't introduce them. Consider the U.S. steel industry, which was once the strongest in the world. In the 1970s, American steelmakers were slow to respond to innovations that might have reduced costs, particularly the basic oxygen furnace process and continuous casting.[13] This slowness left open an opportunity for new steelmakers from other nations to adopt the new technologies, then take markets away from the Americans because of their lower prices.

There were a number of reasons why the established American companies were slow to adopt the new technology. One reason was the structure of the U.S. industry, where one company (U.S. Steel) possessed 60% of the nation's raw steel capacity. This lack of competition had created a structure whose emphasis was not technical development but stability.[14] Innovation was of little concern. If there had been change in the demand for steel, there might have been some change in production; however, relationships with steel consumers were remarkably stable. To some extent this slowness in adopting the latest processes was also a result of unlucky timing. The companies undertook a major expansionary push just before the new technological advances had been made.[15] Having made a major investment in fixed capital, steelmakers had limited ability to make alterations in production processes. It is a reminder of the importance of timing and luck. But, generally speaking, their failure was a result of their past success, which had created complacency at all levels of the industry.[16] The conservative nature of the established American companies created an opportunity for new players to enter and succeed in the market. If you can see these conservative forces at work in an industry, an opportunity might exist for you to enter it.

Government-Political Waves

In the mid-1980s Gordon Wu became one of the first foreign entrepreneurs to invest in China.[17] At a time when few foreigners were prepared to invest significant funds in this market, Wu was a pioneer. His company, Hopewell, built power plants and highways and earned a reputation for successful and profitable completion of the projects that he undertook. These early experiences allowed him to develop a reputation as a credible supplier and also helped him to secure personal relationships with key political figures.

Wu was now in the right time at the right place. China was making significant changes in its economic structure, which was propelling the country on a new growth wave. This meant there was a growing demand for the construction of infrastructural projects in which he had built significant expertise. Wu's early work helped him to catch this new wave. His reputation and negotiation skills helped him to secure favorable terms with the governments he dealt with. He was also careful to make good political connections wherever he invested. It was a deliberate part of his strategy. However, such projects left him vulnerable to changes in policy, and in 1993, a policy change capped profits for companies like Wu's at 12% (which gives an idea of the extent of the profits he had been earning beforehand). This caused him to turn to other parts of Asia. In the middle of 1993, Hopewell began building a $3 billion to $4 billion transit project in Bangkok. He also gained contracts to build power plants in Pakistan and the Philippines. By 1994, Hopewell's market capitalization was $3.764 billion. It continues to ride the growth of Asian economies and is now a cash-rich giant.

Changes in government policy can provide many entrepreneurial opportunities. Not only do governments have large resources at their disposal, but they set the rules by which markets operate. As in the market, exploiting government-based opportunities requires an ability to identify change and the implications of those changes, something the distant observer is not always capable of doing. It requires contacts and keeping your ear to the ground.

A major form of government change that can open up opportunities is shifting government expenditure. Governments have large budgets at their disposal, so it pays to stay aware of them. Many U.S. fortunes were made from government expenditure. For example, although Rockefeller made his mark in oil, his first fortune was made selling provisions to the Union army during the Civil War. He was not the only one to benefit this way. Shipbuilders W. Cramp and Sons took off during the same war building boats for the Northern navy.

Governments also make a significant impact on the market when they introduce regulations on production and consumption. Governments frequently pass laws that affect what consumers can and cannot buy. They are effectively changing consumer tastes by decree and, in so doing, can open and close markets for entrepreneurs. For example, a law requiring all cyclists to wear safety helmets can open up a market for helmet producers. Governments also set rules regarding what producers can and cannot do. For example, in the 1990s many entrepreneurs benefited from a raft of deregulation, which saw entrepreneurs enter areas such as radio and airlines, areas previously reserved for government producers.

Significant opportunities can open when governments change the way they manage their owned resources. Governments own significant resources that have productive potential. Sometimes they own these for noneconomic reasons such as conservation, or sometimes they take over problems that no one else wants to own. Recognizing the true potential of these and opening up negotiations for their use can be quite profitable. In these negotiations you need to recognize that government ownership of these assets is not driven by profit but by other concerns. Changes in these other areas of concern can have implications for entrepreneurs. For example, sometimes opportunities open as more knowledge is made available on the environmental impact of an industry or ways are found to make an industry environmentally safe. This might include opening up a goldmine on government land with environmentally safe mining techniques or a ski field in a conservation park. An assessment of government land can be quite enlightening.

Weidenbaum argues that businesses have three approaches they can take with regard to public policy.[18] The first is passive reaction, in which a business simply reacts to government policy as it occurs. A company taking this approach does not manage its environment. It simply responds to change as it occurs. The second approach is positive anticipation, in which a business is aware that changes are coming and anticipates these changes when it makes its business strategies. Once again, the business does not attempt to influence government policy, but it is more proactive in that it anticipates change in its policy.

The third approach is public policy shaping, in which the business becomes actively involved in government policy formation. A company taking this option tries to shape political outcomes so that they are aligned with its own interests. In this way, entrepreneurs can use the public policy process to create opportunities.

History is full of examples of political entrepreneurs. Many great Japanese companies like Mitsui and Mitsubishi were created by "seisho" merchants (merchants by the grace of political consideration). Similarly, today's Russian resource billionaires have risen to the top by manipulating the political process. Each country has its own political regimes with its own idiosyncrasies. So how do you become a political entrepreneur in the West?

Political entrepreneurs scan the environment for any opportunity where they can apply their skills for political gain.[19] While established players focus on the political status quo, political entrepreneurs actively attempt to facilitate policy change. There are a number of ways of doing this. For example, if an entrepreneur becomes aware that some government officials are interested in developing an idea, the political entrepreneur can offer information and advice that can shape the process. Government officials often have their own agendas and areas of interest. Political entrepreneurs need to keep up with developments in government to know when political interests are converging with theirs or detect a changing mood that can be harnessed.

There are a number of approaches that entrepreneurs can utilize when attempting to shape government policy. Hilmann and Hitt suggest three generic strategies that can be used to affect the political process.[20] The first is information strategy, in which a businessperson seeks to affect public policy by providing policy makers specific information about the options the government officials are considering. It may mean providing information on the costs and benefits of the different options that the government is considering. Information can be provided through a number of means, from lobbying, research reports and surveys, expert testimonies at policy meetings, or simply supplying policy makers with technical reports on the matter.

The second political strategy is financial incentive strategy, in which the entrepreneur targets political decision makers directly and through financial inducements. It may involve providing financial support to political parties or giving generous honoraria for speaking engagements.

The third strategy is constituency-building strategy, in which the entrepreneur works to gain the support of individual voters and citizens, who in turn seek to influence political decision makers. It is often called a bottom-up strategy because it seeks to gain grassroots support of sympathetic constituents. This may include employees, customers, suppliers and others linked to the firm. Mobilizing this support can be done through advertising, public relations programs, press conferences, and economic or political education. Constituency building must be managed carefully. A common technique is to encourage constituents to bombard politicians with faxes, emails and signed petitions. However, these techniques are often ineffective. Such techniques are easy to organize, but they do not indicate how strongly constituents feel about an issue. Signing a petition is something people do in a shopping mall with very little indication of how strongly they are committed to an issue, so governments give them little weight. They are also easy for your opponents to duplicate.[21] A personal letter or visit can be far more effective in portraying commitment.

Many entrepreneurs lack the resources for political contributions and have limited means to engage in constituency building, so they rely on lobbying as their principal political weapon. Of course, entrepreneurs can expand their resource base by joining together with other parties with similar interests. This may mean joining with other small firms or forming an industry-wide coalition. It could involve linking together with suppliers and customers (those in the vertical chain), those in other industries or creating your own coalition.[22] However, in joining with others, you may also be priming future competition and reducing your future rewards.

The lobbying process must be managed carefully. Gaining access to important officials will not necessarily translate into political advantage.[23] Entrepreneurs need to recognize that government officials have their own time and resource constraints.

If you gain a reputation for providing superior useful information, you are more likely to have success.

When presenting information, you may find yourself in three types of argument.[24] The first is a fact-based or science-based argument, in which the entrepreneur presents fact and rebuts arguments put forward by those opposing him or her. It may involve scientific and factual evidence about the subject, in which case the entrepreneur has to present an argument based on the stronger fact—a more rational debate.

A second type of argument rests on economic efficiency, in which politicians will consider the policy change in light of the economic benefits it creates. Will the economy perform more efficiently as a result of this policy change and benefit the nation's consumers, producers and others who may be affected? Finally, you may find yourself arguing in terms of distributional equity and fairness. Some of your opponents may argue that opening up a market will lead to some people benefiting at the expense of others. In which case, you will need to argue that opening up a market will not have a positive or neutral effect on incomes, etc.

Case Study: The Political Entrepreneur

An excellent example of opportunity creation through political management can be seen in the advent of Microwave Communications Inc. (MCI).[25] In its formative years, MCI's strategy was driven by its political strategy as it tried to open an opportunity in the long-distance telephone market. This market was regulated by the Federal Communications Commission (FCC), which had given one company a virtual monopoly. That company was AT&T.

Most economists at the time believed that long-distance telecommunications transmission was a "natural monopoly," which means that, due to the high capital costs in the industry, it would be more efficient to have only one producer. Otherwise, the industry would be burdened with costly duplication of resources. For that reason, AT&T was given the whole market, but it had to comply with the regulations of the FCC.

During World War II, alternative telecommunication technologies were developed, including microwave radio, which made it possible to transmit data without the costly wire connections used by AT&T. These innovations reduced the capital required for the industry and weakened the argument to keep the industry as a monopoly. Although this provided an efficient alternative, the FCC would not open the market to other companies.

In the 1960s, other changes occurred that affected the demand for telecommunications services. These included the increased use of business computers and the associated need to connect computer terminals and transmit data from different locations. However, AT&T did not make it easy for companies wanting to make these connections. Many came to believe that AT&T's monopoly restricted efficiency in the market and stressed the need for competition. These changes would create the momentum to create an opportunity for new service companies.

In 1963, MCI was founded by an entrepreneur with the intention of competing with AT&T using microwave technology. However, AT&T opposed any policy change that would allow MCI and others to enter the market. MCI had embarked on a David-and-Goliath struggle. It was taking on a company whose revenues were equal to almost 2% of the GNP of the United States. In such circumstances, the company floundered. Between 1963 and 1969, it battled AT&T and the FCC but generated no revenues.

In 1968, William G. McGowan became MCI's new CEO, with an objective of turning MCI into a microwave system provider connecting a number of major cities. This strategy required assertive political action, so McGowan moved the company's headquarters to Washington; an indication that political management was central to the company's success. McGowan realized his company was too small to take on the might of AT&T, so he looked for allies. However, few people shared MCI's interests. Those in the industry were anxious not to offend AT&T, which provided all their communications services. Other companies and lobby groups simply didn't consider telecommunications a priority. It fell to McGowan to lead the political attack and open the business opportunity.

McGowan set himself the task of developing contacts, testifying to Congress and promoting MCI's case to the FCC. He became known as the "most politically active CEO in any industry."[26] Together with his two top managers, he became acutely attuned to political trends. McGowan marketed his political package to targeted audiences receptive to deregulation and competition. This included officials in the FCC, the Justice Department and the White House who believed that competition would bring advantages to the telecommunications industry. The arguments could be couched in economic terms, stressing the benefits to customers and the role of competition in stimulating technological innovation. There was also concern with inefficiencies stemming from AT&T's monopoly power and frustration over its lack of cooperation. The argument for change was also couched in terms of broader social goals, and this helped attract post-Watergate reformers in Congress. The debate drew on concerns of economic advancement and consumer welfare. Government officers who shared these concerns became welcome allies for MCI. Finally, in 1976, MCI joined together with a few other small companies to establish the Ad Hoc Committee for Competitive Telecommunications (ACCT), which handled the less glamorous lobbying tasks.

The process of creating opportunities in the telecommunication market was long and fragmented. For example, a decision by the FCC in 1971, the Specialized Carrier Decision, opened the door to MCI but did not clearly delineate the boundaries of its activities, so MCI repeatedly performed activities that tested the limits of these regulations. If AT&T or the FCC attempted to restrain MCI, the company turned to the courts. The 1970s were a period in which a number of legal battles were fought to gain market access, including an antitrust suit against AT&T in 1974.

In the end, political and legal activity opened up the business opportunity that MCI then richly exploited. Key to McGowan's success was the support from FCC regulators and other government officials. McGowan's efficient use of information helped him to develop a reputation that granted him continued access and influence with key decision makers. His persistence and effective political management meant that the final industry outcome chosen was the one most favorable to MCI.

MCI's legal activities had one other positive consequence. It became a marketing tool for the firm. By the time the long distance markets were opened for competition, MCI had already established a name ahead of the other newcomers. This helped MCI raise equity and resulted in it gaining the largest market share among the new companies.

McGowan was a formidable political entrepreneur, changing public policy in a way that opened business opportunities that it later exploited. Of course, MCI could not have exploited those political maneuverings if it did not have the business and technological capabilities to back it up. The political strategy was only one arm of a business strategy, albeit a very important one. You should not be intimidated reading the exploits of McGowan, for political entrepreneurship can occur at all government levels, from central government to small local councils. At all levels, possibilities exist for political entrepreneurs to create business opportunities.

Catching the Wave Too Early

So far, we have stressed the importance of being early to catch changes in the environment. But it is worth recalling the example of the Great Western Steamship Company, which pioneered steamship technology. It moved too early when the technology was not yet feasible and failed. The dangers in being too early are not just technical. Feasibility may be limited by market or government barriers, as Hong Kong entrepreneur Lo Chiu-Hung found out.[27] Lo Chiu-Hung took a brave step of investing in production in China in 1973. At the time, China was still under the influence of the Cultural Revolution and had a very different political-economic environment from today. Lo found that doing business with China's state enterprises was extremely difficult, and she did not benefit from her investments. Lo recalled one painful experience:

> State managers in China after a long time in isolation from the outside world did not know the significance of punctual delivery and quality control. A cargo of the company's finished products was urgently packed to beat the deadline for Christmas Sales in the USA. Later, Lo was told by the country officials involved in the state enterprise that her cargo had not been arranged for delivery because the train had been diverted to transport moon-cakes to Hong Kong for the mid-autumn festival. Consequently, she lost several hundred dollars.[28]

Being a first-mover can be dangerous. There are still many things that have not been tried and tested, and there may be a need for significant learning. In this case, Lo learned that business could still be done in China but not in Shanghai, which was too far from Hong Kong and created communication problems. So, in 1977, she established a processing factory in nearby Fukian and subsequently prospered.

To avoid being too early, it is useful to think in terms of thresholds. Important features in the environment must reach a threshold that will support the business. For example, when the Great Western Steamship Company was launched, the steamship had not reached a technological threshold that made it an effective producer. Similarly in 1973, the Chinese government's knowledge and experience of business had not reached a threshold that would support foreign investment. Most often, the important threshold is demand; consumer demand needs to reach a level where there are enough consumers to support a business. If the environment has not reached those thresholds, the business will suffer. Before launching your business, you should identify those crucial features in the environment on which your business relies and carefully examine whether those thresholds have been reached.

If we define products and services as technology applied to human problems, it is not too hard to grasp the importance of thresholds. For a product to function, it relies on a certain level of technology. For it to sustain a business, it relies on a minimum-size market. Once a demand or technology threshold is met, an idea becomes feasible and an entrepreneurial opportunity is opened for someone to seize.

The importance of thresholds for entrepreneurs can be more easily understood if we define products and services as technology applied to human demand. When technology and demand change, so too do the opportunities to make new products and meet new needs. For example, when the two-stroke engine arrived as a new technology, a number of entrepreneurs built successful businesses by linking the technology to different consumer needs. Some applied it to the forestry industry and built the chainsaw. Others applied it to transportation with the two-stroke motor bike. Others found uses for it in recreation, with the surf ski. Changes in technology enable us to exploit demand. Changes in demand allow us to exploit technology.

Thresholds are not restricted to technology and demand. They are equally important in other environmental forces such as levels of government support and levels of business infrastructure, including the opening of transportation routes and communication channels. A change in any of these can create an opening once a significant threshold is reached that can support a business.

Chapter 4

Technology, New Products and Pioneers

Opportunity is missed by most people because it is dressed in overalls and looks like work.

(Thomas Edison)

The need for light at night is a very basic human value, and over the years, a number of products have been introduced to meet this need. Among the earliest are candles, kerosene lamps and whale oil. At the turn of the nineteenth century, gas lighting became the preferred technology after a method was found for distilling gas from wood and coal. The gas lamp was a popular product, offering five times as much light as a candle, and it gave birth to a number of new enterprises.[1] By 1870, there were 350 gas firms in the United States alone.

The next wave in lighting products came after scientific breakthroughs in electricity opened up new possibilities. However, a number of technological problems needed to be solved before light could be made by electricity, and a number of inventors in England, Germany and the United States all struggled with the problem. The question was who would be the first to realize the opportunity? In the forefront was an Englishman by the name of Joseph W. Swan, who had designed a lamp using a carbonized paper filament inside a glass vacuum. The design worked, but the lamps burned out quickly.

Every advance by one inventor raised the ladder and brought the industry closer to the window of opportunity. Finally, one man put all these pieces of information together and came up with something that crossed the threshold. That man was Thomas Edison, who had previously succeeded with a number of other inventions. This early success gave him the resources to establish an R&D laboratory, where 40 mechanics and technicians worked with new technologies, creating new products. Their quest for lighting from electricity was multifaceted. Not only did they look for a more reliable filament, but they developed a more efficient dynamo for generating electricity, and they developed wiring systems. This team eventually came up with an "electric candle" that could reliably be sold as a product. It was cleaner, safer and more convenient than any lighting technology that had gone before.

Naturally, the gas companies did not like this new product, and one went as far as sending an electrician to sabotage a public display put on by Edison. A more enduring way of combating the electric lamp was improving their own product, and the gas companies undertook a number of product improvements. These included the introduction of the gas mantle in 1883 that glowed more brightly. The new mantle provided a fivefold improvement in gas-lighting efficiency and reduced cost by two-thirds. As a result of these improvements, gas remained competitive with Edison's product. It took 12 years before Edison returned a profit, but the electric lamp also underwent improvements in both the product and the way it was made. In the end electricity had more technological potential than gas, and the gas industry could not compete. The electric candle, now known as the incandescent lamp, had won.

The design that emerged in the 1880s remained the basis for lamps into the twentieth century, but it still enjoyed advances, including a change in the filament to ductile tungsten in 1910, which offered six times as much light over the first filaments and lasted 66% longer. Most important were the improvements in production. The first light bulbs were made by hand and involved more than 200 different steps. With more skill and experience and the introduction of mechanized production techniques, the cost was reduced in 1896 to 20% what it had been in 1880.

The relentless walk of science continued to affect the lighting industry, and in the 1930s a technology arrived that released a new wave of product development; fluorescent lighting. The first commercial fluorescent lighting was actually developed by Edison's company (now called General Electric) and Westinghouse as a collaborative effort. Fluorescent lamps were far more energy efficient than the now-old incandescent lamps. However, neither of the two companies wanted to introduce the new lamps to the market out of fear of alienating the power companies who did not want to see energy consumption reduced. Sylvania was a company that did not care if it offended the power companies. It only had 5.5% of the lamp market and saw no prospects for expansion. To Sylvania the new technology was a window of opportunity that it aggressively seized, capturing 20% of the new and growing market.

The history of the light industry illustrates how advances in science can be applied to improve products and increase the value for money received by customers. This pattern is not restricted to lighting, and waves of innovation, as illustrated in Figure 4.1, have characterized a number of industries. For example, typewriters have progressed from manual typewriters to electric typewriters to word processors and to personal computers with word processing software. Each new product embodies an increase in value for the customer. Each wave of innovation unleashed opportunities for entrepreneurs to commence new businesses.

When a new wave of innovation arrives, producers of the old product often have trouble making the transition to the new technology. They have invested in skills, machinery and ways of thinking that are simply not applicable to the new technology. For example, Royal, which produced manual typewriters, was eclipsed by IBM when electric typewriters came along. A company's ability to adapt to change is dependent on whether its existing business and technical capabilities can be applied

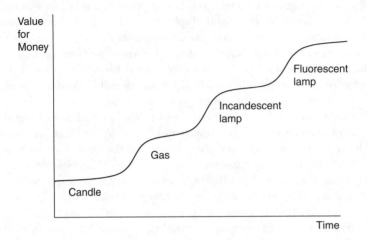

Figure 4.1 Waves of Product Development: Increased Value for Money

to the new technology. With this in mind, innovations have been classified as either competence-enhancing or competence-destroying. A competence-enhancing innovation builds on the know-how that existing firms have. The innovation is not too different from that already in place, and existing firms can easily adopt it. However, a competence-destroying innovation renders all the old skills and knowledge obsolete. Such technologies are radically different from the past, and old firms have trouble changing with the times. This creates opportunities for new players to enter the industry and take over from the old firms.[2]

Technology, Science and New Products

The example of the lighting industry reveals the key role that science and technology play in new product development. Even the simplest products require at least a basic technology to shape them into a commodity that we value. We could in fact define products and services as technology applied to problems.

Not all advances in science result in technological change, and it is necessary to distinguish between pure science and applied science. Pure science deals with basic issues that might not have any relevance to everyday living. It addresses underlying principles and relationships in the scientific world. It is in applied science where these principles are put to work. As its name suggests, applied science is the application of science to specific problems and technologies. Advances in applied science increase our options when it comes to designing products, solving problems and adding value to people's lives.

Given that advances in pure science do not always have an immediate flow-on effect for technology, it raises the question whether it is best to fund pure or applied science. It is common for industry to want university scientists to do more applied research, while, in response, some university scientists believe they should be left alone to advance human knowledge free from commercial influence. These scientists believe that industry should do its own research. Of course, there is a wide range of opinions as to the role of university research, and many scientists enjoy contacts with industry and the chance to do applied research. It is also a good way to earn some extra income.

The interaction between science and product development can be seen in a study by Gibbons and Johnston.[3] They conducted interviews with people directly involved in the technical development of new products in Britain. Their task was to reveal the role of science in these innovations and, in particular, to find out where the product developers get their information from. This research was done before the days of the Internet, which has revolutionized information gathering. Nevertheless, the study clearly illustrates new product development as a process involving information amalgamation.

They looked at 30 innovations and found that, on average, each required 29.6 pieces of information. The type of information needed included such things as knowledge on the existence or availability of equipment, or materials with particular properties. The information sources are broken down into three groups: 1) personal, which draws on the experience and education of the person developing the new product; 2) sources from inside the firm, such as superiors and colleagues; and 3) a wide range of sources outside the firm. A full list is given in Table 4.1.

These are quite technical products, so there is a natural bias toward technical sources of information. The two main information sources were scientific literature and personal contact with scientists. Most of the scientific literature was in the form of reports of original work carried out in universities, which, when originally written, was not directed to any product or innovation. Personal contact with scientists in universities contributed to innovation in a number of ways. They provided information concerning general theories and the properties of materials used. They also played a supportive role, advising on the feasibility of a proposed solution, providing details on where information or specialist facilities could be found and sometimes offering services to help overcome problems. However, in terms of sheer numbers, scientific sources do not figure prominently, as can be seen in the table. One problem with the information in Table 4.1 is that it doesn't indicate how important each piece was. Although the scientific source may have only been used once, it could have made the difference between success and failure.

One example of the role played by pure scientific research and scientists can be seen in the development of an improved tungsten-halogen lamp system. In this case, the person designing the product needed to find a suitable form in which both phosphorus and halogen could be used in the lamp. A search of the scientific literature revealed the existence of a class of compounds called phosphonitrilic halides, which was ideal for the purpose. However, these compounds made the lamps go black. The designer thought this blacking was due to decomposition, but once again, scientists helped to overcome the problem and place the designer on the right track.

Table 4.1 Sources of Information for New Products (Adapted from Gibbons and Johnson)

Outside firm	No.	Inside Firm	No.	Personal	No.
Trade literature	43	Analysis and	183	Experience	255
Technical literature	22	experiment		with company	
Scientific literature	36	Superior	25	Experience	58
Textbooks	8	Colleague	17	with other	
Handbooks	20	Other departments	17	companies	
Reps & customers	20	Other divisions	7	Education	150
Suppliers	39	Company manual	9	Superior	12
Universities	30	Company report	6	Colleague	7
Prof. institutions	3	Library services	3	Trade reps	17
British standards	12			Customers &	45
Exhibitions	2			suppliers	
Consultants	12			Institute	20
Gov't agencies	11			meetings	
Field tests	8			Trade literature	84
Conferences	4			Technical	84
Research assns	24			literature	
Patents	6			Scientific	20
				literature	
				Sales	3
				department	
				Universities	4
				Research	2
				associations	
	300		267		761

A discussion with chemists at a nearby university who had worked with these compounds provided an alternative explanation. They suggested that the blacking may result from impurities, which could be removed by preparing the compound in a different solvent. As part of the solution, the chemists also analyzed samples using their more sensitive equipment at the university.

As this example shows, the role of the scientists was responsive. They were not the ones who came up with the idea for the product, but they played an important role in making the idea become a reality. The scientists responded to problems put to them: sometimes providing information directly, sometimes suggesting ways in which the problem might be tackled, sometimes helping to narrow the options, and sometimes providing equipment and procedures to test the product's feasibility. One important role played by the scientist was that of "translating" the information from scientific journals into a form meaningful to the designer and the problem at hand. All in all, scientists in universities played little or no role in initiating the innovations, yet they frequently contributed to the resolution of technical problems as they arose. Once started on the path suggested by scientists, development frequently proceeded with few major stumbling blocks.

If industrial designers could be described as fishermen fishing in a pool of knowledge, then scientists would be the ones who keep it stocked with fish. Scientists are also able to point out where the fish are in the pool and even present fishermen with suitable specimens. Gibbons and Johnson's study also noted that science plays an important role in educating the staff who become the product designers. The staff provide access to newly generated knowledge. Science also contributes in areas where government, industry and university interaction is more intense, such as aerospace.

In this study, the original ideas for products did not come from scientists. Perhaps the company saw a need in the market for the product, so it applied its technical strengths to solving it. Alternatively, perhaps a technical person in the company had an idea on which the subsequent information and design processes were built. Most R&D efforts start with a need that is recognized to create a product, and the developers then reached back to science to find the tools and knowledge to make it happen.[4] However, a study by Scott Shane noted that one patented technology gave rise to eight different ventures.[5] In this case, the technology came first, and the eight entrepreneurs then recognized how the technology could be used. Each recognized a different opportunity to use the technology, and that use reflected their past experiences. This illustrates that innovations can be both demand-driven in response to customer need and supply-driven as new technologies expand the range of possibilities.

Scientific knowledge opens up new possibilities for entrepreneurs, and the first people to recognize those possibilities will be those with access to that knowledge and the ability to apply it. This suggests that those people with technological expertise are in a better position to develop new products and add value to existing ones. However, opportunities stemming from science are not restricted to technical people. Often a technical change can radiate a wide range of opportunities for nontechnical entrepreneurs. Scott Shane argues that the ability of an entrepreneur to recognize the potential of a technology depends on the entrepreneur's previous experience solving customer problems in related markets.[6] This enables the entrepreneur to recognize the market potential of that technology. Similarly, Hills and Shrader's survey of entrepreneurs revealed that most successful ideas stemmed from entrepreneurs' prior experience of customers and markets.[7]

Developing new products is a common path into business ownership. Each year, an enormous number of products are introduced to the market. According to one study, 25,261 products were released in 1997 alone.[8] That is 69 new products a day. Of course not all new products will be released by entrepreneurs. Many of them will be developed by corporations extending their product range.

Unfortunately, many well-funded and researched products have cost their innovators dearly. A 1993 study of 11,000 new products found that only 56% of the products that reached the market were still being sold five years later.[9] That gives a failure rate of 44%, but even this figure might understate the failures, as it only includes products that made the market. It does not include products that were not released due to design failures or other shortfalls. A common finding is that new products do not live up to expectations in some aspect of performance, whether it be sales volume, profitability, distributor acceptance or its effect on corporate image.[10] Clearly, it is not enough to merely have a new product. It is only human nature to get excited about an idea for a business, but excitement can blur objective judgment. If you love your idea, you need to take a step back and ask yourself:

1   Does your offering satisfy a real customer need, or have you been overcome by wishful thinking?
2   Does your offering have a distinct advantage that makes it a better value for money than existing competition?
3   Does a market exist that is big enough to sustain a business, and what will it take to reach that threshold?

Pioneering New Products and Services

Problems with pioneering a new product can occur when the business model you intend to introduce is vastly different from anything that has previously existed and, as a result, is incompatible with the existing institutional and environmental structure. Pioneering by definition involves breaking new ground. Your idiosyncratic views that have enabled you to perceive an opportunity that others have not yet noticed might be an advantage with opportunity identification, but it can also be a problem when it comes to implementing your business model. To succeed, entrepreneurs rely on others to share their views, but if others do not have the same experiences or interpretations, you can struggle to raise finance, gain regulatory approval, or attract customers. It is ironic that the same reason pioneers succeed is one of the reasons that resistance occurs. Entrepreneurs often come across their informational advantage because they actively search their environment and keep up with the latest advances in various fields. By contrast, legislators and banks do not peruse the environment with the same motives.

The problem is made worse in that institutions are bound by rules that reflect the times in which they were made. An example can be seen in my home country New Zealand, where a law called the Resource Management Act was introduced to safeguard the environment from exploitation and provide guidance on businesses that affect those resources. The law requires that every district council in the country accept submissions on what regulations and standards are appropriate. It is a highly diplomatic process that allows business interests to influence their local laws. Businesses and others in the community can make submissions on what local rules will be implemented. However, no one can represent new ideas that may arise in the future because they do not exist yet. As a consequence, entrepreneurs wanting to start up a new industry will be constrained by rules that were created in the past to assist established industries, but not theirs.

An example of this can be seen in the way the Department of Conservation actively sought submissions on use of the local mountains. It received submissions from farmers, hikers, mountain climbers and everyone associated with the mountain use at the time. No one represented alpine tourism because there was no such industry. As a result, when I wanted to start an alpine tourism venture, I found the rules were highly constraining. Not only were the rules restrictive, but I found that many staff in the government institutions had mindsets that reflected the existing knowledge, not the new possibilities. For example, some years ago an entrepreneur wanted to put a gondola up a mountain but found that, at certain times of the year, winds were too strong to operate the gondola and would leave tourists stranded on the mountain. As a result, staff in the Department of Conservation had adopted the mindset that a gondola was not viable. This outlook was not the result of stupidity or doggedness. The staff members were all educated, and their outlook was built on solid analysis. Even the businesspeople who had the original idea agreed with them. Everyone gave up on the idea as unrealistic, and, when new rules were made, they were made in a way that would not accommodate this business. However, many years later, I researched the industry and discovered that European manufacturers had developed gondola technology that could withstand the winds. The business had passed the technological threshold, but I was left facing a huge regulatory and institutional barrier.

The perception of others is important for the success of your business model. Governmental agencies and other stakeholders may provide resistance, but, in so doing, they may also provide valuable feedback about the use and structure of a business model. This feedback can indicate what barriers you need to overcome and what future research is needed. It can be valuable as it can give an indication on how you need to modify your model to succeed. This feedback can also provide insight into the way that others are thinking. With that information, you can identify the strategies that are needed to overcome community or legal resistance. Entrepreneurs who blindly pursue a strategy and ignore such feedback do so at their peril.

To illustrate the successful management of the environment, it is worth taking another look at Thomas Edison's introduction of electric lighting. Edison is often praised for his technological accomplishments, but Hargadon and Yellowlees believe that his abilities in getting the technology accepted were equally praiseworthy.[11] In fact, the technological advances on this system belong not to Edison but to one of his engineers, Francis Upton. But Edison shone as an entrepreneur in the way he gained acceptance for a system that challenged the institutional mindset.

Electric lighting first caught the public's attention in 1808, and, although the technology existed for more than 70 years, commercial use was scant. In 1878, when Edison pursued his electric lighting system, he faced an environment with an entrenched competitor, gas, and a collective mindset that did not share his optimism. Few people believed Edison's system was even possible, let alone practical or commercially viable. And the early years of the technology justified this caution. Newspaper headlines reading "Another corpse in the wires" did not inspire confidence, nor did the warnings of firemen who, after storms that felled telegraph poles, roamed the streets warning pedestrians about the danger of live wires. Given this situation, Edison would fail unless he conquered the environmental forces around him, and here he proved to be a master.

When Edison first demonstrated his electric lighting system, he chose the business offices of Drexel, Morgan and Company in the heart of Manhattan's financial district and a stone's throw from the newspaper district, both sources of much needed support. Edison was also selective in what information he released. As with many pioneering ventures, his project made huge losses in the early years that nearly led to the plant's collapse. Edison kept these losses secret for fear of dissuading investors or encouraging competing ventures. But even once finance was secured, Edison still had battles to win his ideas over. For example, one of his biggest investors was William Vanderbilt, who argued against Edison's decision to create a centralized electric system similar to gas and other utilities. The dispute reached the point where Edison threatened to resign in order to preside.

To develop his system, Edison needed a pool of qualified laborers, but he could not get them. He lobbied schools to develop training programs and, when that failed, started his own training program. But his biggest battle was convincing customers and society that his system was superior to his competition. When Edison launched his incandescent lamp, the gas industry responded with a technological upgrade. Gas lighting became more efficient in 1885, with the introduction of the Welsbach mantle, an asbestos bag that fit over lamps and provided a clean white light and sixfold increase in power. Edison faced a tough challenge made worse by the fact that electricity was more expensive. In contrast, Edison presented electricity as being superior to gas, as it did not just provide lighting. The same wire that brings the light to a building will also bring power and heat; cook food; and power an elevator, sewing machine and many other appliances. But electricity was a radically different technology. To succeed he had to work within the existing mindset of potential customers.

To conquer the minds in the market, Edison presented his system in a manner that consumers could easily understand and identify with. To do this he based his model on a system with which consumers were already familiar: the gas industry. Instead of differentiating his product from his competitors, he deliberately imitated many aspects of their operation.

He copied the gas industry's system of centralized production and distribution, as this made it easier for the public to understand. To make his system appear less daunting, he hid from view the enormous capital resources and specialized expertise needed to negotiate the uncertainties of the emerging technology. Other utility providers—water and gas—supplied their products underground, so Edison too buried power lines underground, even though it made them harder to maintain. Taking another lead from the gas industry, which used easy-to-read gas meters, he decided to use meters to bill his customers, even though he had not devised a means of measuring electricity usage. As a consequence, his earliest clients enjoyed six months of lighting absolutely free, until a meter was developed.

In this way, Edison triumphed over the gas industry, not by distinguishing his system from the competitors but by adapting his offering to resemble established institutions. In so doing, he ensured his users would both recognize the purpose of the innovation at the outset and know without reflection how to use it in their everyday lives.[12]

Hargadon and Yellowlees's research on Edison reveals how pioneers seeking to introduce change into a stable social and institutional environment must overcome the conflicting mindsets or schemas that exist. Consequently, they state that "prospective innovators must carefully choose designs that couch some features in the familiar, present others as new, and keep still others hidden from view."[13] It is a risky endeavor that involves locating new ideas within frameworks of understanding and patterns of product use while at the same time seeking to present something different. It is a balancing act that marks Edison as an accomplished entrepreneur.

Problems for Product Pioneers

This book has stressed the need to provide greater value for money as the basis of entrepreneurship. However, sometimes superior products lose out to ones that provide less value. Customers can become locked in to inferior products. This notion of being locked in to a specific technology was illustrated by Paul David, who in 1985 noted that people used keyboards with the letters Q, W, E, R, T and Y at the top, even though other keyboards could be used much faster. The problem was that a number of producers and training schools adopted the QWERTY style, making that the industry standard. Any producer offering a different keyboard would find that trained office staff would not be used to them. It is hard to change and improve a product once it has become locked in because so many other parts of the economy are affected. All parts of the economy using the product would need to be changed, and often the change process is just too hard to introduce. For that reason, many good products fail against inferior competition.

Another problem faced by new products is the length of time that it takes for the market to recognize their benefits and begin buying them. People are not going to change their consumption habits just because innovators feel they have a good product. The problems of introducing new products can be seen by contrasting incandescent lamps to the superior compact fluorescent model.[14] The new fluorescent lamp lasted eight times as long and used a fraction of the electricity. At a price of $30, the new lamps saved the customer $64. The new lamps were a true leap in value for money, but sales were slow. The company experienced problems getting through to the customer all of its advantages. It was discovered that, because the old bulbs cost $1.50 and the new product lasted eight times longer, customers valued the new bulb at $12 and were not prepared to pay the $44 price tag. They did not take into account the savings in electricity.

There are clearly learning and perceptual difficulties on releasing new products to customers. Unfortunately, few small businesses have the resources to sit out long periods of time until the market recognizes the value of the product. There are many factors that influence the rate at which customers respond to a new product.[15] They include:

1   **The Perceived Comparative Advantage over Alternatives**. If your product has clear advantages over competing products, you will be more likely to see a quicker switch to your product. This emphasizes the point made previously, that your product must have superior advantages. However, you cannot expect customers to go looking for those advantages. People make a huge number of purchasing decisions every week, and they will not evaluate every possibility. It is your job to ensure that customers are made aware of your product's advantages.

2   **The Perceived Risk**. One reason that customers regularly buy the same product is they know they are safe with a product they have bought in the past. There is always a risk that a new, untried product will not do its job, and the money will be lost. Your campaign must overcome this fear of financial exposure in the event of failure and the uncertainty about whether the product will bear fruit.

3   **Barriers to Adoption**. For example, some products are consumed in association with other products or values that people hold. If such a relationship exists with your product, it could slow the rate of acceptance of your product.

4   **Information and Availability**. Many new product launches have stalled because they have had insufficient product in the marketplace. The product must be readily available for purchase and servicing, and information must be in place to inform prospective buyers of the product and its benefits. Getting the information out there costs money, and it is necessary to budget for this.

Once consumers have become aware of the product and a market has been built, other businesses may try to tap the growing market. This might not be all bad news. In some instances, you can actually benefit from this competition. As other firms enter the market and invest resources, they can actually contribute to the growth of the whole market. Their advertising and distributional efforts help to inform customers about the benefits of the product, and the presence of more than one supplier can make the product appear a safer buy. The obvious downside of this is the potential loss of sales and downward pressure on profit margins.

Pioneers and Long-Term Leadership

Pioneers of new products face large problems in that they are investing in unsteady technologies, and this opens up the high possibility of failure. You must often spend a great deal of time and resources developing a product in which there is no certainty about the demand. Furthermore, even after a product is introduced, pioneers will encounter large and rapid changes as competitors respond to its entry into the market. Customers will refine their preferences and technologies will evolve. It leads to the question, "Is it worth being the pioneer of a new product if so much of your market can be taken away?"

Consider the following quotes from *Financial World* about a company in the restaurant business:

> *"World's Biggest Chain of Highway Restaurants"*
> *"Pioneer in Restaurant Franchising"*
> *"Most Strongly Entrenched Factor and Highest Quality Investment"*
> *"Most Fabulous Success Story in Restaurant Chains"*

One glance at these headlines and you might instantly think of the famous fast-food restaurant chain McDonald's; however, these headlines are not about McDonald's. The pioneer they are referring to is Howard Johnson's Restaurants. So what happened?

Research conducted by Golder and Tellis found that pioneers do not stay leaders for very long.[16] They studied 500 brands in 50 product categories that were launched in the twentieth century and found that pioneers only held market leadership in four of the product categories. Pioneers only had a mean market share of 10%. For the 16 product groups launched after World War II, the market share was only 7%. In this later group, pioneers only maintained market leadership for an average of 12 years.

Of course, an entrepreneur does not have to be the leader all the time to justify launching a product. The enterprise may still be lucrative. In the early years, when the entrepreneur is the sole producer, he or she has the opportunity to collect monopoly profits that could set a person up for life. And even after the entrepreneur has lost the leadership position, he or she could still have a profitable business.

A surprising finding from Golder and Tellis's research was the poor survival rates of pioneers. They found that 47% of pioneers failed. The failure rate for producers of durable goods was highest at 67%, while nondurable production was 28%. However, this analysis only looked at successful products that found a market throughout the century. It did not include those new products that fell over completely.

So if pioneers do not stand out over the long term, who does? The companies that fared best seemed to be those that entered the industry during a period of early market growth. These companies were leaders in more than half the product categories studied, with a mean market share of 28%. This group also had a very low failure rate (8%). These companies imitated the pioneer's idea and captured market share while demand was growing. They entered the market during the early growth phase of the product life cycle, many years after the market pioneer launched the product. They rode the wave of growing demand when more and more customers recognized the value of the product. This suggests that a good strategy for entrepreneurs is to imitate a pioneer, to take his or her product and enter the market as it is about to take off.

Timing of market entry is key. It is notable that those companies that entered the market *after* this early growth spurt also had high failure rate. Enter too early and the market is not ready for the product. Enter too late and someone else has seized the opportunity. The best time to enter is when the product has been established

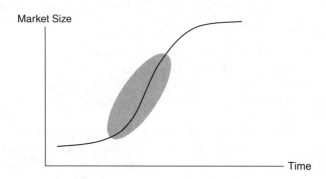

Figure 4.2 The Best Time to Enter a Market (Adapted from Timmons, 1999)

and the market is growing. It seems that this is the best window of opportunity for entrepreneurs, as Figure 4.2 illustrates.

It is very possible that the reason the market enters the growth phase is actually due to the entry of the new companies. They commit large resources to develop the market and consequently benefit from its growth. This finding has been found in other markets where the commitment of adequate resources to large-scale production was more important than entering first.[17]

This strongly suggests that you should let other firms pioneer new products and undergo all the problems associated with development and customer education. Then, when the dynamics of this new market are understood, you can enter and take advantage of their work. This is an imitative entrepreneurial strategy. However, it should also be noted that, in the study by Tellis and Golder, the best imitators were large companies that committed large resources to building and leading the market. One company that has continually exploited this imitative strategy is the Japanese company Matsushita. In fact the company's nickname "maneshita denki" translates to "electronics that have been copied," a reflection of its strategy. Matsushita copies the innovations introduced by Sony, then enters the market exploiting its strength in manufacturing and marketing. Who needs to innovate?

It can be distressing, having spent so much time and resources developing a product, to see someone else make an identical product and capture your market. If an innovation can be easily replicated, a firm faces the danger of bearing all the costs of development for other companies to exploit. A key factor in reaping the benefits of innovation is appropriability: to what extent a firm can appropriate the returns from an innovation (that is, how easy it is to copy the product). The most obvious way of stopping this is to take a patent out on your product. A patent is a grant issued by the government that says only the inventor can make, use or sell the invention. If other people want to produce and sell the product, they must get approval from the inventor. That normally means the inventor gives them a license in return for a royalty payment.

Patents only provide limited protection. First, there is a time limitation. This protection only lasts for a limited period of time: 20 years from the date of application for a patent in the United States. Second, this protection only applies to the country in which that patent is sought. If you want protection in Germany or France, you must also take out patents there. Third, competitors can sometimes get around patent restrictions by making minor changes in the design of the product. Fourth, many small firms simply don't have the finances to take legal action against anyone who breaches their patents. Using the law to protect your rights can be a costly process. Finally, just because you have gained a patent does not guarantee that your product is unique and other business people do not already hold patents for similar products.

However, patents are not the only form of protection.[18] Innovations can also be protected through secrecy or by combining them with some strategic capability you might be able to develop. These include things such as reputation. If you quickly establish a reputation in the marketplace as the reliable supplier, customers will be more likely to buy your product over some new, unproven competitor. This suggests that you should only launch your product when you are convinced of its reliability and back it up with advertising and market information. In so doing, you are educating the customer and defining the market on your terms.

Other forms of protection can be built as a result of being the first to build up production. As you expand your production and gain experience, you can reduce costs. This leads to advantages including economies of scale and experience curves. By contrast, the new competitors will initially have shorter, less economical runs, and they will lack your experience. This will make it harder for them to intrude on your market.

In many industries, it may be difficult for others to get information on how your business operates, and this can make it hard for a competitor to steal your idea. In 1967, Polanyi noted that some tacit knowledge can only be acquired by experience and cannot easily be transferred.[19] This acts as an obvious barrier to late movers attempting to catch up in an industry at a later stage, because they simply do not know what to do.

You may also be able to protect your position through organizational strategy. For example, by investing in a distributional structure, you may be able to make it difficult for new players to get their products to market.

Through these techniques, pioneers can create barriers to entry that make life difficult for new competitors. Studies of the pharmaceutical and cigarette industries show that their tactics can be very powerful forms of protection.[20] However, all of this is no guarantee that other producers will not find a way to produce your product and compete.

Golder and Tellis identified five factors that allow people to retain leadership over the long haul.[21] First, it is not enough to be content with a successful product launch. Even if you are earning a healthy income and are in an apparently secure situation, there is always the opportunity for latecomers to enter the market with superior techniques. If you can dramatically reduce your costs, a late entrant will have trouble competing with you, and you will more likely maintain your position. One of the best ways to reduce costs is through economies of scale, and the only way to achieve economies of scale is through large sales. Consequently, you are more likely to have long-term success if you have a vision of the mass market.

An example of this can be seen in the video recorder market, which was pioneered by Ampex in 1956. Ampex remained the leading producer in this market for several years. Video recorders were expensive to build, so they sold at $50,000 to the professional market, which Ampex dominated. Their only competitors were RCA and Toshiba, whose sales were far behind. Recognizing that the professional market was limited in size, Ampex did little to improve quality or lower costs, preferring to develop other products such as audio and computer products. While Ampex was happy to milk its niche, three Japanese companies believed that video recorders had mass market potential. Following a strategy similar to that followed by Henry Ford 70 years earlier, they realized that if they could reduce costs, the mass market would be open to them. The three companies—Sony, JVC and Matsushita—all made a concerted research effort to bring the video recorder to a larger market. In the mid-1950s, Sony's engineers were told they had to find a way of reducing the price to $5,000, which was later reduced to $500. JVC's engineers were given similar orders. It took 20 years for the companies to realize their goal, but by the mid-1970s they were successful and were catapulted to dominant positions in the industry. Between 1970 and 1985, video sales went from $2 million to almost $2 billion at JVC, from $6 million to $3 billion at Matsushita, and from $17 million to almost $2 billion at Sony. By contrast, sales at Ampex had only increased from $296 million to $480 million. Ampex had lost control of the market it had pioneered.

When trying to design a new product, pioneers often have a breakthrough that allows them to pioneer the market. But you cannot rest on this if you wish to maintain product leadership. Maintaining leadership requires ongoing incremental innovations in design, manufacturing and marketing. This brings us to the next requirement, relentless innovation. For example, to achieve their goals, Sony engineers worked to introduce a number of innovations, including the introduction of color and weight reduction, increasing recording density, and, at the same time, reducing the price by 88%.

You may feel reluctant to introduce further innovations for your product. You may fear cannibalizing your own product. It takes brave people to deliberately make their own product obsolete. A second reason why firms fail to make incremental innovations is because, as they become larger, bureaucratic problems get in the way of innovations. A final reason is they rest on their laurels. Successful companies become satisfied with their progress and feel no need to change. This was one of the prime reasons that Ampex failed to bring video recorders to the home market. They were satisfied with sales to the professional market. Pioneers should never rest on their laurels, for the market will continue to undergo large and rapid changes. These include changes in consumer taste as customers come to terms with what they like and dislike in a product, changes in technology and the arrival of new competitors. To be successful in the long term, you must value incremental learning so you can adapt to rapidly changing conditions and make modifications based on market feedback.

Implementing your vision of a mass market requires ongoing managerial support to ensure your product designers have the resources and time to achieve their goals, and this support must be backed by financial commitment. This can be difficult because it may take some years for results to bear fruit, consuming significant levels of finance in the process. It is easy to let your financial commitment slip because other parts of your business will be crying out for funding. Nevertheless, you must be prepared to supply financial resources and be willing to use them.

The final aspect that Golder and Tellis stress is asset leverage. Many successful late entrants have succeeded in becoming leaders in their markets because they were able to draw on significant resources. This does not just mean financial resources but also other assets such as brand names, distribution, production and managerial expertise. This is an area small entrepreneurs need to be wary of, as they cannot leverage the assets of large companies. For example, in the 1950s, Royal Crown pioneered the diet cola market, selling it to people with diabetes. In 1961, it recognized the importance of the mass market and actually achieved great success in the market. However, when Coca Cola and Pepsi decided to launch their own diet products, Royal Crown was virtually powerless. Even through Royal Crown spent millions to support its brand, it took Diet Coke just one year to gain leadership after its entry in 1982.

This example shows that late entrants are often able to become leaders in some categories if they hold dominant positions in a related category. Clearly, Pepsi and Coca Cola were able to draw on the strength of their brand names as well as their production, managerial and distribution strengths. Another large company to be a successful latecomer was IBM, which could draw on its success with mainframe computers to enter the PC market.

If you are a small pioneer, you should respect the threat of large companies moving in, but you do not need to shake in your boots. After all, as the pioneer, you still have more experience in the new product than the late entrant, no matter how big the company. In fact, many large companies have been seriously hurt when entering new markets.

One large company that suffered from entering new-product markets was Jostens. Thirty-four years of continued growth selling school products had given Jostens 40% of the U.S. market for class rings, yearbooks and other school products. With established distribution channels selling educational products, Jostens decision in 1989 to expand into educational software seemed to make sense. So, the company launched Jostens Learning Corp and then bought out its biggest competition. This brought its share of the computer learning market to more than 60%, but its lack of experience was evident from its strategy. The software it launched onto the market was an integrated system linking all computers to a file system. By contrast, its competitors offered modular step-by-step systems, which had a lower initial cost to schools. Jostens's strategy failed. By early 1992, New York equities analyst Robert Renck Jr. was recommending that investors sell the stock short, saying "these were wonderful guys sitting in Minneapolis who went into a business they didn't know and seemed to have a call on the corporate treasury. That's a formula for failure no matter where you're sitting."[22] In 1993, the company hit the ground with a thump and a $12 million loss.

There is no end of examples where large companies have suffered when moving outside their specialty, although most of them refer to acquisitions. One spectacular example is Borden, a well-run chemical company that achieved continual good results. Looking for a use for its profits, the company made more than 90 acquisitions between 1986 and 1992, buying up among other things small regional food companies. To manage the new acquisitions, staff who had been successful in chemicals took the helms of the food companies. Unfortunately, their chemical production background did not give them a feel for the food business or the nuances of that market. Soon, the nightmares began, and sales fell for 15 straight quarters. As one analyst explained, "To see a major food company of this size go into a Dumpster is just amazing."[23]

If a large company does decide to enter your market, it is not guaranteed success. If it is going to use its assets to enter an industry, those assets, whether they be management capability or brand name, must be able to give it some advantage. This implies that the new product should be closely related to its existing business so that the assets can easily be transferred.

There is another very good reason why you should not fear large companies moving in. They may offer to buy your company out. Many pioneers have received substantial offers from large companies, realizing that buying out the pioneers allows the larger companies to gain all the pioneers' expertise without having to build a business from scratch. In fact, many entrepreneurs find they lose interest as their company grows. The challenges in managing a large business are very different from those in innovating and launching a pioneering company. In these instances, the interest of a large company can be a godsend.

* * *

There are many advantages to being a pioneer. First, pioneers have the first opportunity to strike the market and build expertise, economies of scale and customer loyalty. As a pioneer, you can secure supply contracts, reduce costs, and educate the market to recognize the values embodied in your product.

More important than being first or last is how you shape your strategy once the product is launched. The big profits come when the mass market is tapped. This should be your goal. Given the high cost and risk of pioneering new markets, it would be foolish to settle for the smaller profit level attained from a niche market.

Second, once you have launched your product, be prepared for attack from new competitors. The market you are making will attract other players who will want to enter. You will need to launch your own counter-attack, penetrate and consolidate your position. You must have a long-term vision that will help you stick it out and reach the mass market. Of course, this is easier said than done when restricted by resource limitations and conflicting goals. At the same time that your marketing effort requires resources for developing the mass market through advertising, you will also need resources for product innovation. And there is only so much money and staff to go around. The importance of marketing assets increases as product attributes are more ambiguous and consumers rely on reputation. However, there is no one recipe, and your situation will need constant reassessing.

Most important, Golder and Tellis suggest keeping the five factors suggested previously in the forefront of your planning. To succeed, you will need a vision of the mass market, managerial persistence, financial commitment, asset leverage, and relentless innovation. Without these five factors, when you introduce a new product, you are merely signaling an alarm that a new market has opened for competitors to enter. With these factors, you can enter the market as a late entrant and steal the lead.

Chapter 5

Market Evolution: Niches and Opportunities

Customer needs do not remain static. There is no such thing as a permanent list of customers' needs.

(Joseph M. Juran)

In the previous chapter, we revealed how a product like gas lamps can go through phases of creation, growth and obsolescence with the arrival of electricity. This brings us to the idea of a life cycle for products. The product life cycle (PLC) is an old and well-known concept. Briefly, this concept says that the market for products goes through distinctive stages. The first stage is birth or emergence, when a product is first brought into the world. This is a period when customers are unfamiliar with the product, so demand is small. At the same time, producers are still grappling with the potential of the technology and a number of product variants will exist in what is a rather experimental stage.

This second stage of the life cycle is characterized by market growth, and the number of firms in the market increases. There are also changes in the nature of the product as the characteristics of what people want become more certain and a dominant design emerges. The number of variations decline, and this allows producers to invest in specialized production processes and exploit economies of scale. These more efficient technologies, combined with competitive pressure, lead to a fall in price. The lower price allows larger markets to be targeted, and the market experiences a period of rapid growth.

By the mature stage of the cycle, the product is standardized and customers are familiar with its benefits. But because of the low-cost production structure of the now large businesses, it becomes hard for new players to enter the industry. In the last phase of the life cycle, the product becomes obsolete, just as gas lighting did with the arrival of electric lights. The market gets smaller and smaller as people stop buying the product.

There are clearly limitations with this view of a product's development over time. First, not all products develop like this. Some industries never take off or enjoy a rapid growth phase. For some the growth is slow and steady. Others rise and fall in a pattern that in no way resembles the curve in Figure 5.1. Some industries may

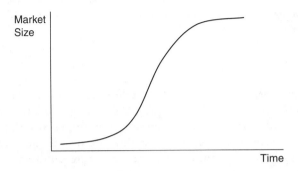

Figure 5.1 The Product Life Cycle   Q: is the product going to meet Ur c

enjoy a long growth phase, while others quickly plateau. A second problem concerns definition and identification. It is not always possible to identify a product as mature or stable. The characteristics of many products change over time, and it can be hard to pinpoint where a product is on the curve. It is particularly hard to gauge modern technologies that change so rapidly.

Finally not all products mature and die. Some products can have their shelf life extended through further development. Alternatively, products may undergo changes to suit diversified markets. For example, televisions can be sold as portable, console sets or projection screens to meet the needs of different market niches. Despite these limitations, the product life cycle is a useful concept and can be used to explain the development of entrepreneurial opportunities.

The Product Life Cycle and Entrepreneurial Options

If people with technological knowledge are in a good position to introduce new products, what does this mean for the non-techie? Are they less likely to become successful entrepreneurs? Murray Low and Eric Abrahamson have suggested that different types of entrepreneurs are better suited for different strategies and timing of the life cycle.[1] This is because, as the market evolves and goes through different stages, different demands will be placed upon the entrepreneur. Each stage requires different strategies and provides different opportunities for different types of entrepreneurs.

Stage 1: The Emerging Product

The first stage of the product life cycle is where the product is brought into the world and where the industry emerges. The entrepreneurs most likely to be pioneers of new products will tend to be creative people who look at business possibilities in novel ways and create "new combinations." The pioneer must have the ability to make the product and understand the consumer problem it solves. If you have an understanding of both the technology and the problem, you are in a unique position to see the potential of making a new business idea.

This stage favors a technical person, but technology is not the only issue to contend with. When a business idea first emerges, there is a great deal of uncertainty over how it will be received in the market. There will be uncertainty about the size of the market, what market segments will respond, what the optimal product characteristics are, the viability of different product and process technologies, and whether any regulatory obstacles need to be overcome. Unsurprisingly, many businesses fail at this stage. Given the high chance of failure, pioneers at this stage are often not motivated by finance, because the financial outcome may not be that great. Instead, they are motivated by the project, which is a goal in its own right, and social motivations such as prestige, affiliation and identification. I suggest pioneering entrepreneurs can also be driven by scientific curiosity, problem solving and sense of adventure.

Although this is a time when little is known about the likely success of the business, pioneers have to convince others that this new business can become a reality. They must create a sense of confidence among financiers and others necessary to launch the business. This involves selling the idea, proving they can be trusted and proving they have the competence to make the idea work. Building confidence may take time and is best achieved through informal mechanisms such as direct personal experience or the recommendation of others. Charisma is a positive attribute for entrepreneurs to possess in garnering support. Belief in the project is the key to success, and this belief helps to bind the participants together and operate in a controlled and coordinated manner.

Stage 2: Growth

During the growth stage, the market begins to take off as more and more consumers recognize the benefits of the product. Fewer businesses are failing. In fact, survival rates are at their highest. This is a good time to enter the market. Entrepreneurs and venture capitalists set up business, attracted by the prospect of superior returns based upon an early-mover advantage. The growth in market is combined with a growth in the number of competitors.

For entrepreneurs wanting to enter the market at this stage, less original creativity is required, and more emphasis is placed on following the example of other firms. Entrepreneurs start jumping on the bandwagon. The sort of person who sets up a business at this stage is not a creative inventor but the keen observer who recognizes the business potential and moves quickly to capture a slice of the action. These entrepreneurs are risk seekers with a bias for action, motivated by the desire to build a business and earn financial returns. They include the type of entrepreneur who does frequent information searches looking for business ideas. They have built large and diverse networks that provide access to information and resources that enable them to identify new business with high-growth potential.

Because the business idea has proven to be credible, the question for investors is not about the product but whether the current attempts to set up a business will be successful. There is more awareness of the product, and entrepreneurs will have less need to pull strings and build confidence. Whereas the pioneer in the first stage relied on informal mechanisms for support and funding, entrepreneurs at this stage are more likely to rely on formal options such as banks and financiers.

With more certainty about the viability of the business, it is possible to plan over a longer time frame. Some of the activities that were previously arranged through suppliers and subcontractors will be brought in-house as businesses seek to secure control of the resources on which they rely. An example of the entrepreneurial company entering the market at the growth stage is Compaq computers. Compaq entered the industry after IBM had established the dominant design for the personal computer. It then set itself the task of building market share by positioning itself as compatible with IBM but offering innovative products of higher quality.

Another group of opportunities comes as a result of changes that occur within the market as the market grows. When the product is young, the market is small, and not many variations in the product exist. At this stage, a small numbers of consumers might want a product with different characteristics from what is available; however, they are forced to either buy the product as it is or not buy it at all. As the market grows, the number of people in this category grows and, at some point, reaches a size where there are enough people of this type to justify making a product specifically tailored to their needs. Once this size is reached, a market threshold has been reached, which presents an opportunity for potential entrepreneurs to seize. There is now a niche market big enough for someone to set up business and make products for it.

This is illustrated in Figure 5.2. The dotted lines represent the section of the market that would like a variation but has to consume the general product. At some point, the market becomes big enough that a sustainable niche exists, as shown by the solid black line. This is the time when an entrepreneur can set up business focusing on that niche. The growth phase is a time of niche-developing potential.

The importance of timing is illustrated in this model. An alert entrepreneur who identifies the rising market and sets up business before the market is of sustainable

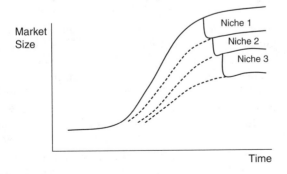

Figure 5.2 Fragmentation of Markets into Niches

size will encounter insufficient demand for his or her product and will struggle to survive. By contrast, an entrepreneur who enters the market after that niche is opened has the demand to exploit. The threshold explains the importance of timing for business success. There are a number of ways that entrepreneurs may be alerted that the threshold has been passed and an opportunity exists. They may discover the opportunity through market research or perhaps they work for a company and hear customers repeatedly ask for a product with different characteristics than that which is currently available. This suggests that someone working in sales is in a good position to identify these opportunities, as salespeople are the ones most likely to hear customer inquiries.

The ability to exploit a niche is not just demand driven and must also consider production technologies. If the product's characteristics are such that mass production results in huge economies of scales, it may be hard to develop a niche that can compete on price. On the other hand, niches can reach a size where they too can exploit economies of scale. This occurred in the automobile industry in the 1920s. Prior to this time, Ford had dominated the market with the Model T, whose production benefited from significant economies of scale. But by the 1920s, demand had grown to the point where it was feasible for other niche manufacturers to take advantage of the production techniques pioneered by Ford.[2] Their niches became so big that they could also exploit economies of scale.

Stage 3: Maturity

In the next stage, the market has stopped growing and has stabilized. There are a number of producers, and competition is intense. Anyone thinking of entering the business at this stage has to face high levels of competition. Not surprisingly, failure rates of new businesses are very high. The sort of person who succeeds entering the market at this late stage is someone who has in-depth knowledge of the business. This person is the sort of entrepreneur who, because of his or her understanding of the industry, has superior information and identifies changes in the marketplace. This entrepreneur uses his or her knowledge to take advantage of any inefficiencies in the market or opening of new market niches. Alternatively, this entrepreneur may introduce state-of-the-art technology and business practices to the industry.

Successful founders are likely to have years of experience with an existing firm in the industry. They spin off to form their own business, their experience being an important factor in their success. They also have well-developed networks in the industry on which they can draw. Their experience and close industry ties make it easier for these people to establish their credibility and attract finance and other resources. Given that the days of fast market growth and large profits are now over, they will most likely be motivated by a number of financial and social goals, perhaps a desire to be self-employed.

In a mature industry, information is more readily available. Previous uncertainties about technologies, design standards, competitors, and customer demand have all been resolved. It is well known what the determinants of success are, and decision making can be more objective and rational. There is less experimentation, and investors and other stakeholders expect a now-standard way of operating. In fact, the new companies could be called "clones," as most of their activity draws on what has been done before.

Foundings of this sort are common in a large number of mature industries and include professional practices, retail, service, construction, transportation and restaurants. Examples of late entrants in the computer industry include Dell and Gateway, which entered the industry after personal computers had become commodity products. By this time, PCs were a well-known product. The two new entrants innovated by developing mail-order distribution channels that enabled them to compete through lower costs.

In a mature market, opportunities for niche opening still exist as entrepreneurs gain more in-depth knowledge of the values that consumers seek. The more knowledge one has on what customers seek, the greater potential exists to create products that can more accurately address those needs. Niches will also come and go as market forces fluctuate. New niches open and close, each demanding different product characteristics. Figure 5.3 illustrates how a mature market may not necessarily be a stagnant market. The more the characteristics of demand change, the more opportunities are created for entrepreneurs who can respond rapidly to the changes. It is appropriate to recall the quotation from John Case of entrepreneurs:

> The structure of a market place shifts, maybe ever so slightly. A new niche opens up. And all at once, people ... who may have never expected to become entrepreneurs are out on their own and amazed by their own success.[3]

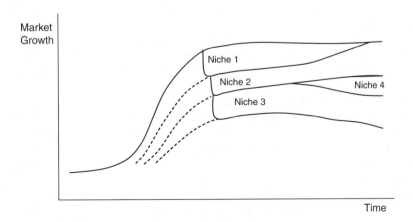

Figure 5.3 Changing Niches in a Mature Market

Niches and Opportunities for the Small Business

In the previous section, we considered the fact that, as industries grow, niches emerge, creating opportunities for entrepreneurs. However, not all industries develop the same way, and this section considers some variations of this idea. A common theme of this research is that, as markets mature, they can become dominated by large companies, and opportunities for entrepreneurs appear in specialized niches.

In 1997, Steven Klepper presented his "industry life cycle," which has many similarities with the product life cycle but contains an important warning for entrepreneurs.[4] He talks of a "shakeout," in which many businesses are forced out of the market, thus spelling the end of many entrepreneurs' dreams. Klepper says that industries go through a series of stages similar to that discussed in the product life cycle. At first there is an embryonic stage, in which the market is still developing. Market sales are low, and producers experiment with different product forms as they try to come up with something that will best appeal to customers. The industry then goes through a growth stage. Producers by now have finally come up with a winning product that customers are buying in increasing numbers.

We previously said that the growth phase was the best time to enter the market, but Klepper sends a warning to would-be entrepreneurs. He says that, as the growth phase nears its end, a "shakeout" of producers occurs. By that he means a large number of businesses are forced to leave the market because they can no longer compete. Why would so many firms be forced to leave a growing market?

Klepper argues that existing firms grow in size and become more efficient. They improve their production processes and reduce their costs. Having developed a good product, they spend most of their R&D not on product development but on how the product is made. As these firms grow, they benefit from economies of scale, making it even harder for entrepreneurs to enter the market and compete with the big players whose costs are much lower than those just starting up. It also means there are many existing firms that can't compete and are forced to leave the market.

The warning for entrepreneurs is this notion of shakeout; the idea that even early movers into the market are forced out of the market. Smaller firms who do not develop low-cost production techniques are pushed out of the market, and many entrepreneurs find that, with insufficient profit, their dreams are brought to an end. Klepper (1997) studied the automobile industry from its inception in 1895 until 1966. Many entrepreneurs entered the market in the early years. An average of 48 firms per year started between 1902 and 1910, with a peak of 84 firms in 1907. However, the number of businesses starting up dropped dramatically after 1910, a time in which Ford had emerged as the industry giant with highly efficient production methods, in particular the assembly line. This signaled the end of opportunity for entrepreneurs. There was a dramatic decline in the number of new businesses starting up, down to 16 firms per year between 1911 and 1921 and, after that, hardly any.

The automobile industry also experienced a shakeout of existing companies. As early as 1909, there were more businesses leaving the market than entering the market. That year, there were 274 car manufacturers, but the industry shakeout saw this number dramatically decline over the following years. By 1929 there were only 30 producers. The industry had become concentrated in three cost-efficient giants. By 1937, General Motors, Ford and Chrysler accounted for 88% of all automobile sales.

Klepper's work still supports the importance of being an early mover. Most of the firms that lasted for 30 years entered before 1905, but no firm entering after 1909 lasted this long, and no firm entering the market after 1922 survived longer than 14 years. Basically, a firm had a greater chance of survival if it entered the market early.

This pattern of industry growth has been found in a number of industries, including tires, televisions, penicillin and typewriters.[5] Of 46 products studied by Klepper, 27 had experienced a shakeout, an ominous sign for entrepreneurs hoping for self-employment until retirement. However, not all industries followed this pattern. Each industry will have its own individual nature, and a key factor may be the technology used and the extent an industry can benefit from economies of scale, which favors large companies.

Steven Klepper also found that, although early entrants dominated their industries, late entrants who did survive tended to fill small product niches. The idea that a small number of large companies dominate the center of the market and small specialist producers fill small niches has been supported by a large number of studies. One of the earliest was Carroll's resource-partitioning model, developed in 1985. Carroll noted that, as the market ages, high competition between generalist firms results in firms dying off and leaving the market. The remaining firms benefit from economies of scale in production and marketing and dominate the market, which is now concentrated in the hands of a small number of large producers. The surviving companies cater to a broad range of consumer tastes by making products or services with a broad appeal. This leaves room on the periphery of the market for small specialist organizations to create and occupy market niches with highly differentiated products. Entrepreneurs then form businesses to cater to these niches in which they appeal to customers with a narrower range of need.

You might ask why the large companies don't move into these specialized niches, but Carroll's resource-partitioning model assumes that firms are limited in their adaptability. His model is strongly linked to biological notions in which organisms evolve to match their environment. In a commercial "survival of the fittest," the firms that evolve to occupy the center of the market are well suited to large-scale production and efficient administration that comes with the large market center. However, surviving in the small niches requires a different business model. The large firms have not evolved in a way that would allow them to compete in the small niche. It is like expecting an elephant to live in the same environment as a chimpanzee. Generalist organizations that produce standardized products and services for the mass market cannot survive in the specialist niches that are too small to provide scale economies.

Second, these large organizations are bound by organizational inertia that can limit their flexibility and ability to capture small niches. The reluctance or the inability of generalist organizations to expand into the specialist niches allows organizations with new specialist business forms to be founded in mature industries.[6] As a result, small entrepreneurs can thrive in these niches because they avoid battling the elephants.

A large number of studies support the idea that, as markets age, a small number of large companies concentrate in the market center. Later opportunities for entrepreneurs come with the establishment of specialist organizations and those specialized firms. The industries in which this pattern has been found include newspaper publishing, automobile manufacturing, beer brewing, film production, microprocessor manufacturing, early telephone companies, medical diagnostic imaging producers, winemaking, banking, airline passenger travel, investment banking, legal counsel and financial auditing.[7]

Another theory with similarities is the niche-formation theory. This theory says that changes in the business environment such as changes in consumer taste or basic technology open new niches. The result of these changes is to create unmet demand for new products and services. Entrepreneurs recognize these potential opportunities and found new businesses to exploit them.

In contrast to the resource-partitioning model, which stresses the structural fragmentation of the industry into specialists and generalists, niche-formation theory says the changes are "exogenous" in that they occur due to forces outside the industry. The types of environmental change that create these niches include new technologies offering improved performance or new product designs, changes in government policy, and changes in consumer preferences that require new product designs and offerings.[8]

These patterns have been observed in the U.S. wine industry. Swaminathan studied the wine industry and found that the number of wineries declined dramatically from 989 in 1940 to 330 in 1967.[9] This period was dominated by firms exploiting economies of scale in their operations and a large number of acquisitions of small- and medium-sized wineries. Although demand grew from 86.1 million gallons in 1940 to 440.9 million gallons in 1990, the market became concentrated in a small number of large producers such as United Vintners, E&J Gallo, and Guild Wineries. The percent of sales controlled by the four largest firms rose from 23% in 1940 to 52.4% in 1990. Economies of scale are very important in the wine industry, so it is no surprise that the large firms reaped most of these sales gains.

However, in later years, the industry experienced a rapid growth in the number of small specialist firms consistent with the resource-partitioning and niche-formation theories. These specialist wineries go by a number of names including "boutique," "chateau" and "farm" wineries. By 1990, there were 1,140 such wineries in the country. This is the area of the market where entrepreneurs thrived.

Farm wineries are often started by entrepreneurs who learned their trade working for one of the large wineries. With limited resources, they start small in converted barns, basements and other buildings, and they lease their production equipment until their sales returns enable them to purchase their own. Their operations are generally based on one vineyard and are typically formed with a distinct niche in mind. In contrast to the large wineries that tend to produce a range of generic wines such as burgundy, Chablis, claret and Madeira, farm wineries limit themselves to small quantities of wine from only one or two grape varieties.

Their small output does not enable them to exploit the mass-production techniques of the large corporations, which means they cannot compete on price; however, they make different offerings to the customer. Farm wines focus on quality and use their smallness to increase their appeal to customers. They use their links to the winery to draw attention to the process of wine making and the agricultural foundation of what can otherwise seem like another product in the supermarket. There is a different sense of culture and identity to farm wines.

Lacking the resources for mass-market advertising, farm wineries rely on tasting rooms on their premises and word-of-mouth publicity, which means they must develop a reputation for quality. Another strategy is to combine their wine sales with the use of their premises for events such as weddings and special-theme tastings. With small advertising budgets, they are very dependent on favorable reviews from wine critics.

The environmental changes that helped create these niches include changes in lifestyle and consumer demand for greater variety. These changes have fuelled the emergence of small upscale niches of relatively affluent consumers. These changes have also affected other industries in the United States. For example, the brewing industry is one that also benefits from economies of scale and has resulted in large brewing companies. However, at the same time that niches in the wine industry were developing, the brewing industry also developed small specialist niches in the form of microbreweries and brewpubs.

Organization sociologists have made some interesting observations in regard to the development of niches, although they do not always use the same language that we in entrepreneurship use. A useful notion is "carrying capacity," which refers to how many businesses a niche can support. They note that, in the early stage, a market niche may have excess carrying capacity, which means that the market can absorb the businesses of new entrepreneurs. As customers, banks and other stakeholders recognize your business idea as a legitimate business model, your business has a greater chance of surviving. Hence, organizational sociologists stress the importance of gaining legitimacy, after which we can see other entrepreneurs emulating the business strategy and setting up businesses in imitation of those that have succeeded. However, organization sociologists stress that at some point there are too many competitors, and some are forced to leave the market. The number of competitors in the market (what they call "density") is the result of two forces: legitimization and competition.

The idea of carrying capacity can best be seen in the wine industry by looking at the link between the number of wineries and incomes across the United States. States with high per-capita income and wine consumption have a higher number of wineries. Government support through such things as farm winery laws has also helped increase the number of businesses formed; however, they have also correlated with an increase in the number of wineries failing. This suggests that state encouragement may lead to a higher number of businesses being formed than the carrying capacity of the niche will support. Hence, many new businesses do not survive.

Resource partitioning theory suggests that large generalist corporations cannot adapt and compete in the smaller generalist niches, but this may not always hold true.[10] Mass producers may be able to introduce brands for niche markets and create an image of high quality through the large advertising budgets they have at their disposal. While this can negatively affect the options for budding entrepreneurs, specialist companies can compete if they share resources such as financing, purchasing, marketing and distribution, in which case they may obtain economies of scale similar to those of the large enterprises.

Another strategy that small firms can use to confront the large firms is to develop "economies of scope." "Scope" refers to the breadth of activities a business operates in, and sometimes a business can achieve more efficient operations by engaging in a number of spheres. Firms in niche markets cannot obtain economies of scale because their niches are too small, but if they operate in a number of niches, they may be able to reduce unit costs as they grow larger. With this in mind, it is no surprise that many firms enter one submarket and add others as they grow. For example, entrepreneurs may establish a steel plant initially performing a small range of tasks, but as they learn from experience, they attempt a broader range of commercial activities. They expand their scope as they age and, as a consequence, older, larger firms can be found operating in a wider range of submarkets than new firms.[11]

A number of changes over the last decade have increased the competitiveness of small businesses vis-a-vis large companies. These include deindustrialization and an expansion of the service sector, where economies of scale are not so important. Demand is increasingly individualized, whereby companies produce custom-made products for their clients, once again reducing the economic power of mass production. New production technologies play a role. The technologies in modern machinery often require a smaller output to optimize economies, while the increased volatility in world markets actually favors small players over large companies with high fixed costs. Finally, there is an increased focus on niches and less focus on the mass market. Consumers do not always want the same as their neighbor.[12]

There is a large body of research linking the success of businesses to the rise and fall of market niches. Klepper and Thompson argue that all opportunities for growth correspond to the emergence of new submarkets.[13] All submarkets have limited life spans, and firms that are specialized in a single submarket can be expected to vanish when the submarket dies. This suggests it is vitally important that entrepreneurs understand the nature of niche evolution, as the life of their businesses may be influenced by factors beyond their control. Klepper and Thompson believe that the central force for change in industry is the creation and destruction of submarkets:

> Firms expand when they are able to exploit new opportunities that arrive in the form of submarkets; they contract and ultimately exit when the submarkets in which they operate are destroyed.[14]

It is notable that they use the word "submarket," not "niche"; however, their description of submarkets suggests substantial overlap. They use the word "submarkets" to refer to how industries are differentiated in terms of the technology they use, the services they provide, the customer segments they target and the geographic areas in which they operate. These different activities are the submarkets. Opportunities arise for entrepreneurs as new submarkets arise. However, submarkets can disappear when technologies become obsolete, as geographic areas decline or as regulations change. When the niche vanishes, firms dependent on them go into decline.

Klepper and Johnson argue that submarkets are the driving force behind the entry and exit of businesses into the market and firm growth. An industry is composed of various submarkets, and the number of submarkets changes over time. If a firm only operates in one submarket, it is niche-dependent and vulnerable should the niche go into decline. Consequently, Klepper and Johnson state that the more submarkets a firm is in, the lower the chance it has of being forced out of the industry.

Klepper and Johnson studied the first 30 years of the laser industry and revealed just how closely businesses' success is linked to the submarkets they are in. The laser industry had an initial burst in the late 1960s but went through a period of relative stagnation in the 1970s. Although a reliable technology, entrepreneurs did not find many applications for the laser in the early '70s. Lasers were "a solution looking for a problem."[15] However in the 1980s, new submarkets were created as the laser found new uses in electronics and medical applications.

The number of firms in this industry increased over time, as did the number of submarkets. Each new application for the laser created a new submarket. The invention of the CD player and rise of the personal computer created laser submarkets for semiconductor lasers. The miniaturization of the helium-neon (HeNe) laser led to the development of handheld scanners. Many of the new companies were founded by employees of laser firms. With knowledge of the technology and awareness of the new market, they left their jobs, spinning off to create their own successful business.

Industry evolution has also seen laser submarkets destroyed. Some applications in printing and surgery have been destroyed because alternative technologies have been improved to the point where they can do the job better than lasers. More common is the displacement of one type of laser by one that is more effective.

Analysis of the firms leaving the industry revealed that the exit rate was highest for firms producing only one laser type, illustrating the danger of operating in only one submarket. More diversified firms had better survival prospects. Klepper and Johnson argue that the importance of submarkets is so great that it can not only be linked with entry and exit of businesses but, in facilitating the growth and decline of businesses, it can greatly influence who the industry leaders are. Growth and decline in submarkets can explain why companies that have long dominated an industry see their leadership abruptly terminated, as younger companies in faster growing submarkets seize their crown.

Case Study: Is There a Niche to Start a Hotel?

This section provides a real-world example of how an opportunity can be found by looking at new niche development. It looks at the accommodation market in an up-and-coming tourist town on New Zealand's east coast. Due to commercial reasons, the town's name has been changed to Seavista. (Yes, this is from a real investment proposal.) We want to know if an opportunity exists for an entrepreneur to start a hotel business. In the early 1990s, Seavista enjoyed rapid growth as a tourist destination based on its spectacular scenery and wildlife tourism. The region possesses a unique geographic and biological endowment, which is beginning to attract tourists from around the world.

To investigate whether an opportunity exists, we need to analyze available data on the number and types of tourists coming to the town. Fortunately, a lot of statistical information is available from the government tourist office. Our goal is to find out when the market has the carrying capacity to support a hotel. We want to find out when that demand threshold is reached and opens up an opportunity for an entrepreneur to start a business.

Statistics from the government tourism office revealed on average how many tourists stayed the night in Seavista. As well as providing data on past tourist numbers, the government also provided projections on future growth rates. These figures are embodied in the second column of Table 5.1, which shows average accommodation demand per night. This tells us the average size of the accommodation market on any night. For example, 518.7 tourists stayed in Seavista each night, on average, in 2006.

Table 5.1 Determining Niche Size

Year	Total Accommodation Demand	Hotel Demand	New Niche (7%)	New Niche (10%)	Total Hotel (7%)	Total Hotel (10%)
1997	235.8	31.4				
1998	239.8	31.9				
1999	271.4	36.1				
2000	314.6	41.8				
2001	352.8	46.9				
2002	376.9	50.1				
2003	372.4	49.5				
2004	404.6	53.8				
2005	463.6	61.7				
2006	518.7	69.0				
2007	530.1	70.5	0.0	0.0	70.5	70.5
2008	541.7	72.0	16.3	16.3	88.3	88.3
2009	553.6	73.6	27.4	27.4	101.0	101.0
2010	565.8	75.3	39.2	56.2	114.4	131.4
2011	578.3	76.9	40.7	57.7	117.6	134.6
2012	591.0	78.6	41.0	59.0	119.6	137.6

We now have to consider what percentage of the market would want to use a hotel if one was opened. To do this, we looked at a number of figures including comparisons with similar nearby tourist destinations. This provides an indication of how big the hotel niche is in the total accommodation market. Statistics reveal that, in 2006, a nearby town had a hotel with 65 rooms available even though the town only received 380 visitors. This is much less than Seavista, which received 518.7 visitors per night. This tells us if a similar percentage of tourists going to Seavista want to stay in a hotel, we could build a hotel with 88 rooms.

We also considered what percent of tourists to New Zealand used hotels or, to put it another way, what percentage of the national accommodation market is in the hotel niche. Government statistics revealed that approximately 20% of visitors to New Zealand stay in hotels; however, we had to consider the differences between Seavista and other tourist markets. Because Seavista did not get any business visitors, we felt that the hotel niche would be slightly lower. After in-depth comparison with other locations, we felt it was realistic to expect approximately 13% of visitors to Seavista to use a hotel if it was made available. On this basis, the third column of Table 5.1 shows how big the hotel niche would be.

This suggests that there has been sufficient market for a 50-room hotel for five years, but no entrepreneurs have seized the opportunity. But this assumes 100% occupancy rates. The hotel will not always be full and, on current cost structures, should be able to produce a healthy profit with a 70% occupancy rate (or 35 units per night). This reveals that the threshold was passed as long ago as 1999. Tourists who might normally stay in hotels were having to choose other accommodations.

The lack of a hotel seems an anomaly, especially given that the nearest tourist town has a hotel in a smaller market. The economist Israel Kirzner said entrepreneurial opportunities exist when people make "errors of pessimism." These are errors made when people think an opportunity does not exist. People also make "errors of optimism": when entrepreneurs think an opportunity exists but it doesn't. An example of an "error of optimism" would be when an entrepreneur acts before the threshold is reached. In the case of Seavista, there would appear to have been an error of pessimism.

Why would people overlook this potential? Maybe there was a perceptual problem. In theory, Seavista had two hotels, but both were very old and in a state of disrepair. Given the choice of financing an upgrade or becoming a backpackers' lodge, the management at one chose the second. It kept the name of a hotel but in reality was in a different market. Another possible reason for this oversight may be the perception of a market as a backpackers' market. It was perceived that the market was one of young, low-budget travelers and that the sort of people who want to stay in hotels are not interested in nature. This is clearly false. New Zealand tourism as a whole is based on exactly these values, so there should be no difference from other New Zealand tourism locations.

This opportunity may have been overlooked for some time, but that is no longer the case. A number of companies are looking at investing in the Seavista hotel market. But this opens the problem first pointed out by Richardson; that is, our unawareness of other people's investment ideas leads to niche overcrowding. An entrepreneur does not want to target the market with a 60-unit hotel only to find three other companies have done the same thing and the market is flooded. To some extent, this is less of a problem in Seavista, as hotel developers must apply for building consents, and if their application does not fit existing rules in some way, they must apply for a resource consent. This means, by observing the consent process, we can see what hotels are planned for the coming years. The immediate investor we can identify is an established hotel group that has applied for and obtained a resource consent for a hotel of 50 to 70 units. This will take much of the pent-up demand and reduce the size of the entrepreneurial opportunity.

Before we consider the effect of competition and the Richardson problem, there is one last issue to consider. So far, this analysis is based on fair share of the existing market and projected market growth. No consideration has been given to the extent that the hotel could contribute to overall market growth. At the moment Seavista is not getting package tours or tour groups. The Tourism and Economic Development officer in Seavista sees the lack of hotels as the reason for this, saying that hotels "will bring the buses." So the placement of hotels in Seavista is likely to open up a new market and contribute to overall growth. Analysis of tour group routes and similar markets in New Zealand suggest that tour groups and package tours should provide a bump between 7% and 10% to tourist numbers.

The growth is shown in columns four to seven of Table 5.1 and in Figure 5.4. When the new niche is combined with projected hotel demand, these figures suggest the size of the hotel market will be somewhere between 114 and 131 units per day on average in 2010, sufficient to accommodate two 70-unit hotels comfortably.

In summary, the market threshold was passed in 1999, and the opportunity laid waiting for someone to discover. Recently, a hotel group has discovered this and will exploit the existing demand. Fortunately, the market is growing and, when combined

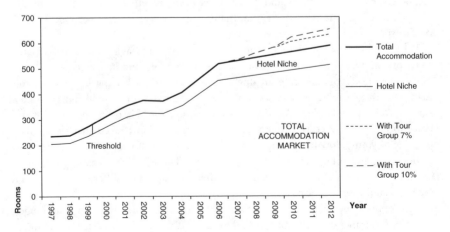

Figure 5.4 Opportunity in Hotel Market

with the new tour group niche, there is sufficient demand for an entrepreneur to enter the market and start a business.

This case study highlights how niches may be sitting dormant, waiting for an entrepreneur to discover them. Opportunities will continue to appear long after a new product or service is developed. They emerge with the evolution of demand and the appearance of submarkets. Entrepreneurs need to consider carrying capacity, when the demand threshold is crossed so that demand is sufficient to support a business. They also need to consider the appearance of competitors in that niche. Finally, they must remember that niches can also close over time.

There are many opportunities during times of technological change, and those with technological skills are in a good position to seize opportunities by applying the technology to human needs and wants. But over time opportunities will open for those less technical as the product is developed. Low and Abrahamson argue that the success or failure of an entrepreneurial venture depends on the stage of the life cycle. It is another way of saying that the environment determines which entrepreneurs and which strategies will succeed. At each stage of the life cycle, different characteristics will be needed to succeed.

Chapter 6

Trajectories and Emerging Niches

The only big companies that succeed will be those that obsolete their own products before somebody else does.

(Bill Gates)

Technological Trajectories

New technologies can provide the missing link that turns unobtainable ideas and dreams into a reality, and often a new product or technology when introduced will have impacts on other products. Think, for example, how refrigerators and freezers changed our attitude about food storage. This led to new food-storage products such as plastic-sealed bags. New technologies enable us to come up with solutions to problems, but they also create new problems. For example, an improved design of an engine, which enables cars to travel at greater speeds, will create a need for more powerful braking systems. The greater use of computers has created a problem of neck and back strain and a need for ergonomically designed office furniture.

New technologies open up new problems. These problems can be opportunities if you can solve them. The types of problems opened by new technologies include new demands and the need for new supplies of resources, machines and skills. In this way, technology has its own momentum, which stimulates further invention.[1] Technology operates like a rolling maul, progressively moving forward, creating a need for new products, bringing death to other products. This suggests that a good way to start looking for new business ideas is to first consider new products introduced over the past five years and then to think about the impact they have had. It means thinking about new products that could be used in conjunction with those products. This applies to both consumer and industrial products.

The idea that a new technology propels innovative activity in particular directions could be seen as early as the industrial revolution, when many improvements were made to textile machinery. One of the first improvements was the flying shuttle invented by John Kay. This increased the speed at which weaving looms operated; however, the looms worked so fast that spinners could no longer keep up. The new looms had been a huge improvement, but their effect had been to create a bottleneck in textile production with the spinners. This led to the need to speed up spinning operations, a problem solved when James Hargreaves invented the "spinning jenny." Once this was achieved, it revealed a shortage of weaving capacity that eventually led to the invention of Cartwright's power loom. These three inventions illustrate how technological innovation can create an imbalance that propels innovation in certain directions.[2]

These examples also show that what is invented in the future is strongly determined by what has been invented in the past. Innovations don't just happen. The technology of the past causes people to look at certain problems and pushes technology into certain directions. This happens not just because of the problems it creates. It also occurs because of the knowledge we build up. When we solve a problem, we draw upon the knowledge and skills we have built up over time. The knowledge we gained in the past determines how we solve problems. To put it another way, our past knowledge determines our future achievements. Any new technology is developed along a path that reflects these endowments built in the past.

Any new technology is based on past knowledge and problems. It is as if technology is pushed along a path. These "pathways" have been called "natural trajectories"[3] or "technological trajectories."[4] These pathways have important implications for entrepreneurs, new businesses and established competitors. A firm invests in workers with specific skills and knowledge. It buys machinery with specific technical applications, and the whole firm builds up knowledge in certain areas. These investments shape the way a business perceives and resolves technological problems. For example, a firm with expertise in chemical engineering will not deliver innovations in electronics, and vice versa. In this way, a firm's future is shaped by the trajectory it travels. Its machines, skills and expertise affect what technological directions to pursue or not to pursue. As a firm advances along a path or trajectory, it gains greater knowledge of the potential of the technology. New opportunities are revealed, pushing development further along the path in a cumulative effect. Advance becomes self-propelling.

As a firm progresses along a technological path and builds up knowledge of the technology, it is in a better position to exploit future technological development.[5] Success breeds success, and a technological gap is opened up between it and potential competitors. This is a major problem for new businesses (and underdeveloped countries). They find it hard to enter new industries where established companies have built up huge experience dealing with technologies.

Who Exploits New Technologies: New Firms or Old Players?

If established companies have an advantage in developing existing technologies, do they also have an advantage in developing totally new technologies? Is technological innovation best suited to large companies or new entrepreneurs? The esteemed economist Joseph Schumpeter used to believe that small competitive entrepreneurs drove innovation in the economy. A few years later, after observing the success of large American corporations with their R&D laboratories, he changed his mind.

Today, most innovations come from small players. Research has also shown that the greater the rate of technological development occurring in an industry, the greater the formation of new ventures.[6]

But this situation is not straightforward. We saw this in the lighting industry, where gas companies improved their competitiveness and made it difficult for Edison to establish his product. Several constraints can make it hard for a new firm entering an industry and exploiting a new technology. These "entry barriers" include the pricing policies of existing firms, excess capacity in the industry, economies of scale advantages of existing players, government regulation, retaliation tactics of current players and access to distribution channels.

However, existing players also have significant barriers that restrict them from exploiting new technologies. Large companies can become bureaucratic with an institutionalized administration that is slow to respond to change. Vested interests inside the company can actively block change, and psychological and communication barriers exist, such as difficulties in getting information and changing mindsets. Finally, change can be hampered by past investments in capital, skill and knowledge that cannot be changed overnight. A gas company cannot suddenly become an electricity company and vice versa. These barriers can keep a company bound to its old trajectory and leave opportunities open for young players.

It is worth recalling the difference between competence-enhancing and competence-destroying technologies. An innovation that is radically different, such as the introduction of electric lights, can destroy the usefulness of gas production investment. On the other hand, if a large company has technological capabilities in an area where an innovation has occurred, it could easily adopt and commercialize the idea. If not, a new player may be better suited.

Research by Sinha and Noble found that large firms are often the first to leap at emerging technologies, and their resource-base gives them a huge advantage when exploiting technological opportunities.[7] However, they have a tendency to restrict themselves to those opportunities close to their core business strategy. This still leaves plenty of opportunity for small firms to pursue maneuvers, as Gordon Moore, founder of Intel, notes:

> We found at Fairchild that any company active on the forefront of semiconductor technology uncovers far more opportunities than it is in a position to pursue. And when people are enthusiastic about a particular opportunity but are not allowed to pursue it, they become potential entrepreneurs.[8]

Niche Commitment and Emerging Opportunities

In a world of ineptitude, arrogance and bureaucracy, it is easy to imagine fresh entrepreneurs defeating bureaucratic Goliaths. But how can it happen when those large companies are efficiently managed, technologically active and well-resourced? Can small entrepreneurs take on these guys and win? Recognizing emerging niches is a case of identifying what customers want and being able to provide the values expected from a product or service. In this section, we explore the development of emerging niches and how existing companies, trapped in their technological and organizational trajectories, leave opportunities open to small players.

Joseph Bower and Clayton Christensen conducted research that showed a relationship between technological trajectories and the opening of new market niches for entrepreneurs.[9] To understand what happens, we need to broaden our notion of trajectories. In this case, companies had trouble moving off the trajectory they traveled, not because of technological limitations but because of the tightness in which they were geared toward their target market. They didn't change, and this led to their failure.

This seems the opposite of everything we learn at business school, where we are told to stay close to our market and cater to the demands of customers. Even though the leading companies constantly invested in new technologies shaped by the demands of their target market, they still suffered. The problem was, in focusing so strongly on their core markets, they did not consider technologies that served smaller, less profitable niches. These vacant market niches left openings for entrepreneurs to start new businesses. These niches provided the beachhead for a later assault that destroyed the established companies. The irony is that the companies often pioneered research in the new technologies that later buried them.

Bower and Christensen studied the disc-drive industry, where this pattern repeated itself again and again. For example, in the mid- to late 1970s, the dominant drive used in the market was 14 inches. The primary market for these disk drives was mainframe computers that required, on average, 200 MB storage capacity. When the 8-inch drive was introduced, it had a capacity of only 20 MB, not enough for the mainframe computers, so the leading companies decided not to pursue it. However, 8-inch drives had other advantages, in particular internal power supplies and smaller size. These characteristics appealed to smaller market niches, and some engineers took the opportunity to set up companies to serve these niches.

This is an example of something that happens quite often. Large companies focus on their core customers and ignore small niches. In their eyes, the small niches aren't worth the trouble or cost, so they leave them for new players to set up business. On this occasion, the new companies then improved their product until eventually the 8-inch drives had the same storage capacity of the 14-inch ones sold by the established producers. When this happened, the new players could take on and defeat the established producers.

The funny thing is, before long, the same thing happened again. A few years later, 5.25-inch drives were introduced, and the leading companies ignored them. When 5.25-inch drives were initially introduced, their capacity was only 5 MB, only a fraction of what was needed by the customers of the day. But once again, these discs had attributes that some people could appreciate, in particular, their even smaller size and low-cost motors. Some new companies set up to exploit this niche, which was not of interest to the larger companies. The new companies also worked at upgrading the capacity of the disc, and by 1986 it had enough capacity for use in the minicomputer market and by 1991 in the mainframe market.

You would have thought by now that the disc-drive manufacturers would have learned the lesson, but no. A few years later, it happened again. One of the young companies to pioneer the 5.25-inch disc was Seagate, based in Scotts Valley, California. An aggressively managed company, it succesfully stormed the market, becoming the main supplier of the drives to IBM and IBM-compatable personal computer manufacturers.

Being an innovative company, Seagate, like other firms, had engineers working on a prototype 3.5-inch disc. However, their principal customers, IBM and other manufacturers of AT-class personal computers, were not interested. Once again, the smaller drives suffered from limited capacity. At the time, Seagate's own earnings from the 5.25-inch disc market was $300 million, while the entire 3.5-inch disc market delivered only $50 million. Understandably, Seagate's managers decided that the new product would not provide the sales volume and profit margins to justify the effort. Yet this was not a conservative company. They continued to innovate and invest in new technology.

Seagate's inaction left the market niche open for others to fill, so former employees of Seagate and other leading companies launched their own spin-off companies. In this way, Conner Peripherals and Quantum were born. As before, these new companies sold their 3.5-inch drives to an emerging market niche, companies making portable computers and small footprint desktop products. Because Seagate had never served this market, it did not see the new company as a threat.

However, the new companies continued to improve their product, and, by the end of 1987, the smaller drives packed the capacity necessary to serve the mainstream personal computer market. It was now obvious that the new company was a competitor, so Seagate introduced its own 3.5-inch product, but it was too late. By 1994, the two new companies, Conner and Quantum, had combined revenues of more than $5 billion. By contrast, Seagate had shrunk to a shadow of its former self.

This pattern has occurred repeatedly over time. Each time, the leaders stumbled with a technological change brought about by the new product. Not that the technologies were beyond their capabilities. In fact, each of the new drives was relatively straightforward. The problem was their technology was also defined by the market they served. These customers wanted attributes that the new products could not provide. So, the companies stayed close to their customers and rejected the new technology because it did not address their customers' needs.

So prevalent is this pattern that no single disk-drive manufacturer has been able to dominate the industry for more than a few years. In fact, not one of the companies that existed in 1976 was standing 20 years later. Nor is this pattern restricted to the disc-drive industry. Bower and Christensen have seen this pattern repeatedly in a variety of industries that have had to contend with technological change.

These waves of technical change create opportunities for entrepreneurs, but the companies were short-lived. When you set up a company, the last thing you want is to see it go under within a few short years. So how do you stop this from happening?

Bower and Christenson have suggested five ways companies can protect themselves from this process. Although these suggestions are aimed at existing companies, they are also of interest to people thinking of setting up a new business. They help us to identify possible new business opportunities.

When assessing future threats, companies need to determine if a new technology is disruptive or sustaining. A sustaining technology is an innovation that builds on existing capabilities. It is good for existing companies. On the other hand, a disruptive technology is good for the new entrepreneur. To determine whether a new technology is disruptive, Bower and Christenson suggest looking ahead at technologies on the horizon to determine future threats. This could be hard to do, but if managers disagree on the importance of certain technologies, it suggests it should be explored further.

When looking at future possibilities, you must consider the rate of improvement of the new technology. You should not compare current performance rates of new and current technologies, as the existing technology may win any comparison. What is more important is the rate at which the products can improve, and here you must trust the opinion of your technological experts. However, it is important not just to consider whether the product will eventually out-perform the old, for in some cases new technologies never out-performed the ones they replaced. What is important is the relationship of the technology to the market (i.e., whether it meets the needs of the market). For example, personal computers do not out-perform mainframe computers in terms of capabilities, but they have succeeded because they meet the computer and data storage needs of many organizations effectively. To determine this, do not focus only on existing customers, as they may not value the technology when it first arrives. It is better to look at customers in the new emerging niche.

Executives must personally monitor intelligence on the progress of pioneering companies. Because the new companies are active in markets that the company does not serve, you will need to create information about such markets. With this information, a large company may be able to imitate the pioneer before it is too late. The one problem with an imitating strategy is that it will invariably create tension between those people in the company pushing the new technology and those associated with the old product. This could destroy any attempt to enter the market late. Consequently, Bower and Christenson suggest that the company place responsibility for building a disruptive technology business in an independent organization, with free reign to realize the potential of their technology—even if it means ultimately killing off the main business.

*   *   *

Bowen and Christensen's study of the disc-drive market is a cause for concern—the fact that companies went into decline despite staying close to their customers and investing in new technologies. The problem was that they focused so strongly on their core markets that they ignored emerging niches. These niches provided opportunities for entrepreneurs and became the beachhead from which they could later assault the larger market. Anthony Ulwick was influenced by this work. In his book *What Customers Want,* Ulwick links failure to the fact that many businesses don't identify what customers truly want, and this stops them from identifying the emerging niches.[10]

Just because a company invests in research and development does not mean it is going to be at the forefront of the market. In fact, the failure rates for R&D research are close to 90%. Companies are repeatedly developing products that no one wants to buy. Consequently, Ulwick believes more care should be given to what customers want before companies invest in new product or service development.

Ulwick believes that traditional market research is very limited when it comes to identifying customer demand. Research techniques such as focus groups, customer visits and needs-based segmentation do not adequately reveal customer demands. There are several reasons for this. First, market researchers do not know what type of inputs they need to obtain from the customer, and neither does the customer. Traditional market research assumes that customers know best; after all, they are the ones whom we want to buy the product. But customers do not necessarily know best. They are not technologists, scientists or engineers, and the solutions they suggest may lead to disappointing outcomes. Although customers are the ones who determine what will be useful to them, they often are not very good at articulating or analyzing those values. For example, they do not know how the features they desire will affect other features in that product. Second, when asked to define features, they often use imprecise terms that are open to interpretation and leave product designers wondering exactly what they meant. Customers might say they want a product that is "strong" or "durable," but does that mean they want a product that lasts longer? Or did the customers mean they want a product that resists bending or maybe one that withstands moisture? In a study Ulwick conducted with Motorola, customers gave 21 different definitions of "easy to use."

The words given to product designers often leave them wondering what customers really want. Researchers need to be aware of these ambiguities and take increased effort to clearly identify the desired outcomes. They must go through the whole process that a customer goes through when using the product. For example, when assessing customer responses to a circular saw, they must move beyond "how well it cuts" to consider the whole process of use, including preparing the saw, adjusting it, operating it, completing the cut and maintaining the saw.

It is hard to identify what values a customer expects from a product, but Ulwick believes it can be done. He argues that innovation is a science—"a systematic process for creating products or services that deliver value to customers—and not an art form that is forever destined to produce random and unpredictable results."[11] Ulwick's approach rests on three tenets:

1   Customers buy products and services to help them get jobs done.
2   Customers use a set of performance measures (metrics) to judge the performance of a product (i.e., desired outcomes).
3   These "metrics" make it possible to systematically create breakthrough products and services.

For entrepreneurs, the task is how to measure customer value. Creating successful products requires identifying what jobs customers are trying to get done and how they measure success. Once these are revealed, a company can identify opportunities in the market and create products and services that are genuinely in demand. To succeed, companies must have a full understanding of which jobs their customers are trying to get done, the outcomes they are trying to achieve and the constraints that prevent them from using a new product or service.

Product development should not occur without knowledge of these metrics. However, creative-thinking sessions in modern organizations are often done in ignorance of these metrics. In brainstorming sessions, employees are encouraged to think outside the box and come up with imaginative ideas. The result is wasted energy, hundreds of useless ideas that do not bring the company any closer to meeting customer requirements. These metrics give direction to the employees' thinking process, which is more likely to result in products that meet the market demand. If brainstorming sessions begin with a list of required outcomes, it channels creative thinking and is useful for evaluating which ideas are best to pursue.

Ulwick states that 80% of innovations come from existing products and services with an existing client base, but this can put companies in a position of vulnerability. Because of their poor understanding of customer requirements, companies make product improvements in areas that are already satisfied or are of little importance to the customer. For example, I have just bought a laptop with a bulb that lights up when my laptop is plugged in. I am still trying to work out why I need it. Many companies make improvements that customers don't need, or, to put it another way, they over-serve markets. When R&D is driven by engineering possibilities, not customer requirements, the focus is on what can be done rather than what should be done.

It is common for a company to move along its technological trajectory while consumer demand moves in totally different directions. The computer market is an obvious example of this. In this market, product values are often defined as hard-drive capacity, memory and screen size, DVD drive speed, and processor speed. They make these "improvements" to match or outperform their competitors on the basis of "specs." But those specifications are often driven by engineering possibilities, not customer values. Instead of over-serving the customer with product qualities that they don't need, the focus should be on requirements that are not being met by existing products. We need to identify where customers are under-served.

An entrepreneur looking for an opportunity in an existing market needs to differentiate between over-served and under-served markets. Over-served markets are those whose products already meet customer requirements and there is little return from R&D. By contrast, under-served markets involve products that do not sufficiently meet customer requirements. Under-served markets provide opportunities for entrepreneurs who can introduce new or improved products that more accurately provide the values that customers seek. These markets provide opportunities for growth.

Over-served markets also provide opportunities for entrepreneurs. The rise and fall of disc-drive manufacturers that we described in the previous section was the result of a market being over-served. Existing companies invested in R&D in an attempt to make a better product, but they ended up providing values many customers did not want. This enabled entrepreneurs to enter the market with an "inferior" product that better met the needs of many.

If opportunities come from emerging niches, the challenge for the entrepreneur is how to identify them. Market segmentation has received a lot of attention from marketing analysts whose approach has changed significantly over the years. In the 1950s, markets were segmented on the basis of demographic characteristics. Customers were divided into groups based on characteristics such as their age, geographic location or gender. By the 1970s, marketers could draw on advances in psychology research and information technology, and they divided consumers into groups reflecting their common customer traits and attitudes toward products and services. By the 1980s, the emphasis was on needs-based segmentation, in which people were grouped on the basis of what product features they sought. At first glance, needs-based segmentation is not dissimilar to what Ulwick is stressing. Both emphasize finding out what are the core values a customer seeks from a product. However, Ulwick argues that the statements used to identify needs were misleading. He recommends job-based and outcome-based segments.

Job-based segmentation identifies customer groups who are trying to get a job done but are unable to do so with current products and services. If an entrepreneur can devise a solution to this problem, he or she can develop an entirely new market.

Outcome-based segmentation is used in existing markets to find customers with over-served or under-served needs. If the products customers are currently using do not provide adequate outcomes, an opportunity exists for an entrepreneur to make a better product. This may include removing obstacles that prevent a customer from doing a job or building in features that help customers perform more jobs. On the other hand, if the market is over-served, an opportunity exists to provide products and services that are both cheaper and do not contain features the customer does not need.

These are the segments of opportunity for entrepreneurs, and the fact that customer requirements continually change means there will always be opportunities in the marketplace. However, Ulwick believes the best opportunities come from targeting the lowest price-point segment. It is far easier for a small entrepreneur to enter an over-served market with a simple product. The customers will be the least demanding segment of the market, and the entrepreneur has the best chance of delivering all the value needed while still making a profit.

*   *   *

I don't want a business that's easy for competitors. I want a business with a moat around it. I want a very valuable castle in the middle and then I want . . . I want a . . . a . . . I want the duke who's in charge of that castle to be honest and hard working and able, and then I want a big moat around that castle, and that moat can be various things.[12]

(Warren Buffett)

When a business seeks a position in the market, it naturally does so by comparing its product offering with that currently provided by others. Because people have variations in what they seek, this enables entrepreneurs to find niches by differentiating their products. However, when businesses make their products different, they tend to use existing industry values as a basis of comparison as to what constitutes a good product. More opportunities may exist by devising products with values currently not considered by the industry. Breaking these restrictions is the logic behind Kim and Mauborgne's bestselling book, *Blue Ocean Strategy*.[13] W. Chan Kim and Renee Mauborgne are professors at INSEAD, a business school located outside Paris. Their approach to finding opportunities involves a total reconfiguration of the product values stressed in the industry. Otherwise, businesses are confined to competing with existing players; a strategy of offering a little more for a little less.

They give the example of circuses, an industry enduring ongoing decline. Circuses traditionally give value on the basis of price, star performers, animal shows, aisle concessions, multiple arenas, unique venues, fun, humor, thrills and danger. Despite the poor state of the industry, one company enjoyed spectacular growth by redefining the values sold to customers. Cirque du Soleil stepped outside the traditional values and, in so doing, stopped competing with other circuses. It created a new set of values and created a market space without competition. Kim and Mauborgne refer to this uncontested market as the "blue ocean" and contrast it to the "red ocean" that other circuses are trying to compete in.

While Cirque du Soleil prospered, other circuses struggled. They tried to create the best circus experience based on existing values and fought for a share of a declining market. To survive, they would do things like attract the most famous clowns and lion tamers, but this merely pushed up their expenses. Cirque du Soleil broke out of this market by offering a new combination of product values. It dropped the emphasis on animals. It borrowed ideas from Broadway shows, so the circus performance had a theme and was built around a storyline. It refined the watching environment and introduced artistic music and dance, thereby combining the best of circus and theater. These new product values appealed to a whole new set of customers.

Such was the success of Cirque du Soleil that it created a market space free from competition. It was almost as if it had a moat around it, protecting it from attack. It is an illustration of the advantages that come when we create a new niche away from existing companies. Finding such a niche involves thinking beyond current market boundaries. Industries can become entrapped in how they define their industry values and customers. Companies end up focusing on being the best within that framework. If you define your market differently, you no longer compete for the same buyers but create new markets. This is a particularly appealing approach for entrepreneurs, as market research used by leading companies does not reveal these opportunities. The customers they survey simply can't imagine the range of possibilities that could exist in the future. However, an entrepreneur may creatively piece together values from synchronicity and observations peculiar to them.

Once a niche is identified, there are still some basic questions that need to be answered: Does the niche contain enough customers to support a business? What price are customers prepared to pay? Can the products be produced at a cost low enough to produce a product? Can the customers be reached economically through promotion and distribution?

*   *   *

Business is about the provision of value to customers, but what are those values? For the entrepreneur, the task is how to measure value. Customers' demands evolve over time as lifestyles change, and new technologies create new needs, making it possible to solve old ones. New niches can provide opportunities for you to set up a business in established industries, while blind spots can prevent established companies from exploiting the changing market. They are frequently trapped on technological trajectories defined by their past organizational and technological investments. It is easy to see how sales assistants in a shop may already have knowledge of these values from their interactions with customers. Every time a customer comes to them asking for products with specific features, they are gaining knowledge that can help them recognize a business opportunity.

In the disc-drive example described in this chapter, the disruptive technologies were designed by an existing company but exploited by ex-employees. This suggests that opportunities like this are most likely to come from people already working in an industry that is experiencing technological change. The employees then spin off to form their own company. In this, there is cause for optimism. If you feel your ideas are rejected by out-of-touch management and you are frustrated by organizational inertia, it may be time to leave your job, start a company and introduce those ideas yourself.

Chapter 7

Industrial Development: Linkages and Opportunities

When we see a change in the environment, the business openings are often obvious to a number of people. But some of the most lucrative opportunities come not from the first entrepreneurial opportunities but from those that stem from them. An example of someone who rode this second wave of opportunities was John D. Rockefeller, who instead of investing in oil wells invested his capital further down the production chain in oil refineries. This strategy started his journey to becoming the world's richest man.

To help understand this phenomenon, we need to refer to the work of Albert Hirschman. In 1958, Hirschman released *The Strategy of Economic Development,* in which he gave a description of how industries grow over time.[1] According to Hirschman, industries grow by creating linkages. They create "backward linkages" to ensure they have supply of goods and "forward linkages" to increase their market.

The concept is not complicated. It is based on the simple realization that if a business does not have access to the necessary supplies it cannot operate. So it develops backward linkages that ensure supply. If a business cannot import the supplies, it will create new companies that can provide them. Similarly, it needs to develop markets in order to be prosperous. So the business will invest in ventures that increase the use of its product. In this way, one business can spark the creation of other businesses. This opens up the possibility for you to create a business as a supplier or further develop the product.

Many industries have grown in this way. It starts with one initial producer, who is then surrounded by satellite businesses. We see it in the car manufacturer who needs tires and forms ties with a fledging tire manufacturer to meet its needs. The companies grow as a result of dependency on each other. Hirschman gives the example of a cement producer who needs bags for packing, and this leads to a "backward linkage" with the creation of a "multi-wall" bag manufacturer. A "forward linkage" from the cement industry could be a producer of cement blocks. The producer uses the cement from the first industry and creates a new product, thereby expanding the market for both.

Obviously not all new companies create satellite businesses, so it raises the question, "What sort of businesses are likely to have this effect?" The most likely are new industries where supplies are not yet readily available and potential markets are not yet exploited. Another influencing factor is the level of import barriers that protect local production. If there are no barriers to imports and cheap supplies can be brought in from elsewhere, it will be hard to establish a backward linkage. However, if trade barriers exist or if it is a new industry, local production can be a viable option.

The birth of the first company can also encourage new businesses where the links are not so strong. For example, the setting up of a multi-wall bag factory might encourage the creation of a pulp and paper industry. In this case, the bag factory is not a major user of the paper, but the fact that it will buy the paper makes investment in the pulp and paper industry easier. Another example might be the stimulus given by the establishment of an iron and steel industry to the development of metal fabricating businesses. In these cases, the linkage is less direct, but they do encourage entrepreneurs to invest in new businesses.

It is through these linkages that "industrial clusters" are created, where a number of companies are born in the same region. Businesses in industrial clusters benefit from their close relationship to other companies in the region. They develop a regional expertise that helps them compete against companies that aren't in similar clusters. These advantages include the availability of trained staff, free flow of information between companies, and shared infrastructure and training facilities.

It is the lack of these linkages and clusters that has been a key problem for many underdeveloped countries. In these countries, the main industry is subsistence agriculture, where peasant farmers produce food for their own consumption. Linkages do exist, but they are small in scale, and they are limited in number. If an underdeveloped country does modernize its agricultural methods, it increases the range of inputs for fertilizers, insecticides, machines and vehicles, but because these countries are late developers, most of these inputs can be imported much more cheaply from countries that have already established these businesses. This means they probably will not develop these industrial linkages.

In underdeveloped nations, there are also fewer forward linkages stemming from agriculture, as a large proportion of agricultural output in underdeveloped countries is destined directly for consumption or export. There are few domestic linkages. Another industry that is common in underdeveloped nations is mining, and here the same problem is apparent. Mined resources are bought directly by Western producers.

Of course, the economic benefits of a new industry can go beyond these linkages. A new industry brings jobs and income to an economy. When people have more money, new business opportunities open up in areas like retail and real estate. Workers like to go to the movies and drink in bars, and this provides opportunities for entrepreneurs in entertainment. It is as if someone throws a stone into a pond, and the economic ripples radiate outward.

*   *   *

This chapter looks at the entrepreneurial opportunities opened through forward and backward linkages. It is not possible to identify all the types of linkages, for every industry is different. However, if an established industry is coming to town, it might be wise to consider what linkages exist in that industry in other locations. With brand new industries, it is less easy to predict the linkages, and you may be able to shape their development. Another factor to consider is the way these linkages vary as technology changes. An innovation in the master business can send a wave of activity up and down the industrial chain, affecting all the interrelated businesses. You must be sensitive to these changes.

This chapter builds on a paper by Stephen Mezias and Jerome Kuperman, who examined the formation of the movie industry.[2] Technological change in the movie industry was relatively slow compared with industries that emerged at the end of the twentieth century. Nevertheless, it is a useful example to illustrate the development of linkages and the entrepreneurs who built them. This is an industry that everyone knows. We have all consumed the product, and we all have some awareness of the different production, distribution and exhibition stages. We also know some of the names that built this industry. Not only is it informative, but it is interesting.

The paper by Mezias and Kuperman built on the idea that entrepreneurs do not exist in isolation. They exist as part of larger communities, and in many respects their success is determined by this social system. Their success is interdependent with other entrepreneurs. You may be more successful if you recognize some of the ways in which your success may depend on the actions of entrepreneurs throughout this community. Producers, distributors and exhibitors are all part of the value chain in this industry. The actions of one can affect the opportunities for others.

This chapter goes a step further than the article by Mezias and Kuperman and looks at the profiles of some of those entrepreneurs. It supports the idea that different stages of industrial development and different links required different skill sets from people wanting to start businesses. The pioneers were originally technical people. Once the technology had stabilized, a new wave of entrepreneurs imitated their success and had skills that could add value to the final product. Forward linkages were created by people with business skills.

This chapter also helps to illustrate the effect of technological change on linkages and how they open up new opportunities and force change on existing players. We frequently exaggerate the stability of industries. In reality, they are a moving target with waves of innovation running down their spine. These changes open doors for some types of entrepreneurs and close doors for others. As you read this history, keep your eyes open for the types of change that affected the various businesses.

The Movie Industry

In the same way that the lighting market has incurred a number of value improvements over time, so too has the market for visual stimulation. Movies are just one in a long line of such products. The movie industry did not just appear at the end of the nineteenth century. It evolved from a series of products that have given people mental and visual stimulation.

The earliest visual entertainment products included paintings and sculpture, but these were static images. One of the earliest products to provide moving images was the magic lantern. First constructed in 1659, magic lanterns used oil lamps and recent advances in optics. The lamp lit a slide that would create an image that could be focused on a screen. Mechanical slides with moving parts helped to create simple moving images.[3] Magic lanterns became very popular in eighteenth-century Europe, popularized by showmen who walked from town to town with lanterns on their backs.

A more sophisticated step in moving images came in 1832 from the Belgian Joseph Plateau, who built what he called the phenakistiscope. This device used a rotating disc with a number of drawings on it of figures in various stages of movement. When the disk was spun around, the figures merged into one and produced images that seemed to move. This illusion of movement came about as a result of the way humans perceive things. For some reason, the human eye supplies the missing motion between a series of still pictures. This phenomenon is called "persistence of vision," and its discovery was crucial for the development of motion pictures, for movies also work on the basis of rapidly played stationary pictures. But that would not be for another 60 years. In the meantime, other entrepreneur-inventors came up with products that exploited this perceptual weakness.

These early products all relied on painted images. Each figure had to be drawn or painted on the drum individually. The alternative to painting was photography, which owes its origins to the Frenchman Joseph Nicephore Niepce. The earliest photographic images used a compound of silver to reproduce an image on a pewter plate. However, it took eight hours to make the copy, severely limiting its use. No model or actor was going to sit in one place for eight hours while the image was exposed. Over the following years, a number of people worked at perfecting the technology, and by the 1870s the time required to take an image had been reduced to just 1/25th of a second.[4]

At this point, the technology became a useful tool for scientists studying motion. In 1873, the British photographer Eadweard Muybridge was commissioned by a former governor of California, Leland Stanford, to settle a wager on whether all four feet of a horse were ever off the ground at the same time as it ran. Muybridge eventually devised a method of taking successive photographs of animals to show how they moved. If he displayed the photos in rapid succession, Muybridge could take advantage of the "persistence of vision" phenomenon, and re-create the sense of movement. Thus, for the first time, a series of still photographs were used to create a moving image.

A big step forward in making moving images occurred when Muybridge went to Paris, where he met the physiologist Etienne-Jules Marey, who had been analyzing the flight of a bird. This meeting inspired Marey to develop a camera that used the mechanism from a Colt revolver. This "photographic revolver" could take 12 pictures per second and was later raised to 100. Universities also helped advance the technology. In the 1880s, Muybridge was supported by the University of Pennsylvania in his research, while Marey was a professor of natural history at the College de France.

The earliest images were reproduced onto glass plates, a difficult material for capturing repeated images. A stronger, more flexible medium was needed. Celluloid was first invented by a company looking for a strong material to manufacturing printer's rollers, but it was soon found to have wider uses. In the late 1880s, the photographic firm Carbutt of Philadelphia used it as an alternative to glass. George Eastman, who had previously marketed paper rolls of film, quickly recognized the benefits of this new material and began marketing rolls of celluloid with his company, Kodak.

Now all of the technologies were in place to create the movie industry; the creation of the photographic process, the invention of the celluloid film and the discovery of "persistence of vision." These three developments had raised knowledge to a threshold where it was possible to make the next step and piece them all together. A window of opportunity was open. All it needed was someone to make the connections and create a new industry.

Given that Muybridge had already exploited "persistence of vision" with photographic technology and the celluloid film was developed for use in photography, it did not require a genius to have the final idea. The idea was out there, although not everybody had access to the relevant information. However, more important than having the idea was having the capabilities to make the idea work. The successful person had to make a machine that embodied all these technologies (in yet another reminder of the saying "an idea is nothing more than a tool in the hands of an entrepreneur"[5]).

One person had the necessary skills and capital to exploit the opportunity. That man was Thomas Edison, who had previously invented the electric light bulb and phonograph. He was building a company called General Electric and was funding a number of areas of research. Edison was also fortunate enough to meet both Muybridge in 1888 and the Frenchman Marey in 1889. In fact, it is possible that Marey gave him one of the most important pieces of information to bring the idea together: putting perforation in the edge of the film.[6] In 1894, Edison wrote to Muybridge:

> I have constructed a little instrument which I call a Kinetoscope, with a nickel slot attachment and some twenty five have been made out. I am very doubtful if there is any commercial future in it and fear that they will not earn their cost.[7]

The Kinetoscope was a box in which film was rolled past a light. Viewers looked into the box to see moving images, like a peep show. Much of the development work was actually done by Edison's assistant W. K. Dickson, who, as well as working on the new machine, also worked on the films that would be seen in it. In a specially built studio, Dickson shot simple films of acts by leading music hall and circus stars, including Annie Oakley and Buffalo Bill. Other films included slice-of-life or odd sights. They were simple unedited films lasting less than a minute.

The Kinetoscope was first revealed to the public at the Chicago World Fair in 1893. The following year, ten coin-operated Kinetoscopes were in a New York City amusement arcade. Its launch was not free of criticism. Some of the films, such as

How Bridget Served the Salad Undressed, were criticized for being too suggestive. But, overall, the new product became popular and profitable.

The new product opened up opportunities for many people to start their own businesses. The first spin-off entrepreneurial venture in the industry came in 1895, when W. K. Dickson, who had done so much work developing the technology, left Edison's factory to start his own company. Together with members of the Latham family, they formed the American Mutoscope and Biograph Company (later known simply as Biograph). The company developed its own projector with which it gave what is probably the first projected movie show in America, scenes of boys playing in a park and a man smoking a pipe.[8]

The "chance" element to entrepreneurial launch is illustrated by the activities of J. Stuart Blackton. While working as a journalist and illustrator for the *New York World,* Blackton interviewed Thomas Edison. During the interview, Edison had the opportunity to see some of Blackton's drawings. These drawings became the subject of a film for the Kinetosope. This baptism gave Blackton the introduction to the industry during its early growth period. He became fascinated with the industry and in 1897 formed the company that would later be known as Vitagraph, with his friend Albert E. Smith. Their first movie, *The Burglar on the Roof* featured Blackton as the thief. Vitagraph, Biograph and the Edison Company were the major American movie production companies of the industry's first decade.

Often with new product technologies, a number of options are developed before a dominant design is established.[9] An alternative to Edison's peep shows was to project films onto a screen. It is an idea that borrows from the old magic lantern technology. In Germany, Britain and the United States, a number of aspiring inventors were looking for ways to project film, but it was in France where the final breakthrough came. Louis and Auguste Lumière had built a profitable factory in Lyon, which in 1895 employed 300 workers manufacturing photographic plates. When they had the opportunity to see one of Edison's Kinetoscopes, they were inspired to develop their own product. The result was a combination camera-projector, which they called the cinematographie (from which we get the word "cinema"). The Lumières gave the first commercial exhibition of projected movies at the Grand Café in Paris 1895. The show included the first comedy: a prank played on a gardener who is squirted with his own hose.[10]

The Lumière brothers had an acute business sense and could draw on their experience as producers of photographic plates. They did not rush their invention to the market but gave it a strategic launch. They waited almost a year after gaining a patent before giving the first public demonstration. This gave them time to build more machines, train camera operators and be ready to exploit the device's success. They guarded each of their machines and organized their own worldwide film shoots and screenings.[11] By 1900, they had produced about 2,000 films.[12]

Not everyone entering the industry succeeded, and the importance of business skills can be seen in the case of two Americans, C. Francis Jenkins and Thomas Armat. They developed their own projection system not long after the Lumières, but while technologically creative, they appear to have lacked the necessary entrepreneurial skills to exploit their invention. They lost money, sold their patent to Edison, and went their separate ways.

The Lumière brothers' machines had a number of advantages over Edison's product. Compared with Edison's bulky machine, the cinematographie was portable and included a camera. But most importantly, the French machine projected a movie onto a screen that many people could watch, whereas Edison's machine allowed only one person at a time to look through a peephole. However, the spread of projection was restricted by a lack of regular places to screen the movies in front of large audiences. By contrast, Edison's machine required no special venue. Consequently, in the early years, both technologies were used.

Projected films were exhibited anywhere an audience could be housed, including church socials, fairs, music halls, penny arcades and travelling road shows. Film producers realized that if their industry was to enjoy stable growth, they had to find more reliable outlets to exhibit their films. In 1899, Biograph pioneered a forward linkage that caused a critical change in the industry's dynamics. The company began marketing its product to vaudeville theaters. The short films became one act in an evening of vaudeville entertainment and stabilized the demand for films. The linkage between moving pictures and vaudeville was quickly established with films now viewed regularly by mass audiences.[13]

Gradually, amusement arcade managers also began to set aside areas to screen projected films. The first entrepreneur to set up a theater showing movies exclusively was Thomas L. Tally. In 1902, he set up Thomas L. Tally's Electric Theater in a storefront in Los Angeles.

Entrepreneurial Opportunities for Those Who Can Add Value

In the next stage of development, many of the successful entrepreneurs who entered the industry at the production end were those who had skills that they could use to add value to the core product. They could improve product quality and market reach.

Although the basic technology for making and showing films was in place by the end of the nineteenth century, the quality of the product left much to be desired. Early movies were nothing like those we see today. There were no specialized directors, actors and camera operators who were masters of their craft. It was not uncommon for the producer to also be the actor in the movie. And most films did not even have a story. Most were slice-of-life shots, relying on their novelty. They included shots of an approaching train, a passing parade or, at its most elaborate, a current event like a heavyweight title fight. And the films did not last long: somewhere between 15 and 90 seconds. It was not a product that justified investment in large theaters.

Over time, creative producers began to see how movies could offer unique ways to tell a story. With the use of movie technology, they could create effects that could not be employed on the stage. For example, in 1895, the Edison Studio used trick photography in *The Execution of Mary, Queen of Scots.* For this film, the camera was stopped during the beheading scene, the actress was replaced by a dummy and the dummy's head removed. This movie lasted 30 seconds.

It was the French who added the most value to the technology in the early years. George Méliès was a conjurer and an illusionist who also worked with stage puppets and magic lanterns. After seeing an exhibition of Lumière's projectors, he realized their potential for use in his shows. At first, he used films made by others as part of his shows, but eventually he started making his own films. His previous profession gave him the experience and skills he could use to add value to the films, and soon he was creating illusions with the camera. In 1897, he set up a studio where he created films of fantasy, including *The Melonmaniac,* in which he played a character who removed his head, had it replaced by another and then threw the discarded head on a telegraph wire.[14] In *The Man with the Rubber Head,* he used double exposures to give the impression that his head was inflated to a massive size. His 1902 narrative movie, *A Trip to the Moon,* pioneered special effects and included a rocket plunging into the face of the "man in the moon." (This movie was more recently given new life with the music video "Tonight, Tonight" by the Smashing Pumpkins.)

The leading company in the world during these early years was Pathé Frères. Its success illustrates entrepreneurs who expanded into activities that complemented their existing business activities. The Pathé brothers were café owners in Paris. To attract customers, they had installed a new phonograph in their café to play music. Soon customers were asking if they could actually buy the phonograph. In yet another example that illustrates the importance of customers in producing business ideas, these requests brought the Pathé brothers to the realization that there was a market for the phonograph. Initially they tried importing them from Edison but couldn't get any, so they got a local engineering firm to create a similar one. Before long the company was making and selling phonographs and recordings.

When the brothers had the opportunity to first see motion pictures, they were attracted by its potential and diversified into filmmaking. Entering the industry at a time when many of the technological problems were solved, they could make the most of their business skills. By the middle of the first decade of the twentieth century, Pathé Frères was producing, distributing and exhibiting films. In doing all three tasks, it had become the first integrated company in the industry. Pathé Frères was also one of the first exporters of films. By 1908, Pathé Frères was the largest single source of films in the United States, larger than any American firm. By 1914, it had 42 offices around the world. Within a very short time, superior French entrepreneurship had created the most successful film company in the world, a vertically integrated giant.[15]

Another French company, the Société du Film D'Art, was formed to produce art films linked to a classical theater, thereby gaining access to the top actors of the day. One of its films, *The Assassination of the Duc de Guise,* even had a score written for its accompaniment by Camille Saint-Saens.[16]

The quality of American films was well behind the French, but advances were being made. J. Stuart Blackton, a founder of the Vitagraph Company, drew on his previous career as a newspaper illustrator to produce *Humorous Phases of Funny Faces*. This movie is generally recognized as the forerunner of the animated cartoon. Over the following years, he introduced a number of value-adding innovations, including the close shot, editing techniques, two- to three-reel comedies and adaptations from Shakespeare's plays.

At the Edison studio, the chief of production, Edwin S. Porter, continually looked for new ways to improve the quality of product. In his movie *Life of an American Fireman,* he was no longer content to move from one scene to another. He used creative editing techniques that included cutting from place to place, from the inside to the outside of a house on fire, thereby increasing his ability to tell a story (although there is some doubt whether he was the first to use these techniques).[17] Porter also used these techniques to create a narrative in the first Western, *The Great Train Robbery,* a film that lasted 12 minutes.

Quality improvements were also a result of technical advances. For example, the team at Biograph invented a three-blade shutter that reduced the amount of flickering on films. Another important technology was the introduction of mercury lamps, which made indoor shooting practical, making it easier to put together interior and exterior scenes to tell a complete story.

At a time when most films were nonfiction "slices of life," Biograph became increasingly committed to fiction, or "story" films. In 1908, it employed J. W. Griffith, who, more than any other director, contributed to the advance of American production. For example, until this time, films were made with the camera placed in one position, normally at 12 feet from the actors at right angles to the scene. Griffith introduced more variation, altering camera angles and breaking scenes into multiple shots. By 1909, his movies were being compared to French movies. The *New York Dramatic Mirror* said of his *A Fools Revenge:* "this is the first American film that we have felt justified in pronouncing the equal in smoothness of construction and power of dramatic action of any of the Pathé 'film d'art.' "[18]

Barriers to Growth

A major barrier to industry growth that limited the opportunities for people wanting to enter this industry was the restrictions placed on the use of movie cameras. Edison's company held most of the patents for the equipment used in the industry and took legal action against everyone. Edison launched legal battles against equipment manufacturers, film producers, distributors and exhibitors. Some film companies such as Vitagraph and Maguire Baucus capitulated and became Edison licensees. Others, like the American Film Company, shut down operations. Edison's stature, combined with his deep pockets to finance legal battles, intimidated the fledging community, and this stifled investment.[19]

Some companies felt they could take Edison on. Sigmund Lubin and Edward Amet were based in Chicago. Knowing that any legal battle would occur on their home turf, they accepted the challenge of Edison, who was forced to back down.[20] Biograph, one of the original three big companies, responded by counterattacking

Edison in the courts. In particular, it accused Edison of breaching the patent it held for the three-blade camera shutter.

Given the effect it had on investment, this episode raises an interesting question about the role of intellectual property and industrial development. Economists generally recognize that patents protect inventors and encourage innovation and economic growth. However, when restrictions are placed on the use of capital goods, it can inhibit industrial growth.

In another area of the industry, there was a definite need for greater legal protection to generate economic growth. Many producers found that their films were being copied by other firms. This discouraged companies from investing in expensive, quality productions as the rewards would go to other people. It was not until a court decision addressed a movie based on the book *Ben Hur* that legal protection was provided. The court decided that the film producers breached copyright by making the movie without the permission of the publishers, who owned the copyright for the book. Although the film producers lost the case, this decision meant that, from now on, the content of movies was covered by copyright law. It was only after this 1911 decision that producers could invest in films knowing they would be protected by copyright, and the industry experienced a rapid increase in quality. These intellectual property arguments directly relate to today's technologies; for example, the copying of music on the Internet.

Many management theorists stress that the growth of any industry is hampered in its early days by the need to gain legitimacy, and in the early days the movie industry was far from respectable.[21] Some society groups, such as Boston's Twentieth Century Club, saw it as a "less desirable form of recreational amusement." The New York Society for the Prevention of Cruelty to Children attacked movies for showing children how to commit crimes. Stage actors did not take films seriously, disparagingly referring to them as "the flickers" on account of the annoying flickering that characterized early movies.[22] However, this lack of respectability did not stop growth. Actors might not have thought much of them compared to the stage, but this did not stop them from working in them, especially in the summer months when Broadway took a rest. Whether the industry would have grown faster without legitimacy problems is another question. There is much to suggest that legitimacy did not affect growth, and what we have is a product that initially appealed to a niche working-class market before quality improvements spread its appeal to the general market.

Opportunities from the Next Wave of Forward Linkages

In 1905, a Pittsburgh-based vaudeville magnate and real estate speculator, Harry Davis, opened a movie retail outlet that would become the industry norm for the next five years: the first nickelodeon. These small theaters had seating for less than 200 viewers, who could enter for a nickel (from which they get their name). They were located in storefronts and showed films with piano accompaniment. They gave

12 to 18 performances a day, seven days a week. The films shown in the nickelodeons were contained on one reel of film; hence, they were known as one-reelers, or shorts.[23]

Nickelodeons were the retail end of the industry, a forward linkage from the producers. For business people to invest in this end of the chain, they needed to have confidence, and it is probably no coincidence that the first movie shown was Porter's innovative *The Great Train Robbery,* which raised the quality of the product. Confidence must also have been gained from the growing urban audience, fuelled by immigration. With improving product and a growing market, a window of opportunity had opened in the industry for entrepreneurs to take the product to the people. Soon other entrepreneurs were imitating the success of Davis and opened nickelodeons.

Nickelodeons required the skills of businesspeople willing to take a chance on something new. Unlike the other parts of the industry, these entrepreneurs did not need technical or theatrical skills, but business skills. Businessmen who seized the opening and later made a name in the industry included Adolph Zukor, a furrier; Marcus Loew, the owner of urban amusement arcades; Jesse Lasky, whose resume listed gold prospector and vaudeville performer; Sam Goldwyn, a glove salesman; the Warner Brothers, who operated a bicycle repair business; William Fox, garment manufacturer; and Louis B. Mayer, who literally sold junk.[24] Many of the nickelodeon entrepreneurs were ex-vaudeville managers who knew the entertainment market, a reminder that business knowledge can be an advantage to those finding business opportunities.

Within months of the first opening, nickelodeons were springing up all over the country. They were very popular with immigrants and working-class audiences, and it is probably no coincidence that many of the successful entrepreneurs were immigrants themselves. They could identify with their audience, and this must have helped guide their investment decisions. Many of them were Jews, outsiders in a predominantly gentile society, and they were not afraid to be associated with an industry still just outside the realms of respectability.[25]

New business opportunities were also seized in ancillary industries. In 1906, the *Views and Film Index,* the first industry trade paper, was published, followed by *Moving Picture World.* In 1907, *Variety,* the "bible of show business," began publishing its first film reviews.

The introduction of nickelodeons created a quickly growing wave for entrepreneurs. In 1907, the *Saturday Evening Post* reported that daily attendance at the nickelodeons had broken the $2 million mark. That same year, *Moving Picture World* estimated that 2,500 to 3,000 nickelodeons were in existence. By 1910, the number had grown to approximately 10,000. Because of the growing audience, the spread of nickelodeons also created opportunities at the production stage. The rising number of exhibition outlets encouraged investment in film production. The total amount of film being turned out increased from approximately 7,000 feet per month in January 1906 to 30,00 feet per month just 20 months later in August 1907.[26]

Opportunities in Distribution: Another Link in the Chain

In the early days, film producers sent mail-order catalogues to the owners of amusement parlors and managers of vaudeville houses, who in turn would order films directly from the company. This system of distribution changed in 1902, when Henry Miles set up the first film exchange in San Francisco.[27] The development of exchanges as middlemen was a natural result of growth in an industry that required more organized distribution. Exchanges became a new link in the industry and opened up a new wave of opportunities for entrepreneurs.

These exchanges acted like libraries. Exhibitors would rent films instead of buying them, and that made it easier and more affordable to change shows more often. This was very important at a time when the quality of the product was not high and the potential audience was quickly exhausted. The only way to continue to attract audiences was through rapid turnover of films. Exchanges enabled exhibitors to turn products over relatively quickly. For producers, exchanges had the advantage of increasing the market reach of their product (although they were rentals, not sales).

Many of the exchanges were actually started by nickelodeon owners, such as Harry Aitken, who owned five nickelodeon theaters in Chicago.[28] He teamed up with John Frueler, who owned nickelodeons in Milwaukee, to form the Western Film Exchange. It quickly expanded to include branch offices in Chicago; St. Louis; and Joplin, Missouri. But not all exchange owners came with this background. For example, Carl Laemmle started an exchange in 1906 after managing a clothing store in Wisconsin. His introduction to the industry came one night in Chicago:

> "I dropped into one of those hole-in-the-wall five-cent motion picture theaters. . . . The pictures made me laugh, though they were very short and the projection jumpy. I liked them, and so did everybody else. I knew right away that I wanted to go into the motion picture business."[29]

While the new distribution system might have been good for the exchanges, times were not so rosy for the producers. As the decade came to an end, the audience began to tire of the novelty of these films, and demand began to slow. Another problem for producers was the influx of imported films. In 1909, approximately half of the total industry production was by foreign companies. Distributors and exhibitors were still making healthy profits, but American producers were being squeezed.[30]

This was before copyright protection for films had been introduced with the *Ben Hur* court case. Lack of copyright protection discouraged investment in quality as producers knew that their innovations would soon be copied. The films of the day were basically commodity products. Producers made films of similar content, sold their product to the same exchange markets and had their products exhibited in the same nickelodeons.[31] In effect, there was very little to distinguish between the competition. Commodity products are easy to reproduce, and a number of entrepreneurs jumped on the bandwagon, spawned by the spread of nickelodeons. Scores of small, independent firms now existed in the industry. The industry was experiencing the eternal problem of investors making decisions without full awareness of the actions of others. The result was an over-supply situation, where producers were squeezed. It is a pattern that has occurred again and again in business history, and the solution invariably involves amalgamation of producers. The American movie industry amalgamated, resulting in the formation of a trust: a common solution in the American economy at the time. Many industries from oil to steel had formed trusts to gain greater control of the market.

The trust was a cartel called the Motion Picture Patents Corporation (MPPC). The companies involved were Biograph, Vitagraph, Essanay, Selig, the Edison Studio, Kalem, Lubin, the two French companies Pathé and Méliès, and an importer George Kleine.[32] The cartel was organized as a holding company with shares equally owned by Edison and Biograph, the companies who owned most of the patents.

The cartel brought stability to the industry as members agreed to coordinate production quotas and scheduled release dates for each member company. The cartel also wanted to bring an end to all competition from outside the cartel. It took legal action against non-member producers for patent violations, and if the lawsuits did not work, the cartel would resort to violence, sending goons to break up any filming. It also persuaded Kodak to sell film only to member companies, thereby putting a big barrier in the way of other producers.

To increase the market power of member companies, the cartel began licensing exhibitors and distributors. It would only distribute films to businesses that held a license and agreed to their terms. This meant that the exchanges had to accept the price set by the cartel and not accept product from companies outside the cartel. This put exhibitors and distributors in an awkward situation. Without product from MPPC, their biggest supplier, they would go out of business. Many signed up.

As more and more exchanges signed up, independent filmmakers were in danger of having no one to distribute and exhibit their films. To avoid being shut out of the industry, they had to demonstrate to the still-independent exchanges that they could supply them with sufficient product to keep them in business.[33] To do this, they created a new distribution organization called the Motion Picture Distribution and Sales Company. Formed in 1910, its role was to take a product from the independents and distribute it.

Although set up as a defensive action, this new company had the added advantage of creating a more organized and efficient form of distribution. In recognition of its strengths, the MPPC created a similar organization to distribute its product and manage the exchanges it had licensed. Under the name of the General Film Company, it bought out the previously independent exchanges handling distribution, putting the movie distribution and production business under one roof, a model for the coming Hollywood system.

There were other defensive responses to the actions of the cartel. Many independent distributors started to make their own films. For example, theater chain owner William Fox began to make pictures, thereby giving birth to the company that would one day become Twentieth Century Fox. Another to respond this way was

Carl Laemmle. He also integrated backwards into film production, thereby ensuring a steady supply of products. He set up his own Independent Motion Picture Company (IMP). Not being able to buy film from Kodak, he imported film stock from abroad. His company grew to become the core of Universal Studios.

In the Midwest, exchange owners Harry Aitken and John Frueler also began making their own films under the name the American Film Manufacturing Company. However, when the MPPC heard of the venture, it went as far as hiring snipers to shoot at their cameras during filming. Consequently, the independents decided to shift their entire production facilities to Santa Barbara, California. California had other advantages, including a climate that allowed year-round filming, and was close to the Mexico border should they need to escape the MPPC. Aitken and Frueler also formed a second studio called Majestic Film, whose stable of actors would include Mary Pickford, Gloria Swanson and Douglas Fairbanks.[34]

The independents also introduced new methods of marketing their films. Until 1910, film companies did not bother to name their actors and actresses, partly out of fear that they would then demand higher salaries, as was the practice of stars in the theater. The pubic recognized the actors' and actresses' faces but knew them only by the name of the company they worked for. For example, Florence Lawrence was known as the "Biograph girl." Laemmle broke with convention by naming artists, and he did it in the most dramatic fashion. Laemmle signed the "Biograph girl" to his studio in 1910. He then spread a false newspaper story that she had died, before following it with an angry rebuttal in advertisements.[35] The strategy worked with healthy returns at the box office. Stars became "brand names" that helped sell movies, but unlike other brands, humans can negotiate higher salaries once they acquire market power. For example, Mary Pickford joined the Majestic Company for $275 a week. In 1913, she joined Zukor's Famous Players for $500 a week, which was raised the following year to $2,000 a week.[36] The pulling power of stars became so important that, by 1917, it was estimated that only 5% of American features were without the protection of a star name.[37]

Through these combinations of strategies, the independents managed to withstand the threat of Edison's trust. As early as 1910, Kodak realized it was not in its interest to restrict sales to the patents company, and it resumed selling film to anyone who wished to buy it. By 1912, production by independent film companies was nearly equivalent to total MPPC production. In addition, during the same year, the first suit under the Sherman Anti-Trust Act was brought against the MPPC, charging that it was a restraint of trade.[38] To make matters worse, the following week, a U.S. circuit court ruled that the MPPC did not have a claim to exclusive rights on the mechanism used in movie cameras, the base of its patent actions. It was the beginning of the end for the cartel.

Despite these legal losses, MPPC might have been able to maintain its hold on the market if it were not for one important fact: the market was losing interest in its product. It seemed the only members of the cartel that realized this were Vitagraph and the French company Pathé. According to Albert Smith, the cofounder of Vitagraph, "Public apathy toward 'galloping tintypes' daily became more marked: some sort of move had to be made."[39] The one-reel shorts no longer had novelty value for the audience. It was an obsolete product that most members of the MPPC vigorously clung to. In fact, MPPC rules stated that they would only distribute one-reel films.

Entrepreneurial Learning: Consumer Response to a New Product

Many entrepreneurs yearn for a period of stability once they have set up their business, but once you have set up your business, you must be prepared to continually learn from your customers and make changes to your operations and products in light of what you have learned. In the next stage of the movie industry, this process of learning was very important for success.

In 1909, Vitagraph pioneered a new product strategy. Its movie *The Life of Moses* was released in pieces, as a series of short films. They were released one reel at a time. By building bridges across the films, maintaining characters and building more complex story lines than could normally be accommodated, these serials captured large audiences.[40]

Given the positive audience response to these serials, it was not a big mental leap to realize that films longer than one reel would also be popular. Soon multi-reel films were being produced with complicated story lines and all the characteristics of what is today called a "feature film." The first four-reel feature film was made in 1912, but its popularity was such that it soon became the industry norm. Within only two years, the number of companies making features had grown from 1 to 114.[41]

At first, most producers were reluctant to make serial films; the MPPC companies were particularly resistant. As late as 1913, the management at Biograph was appalled when its leading director, J. W. Griffith, produced the movie *Judith of Bethulia*, a four-reel film coming in at double the budget. Griffith was relieved of his directing duties, so he joined the newly formed Mutual, taking with him his cameraman and company of actors.[42] Mutual obtained his services by promising him the right to make a long film of his own each year. However, his first film, the historically-based *The Clansman*, was running into 12 reels, taking 120 minutes. Harry Aitken addressed the company's board saying the movie would be a historical landmark and would be highly profitable for the company. However, the board was dominated by conservative bankers and financiers who would not support it. So Aitken raised money and launched the film independently. The film, which was renamed *Birth of a Nation*, was a huge success with staggering returns. The board at Mutual was furious at missing out and fired Aitken, who, with the profits from the film, created a new studio called Triangle. He took to his new business much of the old company's talent, leaving it in a depleted state from which it never recovered. Mutual went into a steady decline before shutting down in 1918.[43]

Having learned from the success of the last film, the new company launched another expensive masterpiece, *Intolerance,* a film lasting three and three-quarter hours with four stories running parallel. Unfortunately, the movie was a colossal flop. Money became tight, and, one by one, the company's talent left for other companies.

Triangle was eventually shut down, and its facilities were sold to Louis Mayer, who established MGM. This experience illustrates the difficulty in reading consumer demand for products that are new. All new products and industries must go through a period of learning which product characteristics customers want. Entrepreneurship can be a process of trial and error, in which error is brutally punished.

These new multi-reel films were not popular with the two distribution cartels.[44] Even the distribution company established by the independents did not want to handle them. Once again, the refusal of established companies to adapt to change created an opportunity for new businesses to be established. Their refusal to handle the films created a window of opportunity for new entrepreneurs, and two new forms of distributors appeared to fill the void. They were road-show operators and states-rights distributors. Road-show operators were companies that toured the country and played the feature films as special attractions in local opera houses, town halls and theaters. They stayed in each town for as long as the business was there to support them and then moved on to the next town. If a film was not on a road show or if the tour had come to an end, the states-rights distributors would step in. These individuals and small companies would attain the rights to exhibit the film in a specific territory and charge the public whatever price they thought the market would bear. These two forms of distribution were yet another forward linkage from producers of the new product to ensure that serials and multi-reels reached their market.

The development of feature films also caused changes in the next link in the industry chain. Because the movies were longer and had customers sitting for longer periods, an increased emphasis was placed on the comfort of the exhibition hall, in particular the quality of the seating. The old nickelodeons were no longer good enough, so new opulent theaters were built, such as the Strand Theater in New York, which opened in 1914. To cover the increased costs of such theaters, admission price was raised to a dime, but it did not negatively affect the industry's growth, which gained a new respectability and opened the burgeoning middle-class market. The size of these movie palaces, which could seat thousands, offered other economic advantages, in particular, increased economies of scale for each viewing.

The move to multi-reel films is one of those moments in business history where established companies fail to respond to a new product development and suffer as a consequence. In a situation very similar to the development of smaller disc drives mentioned in the previous chapter, the companies were rigidly devoted to their old trajectory. It is noteworthy that only one of the MPPC producers went on to become a major producer of features (Vitagraph).

We often blame failures of large companies on complacency, while independents are praised for being more flexible. But this is not the case here. Edison went on to introduce more innovations. For example, in 1913, the Edison Company introduced a new technology that synchronized a phonograph record with a film. This innovation would have revolutionized the industry and brought an end to the silent movie. However, the process was still in its technical infancy and did not always work well. On March 21 of that year, *Variety* reported that the films were booed at a New York theater.

Nor could it be said that the new wave of entrepreneurs were any more open to change. For example, in 1914, Carl Laemmle declared in the *Universal Weekly* that feature-length films were a fad. He preferred serials, as it meant that customers kept coming back for the next episode.[45]

One reason why established companies had trouble changing is because the new product required different production processes. Multi-reel films required different production techniques from the short films of the previous decade. While shorts had been easily created like commodities on a production line, each feature film was treated as a unique product and had its own organizational and creative requirements. New tasks appeared, and old tasks became more specialized. These included learning new approaches to tasks such as scriptwriting, directing, acquiring and developing talent, keeping within budgets, and promotion. This was a period in which the U.S. movie industry dramatically enhanced its skill base and developed capabilities with which it became world leaders.

Multi-reels required a new way of thinking about film structure and composition, and some producers of shorts seemed to lack the ability to think and operate at the level of complexity needed to produce serial shorts or multi-reel films. One producer who seems to have had trouble making the transition was Edwin S. Porter from Edison, although he was certainly aware of the qualities of the films. In fact, he had earlier suggested to Adolph Zukor, the future head of Paramount Studios, that he import the four-reel *Queen Elizabeth* from France. But Porter was at heart a technician and had trouble making the transition to multi-reel films. The industry change favored entrepreneurs with different skills.[46]

While some people had trouble making the transition, many new entrepreneurs rose to prominence by building on their previous skills. Biograph suffered from the transition to features, but it had been an important incubator for future entrepreneurs and talent. One spin-off entrepreneur from this company was Mack Sennett, who joined the company as an actor, having previously been a vaudeville performer. At Biograph, he learned some directing skills under the tutelage of D. W. Griffith. In August 1912, Sennett spun off from Biograph and formed the Keystone Film Company. This was bootstrap entrepreneurship with very little resources.[47] Their first films used a house that a good-natured local lent them. They had intended to use a hired car, but the price was $20, more than the whole wage bill ($15). To get to the location, they had to use public transport. The crew boarded local streetcars: the cameraman carrying his camera, actors carrying the props and Sennet carrying the scenery on his back.

The company eventually moved to Los Angeles. Here the company filmed many of its enduring products featuring the Keystone Kops. In 1913, Keystone signed an aspiring performer by the name of Charlie Chaplin. Within a few years, Chaplin created his own spin-off enterprise when he joined Mary Pickford, Douglas Fairbanks and D. W. Griffiths to form United Artists, the company that today brings us James Bond.

Keystone was not the only company moving to California. Many companies were moving West. Until this time, the major studios were headquartered in the East.

The first film company to film in California was the Chicago-based Selig, which filmed *The Count of Monte Cristo* on the beach in Santa Monica. In the years to come, others would follow. Some independents moved there to escape the clutches of the MPPC. Others moved there for the weather, which allowed year-round filming, while some found it a better place for filming Westerns. On April 8, 1910, it was reported in the *Moving Picture World* that "Los Angeles within the short period of two years has reached a position in the moving industry where it is second only to New York."[48]

Once a region develops an industrial beachhead, it soon generates other advantages for attracting more firms. Entrepreneurs setting up business in an area with similar producers can benefit from "external economies" of location. For example, in Los Angeles and New York, entrepreneurs had easy access to actors, technicians and directors, and these people frequently moved between employers. Businesses could also form cooperative ties with other firms in the same area.[49] In these ways, the environment contributed to more economical operations for individual businesses.

Many of the new film production companies appearing at this time had been created by owners of distribution companies. These backward linkages created companies that both produced and distributed films. A strong relationship between production and distribution made it easier to coordinate promotion and distribution efforts. This led to a flurry of corporate maneuvering. In 1914, Carl Laemmle merged his company IMP with several other independent studios to form the Universal Film Manufacturing Company, the first major Hollywood studio. That same year Fox Film Company, the predecessor to Twentieth Century Fox, also vertically integrated into distribution. In 1916 Adolph Zukor merged his company, the Famous Players Film Company, with the company's distributor, Paramount Pictures, to create what would become the dominant company in the industry for the next 30 years. In 1924, Metro Pictures took over Goldwyn Pictures, recruited the talents of the successful executive Louis B. Mayer and created Metro-Goldwyn Mayer (MGM).

Having consolidated control of production and distribution, these companies then started investing in exhibition. With the help of Wall Street finance, they began to acquire chains of movie theaters. By the mid-1920s, the industry had emerged as an oligopoly, with a handful of powerful firms controlling every aspect of the industry. These mergers and takeovers could only be achieved with finance, in which Wall Street performed a key function. From that point on, bankers and financiers began to dominate the boards of movie industries. The industry was becoming dominated by a few powerful players, bringing to an end the period of the entrepreneur.[50]

Breaking into the big five was an almost impossible task, but one company managed to do it, although it can hardly be considered a newcomer. Albert and Harry Warner launched their first theater during the nickelodeon boom in 1907. They made their first movie in 1919, and in 1925 bought out the once-great Vitagraph with the backing of the New York financiers Goldman Sachs. They were also negotiating with a company by the name of Western Electric, which had been experimenting with sound on film. The Warners acquired a license to use their technology and in 1926 were the first company to release a film with a synchronized music score.

The results at the box office were positive, so they backed it up with the release of the movie *The Jazz Singer,* which was a huge success.[51] This propelled the Warner brothers into the big time. The big companies soon imitated their success and began making sound movies. This was not a disruptive technology of the type mentioned in the previous chapter, as it appealed to the same customers, and the major companies had no trouble adopting it.

The Warner brothers succeeded because sound-synchronization technology had reached a level acceptable to the public. But the company was very aware that the results could have gone either way. It demonstrates that this technology had to reach an acceptable threshold before an entrepreneur could exploit it. How different the structure of the industry would have been if the technology had been ready in 1913 when Edison first tried to introduce sound.

With the arrival of these big integrated studios, the day of the entrepreneur had come to an end. From this time on, it was an era of oligopoly. It remained this way for decades until a 1948 antitrust decision forced the studios to divest of their theater chains.

*   *   *

One of the important aspects of this chapter is that, unlike many motivational books that place emphasis on your own activities, an industry study like this shows a far more complex picture. In reality, businesses come and go, victims of change that may happen some way up the production chain. The market is in a state of continual flux. The lesson is not just to set up shop but to stay in business and respond to the changes that may be thrust upon you, no matter how distant.

It would be wrong to write about entrepreneurship without also talking about the failures. Yet history has a habit of writing biographies and success stories of those who we recognize. It is harder to obtain information about the failures who disappeared from the industry, yet they more than outnumber the winners. Whether we should call them failures is another question. Just because they were forced to vacate the industry does not mean they did not make a healthy profit for many years, and some still managed to have successful careers in the industry after their enterprises ended, albeit in the employment of others. Nevertheless, we can report on some.

Standing out among the "failures" is the Edison Company, which trailblazed the industry. As the leading light in the MPPC, it had been slow to adapt to feature films. However, the company was not blind and soon realized feature films' importance. In 1911, the company responded by imitating its competitors. It established a stock of company actors and made a number of films based on historical dramas and literary works. However, Edison's company was riding a different trajectory from the rest of the industry. His company's focus was on technology, not drama, and he could not keep up with his competitors. The studio was sold in 1918.

Edwin S. Porter, who learned his skills at Edison's company, was also a technician at heart. He created his own spin-off company with Adolph Zukor, the force behind Paramount. However, he clashed with his partners and left in 1916 to spend his time inventing and improving film. He flourished until the 1929 stock market crash. His death went virtually unnoticed by the film industry.[52]

One of the saddest stories was George Méliès, the Frenchman who pioneered trick photography. He appears to have lacked copyright protection and suffered from plagiarism. He was declared bankrupt in 1923. He eventually married one of his former stars, and together they worked selling toys from a street kiosk. He died in 1938, just after being recognized by the French government for the contribution he had made to early cinema.[53]

*   *   *

This chapter shows that entrepreneurship in one part of the community often creates opportunities for entrepreneurs in other parts of the value chain. For example, the development of projectors by technical entrepreneurs increased the options available for entrepreneurs at vaudeville shows. The development of nickelodeons created opportunities to create distribution and exchanges, and the development of feature films resulted in more investment in theaters. The challenge for you is to recognize changes in an industry that create opportunities further down the chain and to act on them.

Not only are openings created by these relationships, but the long-term success of an entrepreneur is frequently dependent on these other links. Other parts of the chain open markets or provide product. An innovation in any part of the chain could have implications for others further down the chain, and this industry experienced many waves of innovation that affected the success of the entrepreneurs. We would expect this type of variability to occur in industries experiencing high levels of change.

Chapter 8

Environments of Constraint and Abundance

Entrepreneurship will flourish if potential entrepreneurs can find opportunities in the environment and if conditions in that environment suggest that those opportunities can be seized successfully. If environmental conditions are unfavorable, you will find it a lot harder to start your business. The need for a conducive environment is greater for young businesses because, unlike large established companies, they have little control over their environment.[1]

The idea that your ability to develop a business is limited by aspects of the environment goes against everything the motivational speakers tell us. So, to illustrate the importance of the environment, this section looks at an extreme example. We consider entrepreneurship in a developing country and examine periods in the history of the West that have provided strong environments for new business growth. In the developing country case study, we can see how potential entrepreneurs in poorer, developing countries are hamstrung by the conditions in which they operate. People have less income to spend, and what they do have is spent conservatively. They simply cannot afford the risk of buying a new product only to find that it does not work adequately. Consequently, it is not a healthy environment to launch new products.

Low incomes also reduce the capital available for investment. Education levels tend to be low, and this affects the pool of labor that entrepreneurs can draw on. Governments frequently create many barriers in developing countries. Poorly trained staff and poor-quality equipment make planning processes for new businesses long and tedious, and it is frequently hard to get quality business information.

The few companies that do exist are normally low in technology, and this reduces the opportunity for new product development through employees spinning off. The slow pace of technical change even makes it hard to imitate overseas products, as most entrepreneurs are only comfortable with technologies they know. For these people, adapting modern technologies is tantamount to a leap in the dark, and it is a very risky maneuver.[2] The result is an environment lacking in dynamism, and yet it is change that is most important for producing entrepreneurial opportunity.

These countries are in a catch-22 situation. They are poor due to a lack of entrepreneurial producers, and entrepreneurs have few options because the nation is poor. That is not to say that entrepreneurship cannot occur in such environments, but the number of options are limited. You are about to discover that entrepreneurs in developing nations can be just as creative and resourceful as those in the West, but there are fewer openings and the returns for the effort is dramatically reduced.

Case Study: Entrepreneurship in a Constrained Environment

An interesting study of entrepreneurship in a developing country was conducted by Sarath Kodithuwakku and Peter Rosa.[3] This study is of interest to us for three reasons: First, because we are looking at commerce in a simple environment, it reveals some of the basic processes of entrepreneurship. It is almost like looking at entrepreneurship in a laboratory where the setting is simplified and we can explore entrepreneurs at work with limited distortion. Second, it illustrates the importance of the environment in defining opportunities. Finally, it illustrates how those with entrepreneurial skills quickly gained dominant positions in the economy.

The study focused on a region of Sri Lanka where a change in the environment had opened up new resources for development. A series of dams had been constructed along the Mahaveli River, which made it possible to irrigate the surrounding land. Under a government scheme, people were settled on this land in 1984. Poor families with no previous assets were each given two and a half acres of land. To overcome difficulties while establishing the business, the settlers were given rations to live on until they had their first harvest. They were also given an allowance to build temporary housing, free agricultural implements, and seed paddy to start their cultivation activities. Loans were also arranged for other needs such as farm power, fertilizer and agrochemicals. The government also provided advice on planting crops.

Each of the settlers started from an equal position of wealth and opportunity. However, within only 10 years, the village had become polarized into rich and poor. The unsuccessful ones had entered a cycle of impoverishment, running into debt. Many had lost control of the land they had been given and were having to work as wage laborers. By contrast, the succesful ones had shown great entrepreneurial ability, starting a number of ventures.

By "entrepreneurial ability," we do not mean the ability to find opportunities. In fact none of the ideas was new. These businesses could be seen in the surrounding villages, and all the settlers would have been aware of them. A full list of entrepreneurial options is listed in Table 8.1. For example, bullocks used for plowing can be rented out, as can tractors. Those entrepreneurs with negotiating skills can gain better prices or can become brokers representing others. The strategies to maximize revenue are well known. To get a higher price, farmers can plant their crops early or store their rice to avoid the harvest glut. If the rice is partially boiled, it can be sold at much higher prices than processed rice. To extract more value from their land, entrepreneurs can "inter-crop," planting vegetables, gherkins or chilies.

Many of these enterprises required capital the entrepreneurs did not possess. For example, processing rice requires special machinery for boiling. Bullocks, tractors, shops and warehousing facilities also required significant funds. Lack of capital was a very real barrier to starting a business, but some managed to overcome it through

Table 8.1 Different Entrepreneurial Options (Adapted from Kodithuwakku and Rosa 2002)

Activity	No. of Families
Keeping village boutiques	16
Bakery	2
Rice processing	11
Buying and reselling paddy	6
Acting as paddy brokers	2
Rice milling	5
Renting out bullock carts	2
Renting out tractors	17
Renting out draught animals	10
Selling agrochemicals	2
Contracting paddy harvesting	3
Money lending	6
Fishing	2
Animal husbandry	
(a) Keeping dairy cattle	7
(b) Goat keeping	2
Carpentry	1
Ready-made garments/tailoring	3
Short eats and confectionery	3
Making and selling spice packets	1
Contracting irrigation channel maintenance	4
Bicycle repair shops	1
Makeshift tearooms	2

a combination of persistence and creativity. In fact, there was far more creativity and innovation devoted to raising resources than in the spotting of new opportunities, a reminder of the importance of resource mobilization in the entrepreneurial process.

Successful farmers showed that not owning resources is not a barrier to entrepreneurship. They mobilized resources through the use of social networks, forming relationships with others to gain access to resources they did not own. The form of the relationship varied, depending on the nature of the resource. For example, those starting boutiques used social contacts to purchase goods on long term credit. One couple lived together, without getting married, in order to meet the legal requirements that enabled them to get two land allotments. Some formed social contacts with traders that allowed them to store paddy and sell it at a later date to obtain higher prices.

In one very successful family, the brother and sister formed contacts that dramatically extended their range of commercial activities. The brother bought rice paddy from fellow settlers during the harvesting season and then sold it to outsiders for a small profit margin. He also obtained agrochemicals and fertilizers on long-term credit, which provided him with stock to sell back to the villagers. While he was establishing contacts in the distribution business, his sister operated in the financial sector. She obtained a bank loan that enabled her brother to purchase the paddy from the villagers. She also obtained loans at a low rate that allowed her to lend at higher interest rates to fellow visitors. Debt was a major feature of the local economy due to the seasonal nature of harvests. However, there was always a danger of defaulting customers, but the sister overcame this by forming relationships with other lenders in the village and sharing information on credit-worthiness. With her brother's marketing/commodity expertise and her financial acumen, this family became significant players in the village. With such entrepreneurial acumen, one can only wonder what they would have achieved in a more prosperous environment.

In some cases, luck was a factor in success. For example, one family planned to raise a loan and purchase a rice mill. A mill owner in a nearby village had recently closed down his business, so an arrangement was struck whereby the family would acquire the mill but only pay for it if the business was a success. Otherwise the mill would be returned to the owner. This drastically reduced the capital required for starting this business and reduced the monetary outflow that would have otherwise gone on interest and loan repayments. It also eliminated the need to provide collateral for a bank loan.

Raising capital was made easier through tight control of expenditure. Successful families were very miserly, preferring to use what little money they had to invest in their business. This attitude stopped them from running into debt and helped them to slowly accumulate capital. Having even a small amount of capital expanded the entrepreneurial options available to them. By contrast, unsuccessful families fell into a debt trap very early, and two reasons contributed to this. With little income, the farmers had to go into debt to pay for the following year's plantings. Other farmers had a good harvest and obtained a good price but made the mistake of spending their money on nonessential items. As a result, they too had to borrow money to finance the next year's crop. As a result, these farmers got caught in a debt trap from the outset. Many had to find extra work to earn wages, and many had to mortgage their property, eventually losing control of their land to the successful families.

Other attributes of successful farmers included recognition of the value of time, the value of hard work and socially acceptable behavior (e.g., abstinence from gambling and alcohol). Consistent with our image of entrepreneurs as relationship builders, these people demonstrated a wide range of social qualities, including trustworthiness and an ability to build relationships that lay at the core of their social networks. But raising capital and trying out new ventures was not a sufficient quality for success. Some farmers had all the successful values, social skills and entrepreneurial qualities but lacked basic management skills. They started off successfully but ended up failing, an illustration that both entrepreneurship and management skills are needed.

Successful entrepreneurs still made mistakes, but they were quick to learn from them, a reminder that entrepreneurship is a learning process. By contrast, the failing farmers blamed their fortunes on unfavorable rainfall distribution for causing crop failures or claimed that there was no one there to help them, a problem others overcame by building relationships. However, the time for learning was very short. Those who had started successfully but then suffered setbacks found it difficult to bounce back once they had fallen behind. Windows of opportunity are only open for short periods, and one must learn quickly. When first-mover advantages exist, you must learn quickly.

Although all started with the same allocation, after 10 years the village had polarized into 40 successful families and 260 unsuccessful ones. About 55% of the families had lost control of their land, either completely or partially, to the successful ones. Due to their debt, they now had to work for the successful families. In effect, they had become locked into a master-worker relationship. Some became the capitalists controlling large land units, while the others were their laborers. In this way, entrepreneurial abilities created a class structure. The irony is that this program was inspired by socialist government policies aiming to achieve equality. It took less than 10 years for this society to become stratified. The vast majority of children in this village will inherit debt burdens that will restrict their ability to break out of the impoverishment.

These entrepreneurs did not have access to the markets, technologies and skilled workers that we possess in the West. Consequently, even the richest of the villagers would be considered poor by world standards. Nevertheless, a range of opportunities was revealed that enabled some to obtain significant wealth and status within their village. These opportunities only became available after a dam was built, which made new land available. It was this change that allowed these people to advance.

In this primitive commercial environment, several characteristics of successful entrepreneurs stand out that have relevance to you in the twenty-first century. These include the ability to learn quickly, build relationships, raise capital, and tightly control expenditure. Entrepreneurs without those qualities were less likely to succeed when the opportunities were presented.

Techno-Economic Shifts and Opportunity

We have to be careful how we access entrepreneurial environments. We think of the United States as a great place for entrepreneurs, but there are proportionately fewer there than many other countries. For example, Turks are four times more likely to start a business than Americans.[4] Although entrepreneurship in wealthy countries may generate higher returns than other nations, on average people are less likely to be entrepreneurs because they can earn a good income working for someone else. Higher wages in the West means an entrepreneur is foregoing an attractive income. This makes self-employment less attractive than in nations where there are fewer employers offering good wages.

Although the returns for entrepreneurs can be higher in the West than developing nations, the returns for self-employment are not as good as the motivational experts would have us believe. In fact, the average self-employed person earns a lot less than the person who works for someone else. The median income for people running their own business is 35% lower than what they would have earned working for someone else.[5] Not only do the average entrepreneurs earn less, their businesses do not necessarily last long. Research suggests only about 10% of new firms are still around and have grown 10 years after their founding.[6] These figures are not what we are led to believe when we read magazines saluting the exploits of business heroes.

This does not negate the importance of self-employment as a form of social mobility. Households that own businesses are more likely to move up to a higher wealth category than households that don't.[7] The problem is the nature of most businesses. They are often in industries that don't grow or industries that are easy to enter; hence, they are exposed to high levels of competition. The industry you choose plays a big bearing on whether yours will provide you the social mobility you seek. One factor of importance is the extent of technological intensity. Businesses with a high use of technology that are hard to imitate are more likely to do well, especially those protected by patents. Other factors of importance are the industry growth rates and the increasing rate of demand. Here is one problem with choosing the industry you know best, something we have stressed throughout this book—your industry may be an industry with a mature market and limited growth potential. In which case, you will end up competing in a tight market with little room for growth.

There are particular times in history when the business environment has favored the creation of fast-growing companies, and they are linked to periods of substantial technological change. Some technological changes are so substantial that they have widespread consequences for all sectors of the economy. A change of this nature involves not just one innovation but a cluster of innovations. In such instances, we have a change in the techno-economic paradigm, leading to a new range of products, services and industries—all presenting opportunities for entrepreneurs. Old industries are also affected, either directly or indirectly, and this can provide more opportunities for entrepreneurs to enter established industries with new business methods. These are the periods in which opportunity is at its greatest.

Such overhauls of the economy do not happen very often. Only five have been counted in the past 200 years. These waves are linked to a key factor that was used as an input for business during each period.[8] For example, in the industrial revolution, the economy was transformed by the use of iron. The second wave occurred in the middle of the nineteenth century and was driven by the use of steam power and railroad transportation. The third wave came at the end of the nineteenth century with the advent of steel and electricity, while the fourth wave arrived 40 years later and involved techniques of mass production. The last wave began in the 1980s and saw the wide use of microchips.

Although these five waves are widely recognized, it is possible to go back further in time and see more examples of such economic overhaul. They would include the proto-industrialization of the Dutch economy from the late sixteenth century, the revolution of early modern trade when the oceanic trade routes were opened, and the Confucian-market paradigm of China during the T'ang and Sung dynasties. We might even go back to include the Bronze, Iron and Stone ages. Each period involved a revolution of the economy.

Each new wave opens up opportunities for entrepreneurs as new products are produced and traded, increased wealth makes more capital available for investment and people have more money to spend. The names of some of the most successful entrepreneurs from each period have come down to us and are listed in Table 8.2. For example, the development of ship technology in the late Middle Ages enabled

Table 8.2 Long Waves and Economic Change (Adapted from Freeman and Perez, 1988)

Period	Description	Main Carrier Branches & Induced Growth Sectors	Key Factor Industries	Entrepreneurs
1980s–?	Information and communication	Computers Electronic capital goods Software Telecommunication equipment Optical fibers Robotics FMS Ceramics Databank information services	"Chips" (microelectronics)	Kobayashi Uenohara Barron Benneton Noyce Gates
1930s–1980s	Ford-style mass production	Automobiles/trucks Tractors Tanks Armaments for motorized warfare Aircraft Consumer durables Process plants Synthetic materials Petrochemicals Highways Airports Airlines	Energy (especially oil)	Sloan McNamara Agnelli Nordhoff Matsushita
1880s–1940s	"La Belle Epoque" Electrical and heavy engineering	Electrical engineering Electrical machinery Cable & wire Heavy engineering Heavy armaments Steel ships Heavy chemicals Synthetic dyestuffs Electricity supply and distribution	Steel	Siemens Carnegie Nobel Edison Krupp Bosch Ford

Table 8.2 (Continued)

Period	Description	Main Carrier Branches & Induced Growth Sectors	Key Factor Industries	Entrepreneurs
1830–1890s	Victorian prosperity Steam power and railway	Steam engines Steamships Machine tools Iron Railway equipment Railways World shipping	Coal Transport	Stephenson Whitworth Brunel Armstrong Whitney Singer
1770s–1840s	Early mechanization Industrial revolution	Textiles Textile chemicals Textile machinery Iron working & iron casting Water power Potteries Trunk canals Turnpike roads	Cotton Pig iron	Arkwright Boulton Wedgewood Owen Bramash Maudsley
1550–1720	Proto-industrialization	Ship building Shipping Ceramics Textiles	Energy (wind & peat)	Stuyvesant Francis Drake Walter Raleigh
1400–1600	Early Modern Trade	Ship building Shipping Ceramics Textiles Craft industries	Sea transportation	Columbus Henry the Navigator Virji Vora Abdul Ghafur
1000–1400	Confucian market	Agriculture Hydraulic Engineering Ceramics Paper making Textiles	Water Fire Animal and human energy	
	Bronze Age	Agriculture Weapons Implements	Bronze	
	Iron Age	Agriculture Weapons Implements	Iron	
	Stone Age	Agriculture Weapons Implements	Stone	

Christopher Columbus to launch his "enterprise of the Indies," making himself and many others rich in the process. In the nineteenth century, the development of the steam engine opened up opportunities for entrepreneurs in manufacturing, rail and steamships. However, for each great name listed in Table 8.2, there are hundreds of nameless entrepreneurs who began new ventures and earned a healthy income.

At the moment we are in the middle of the fifth wave since the industrial revolution, although it could be argued that the recent Internet revolution is a sixth wave. Underlying this wave is the spread of digital technology. With digital technology, all kinds of information, whether it be numbers, text, sound or video, can be stored, processed and communicated through a computer. When combined with advances in the processing capabilities of computers, a commercial revolution has begun, which is changing the lives of employees and consumers and opening up new possibilities for entrepreneurs.

We have become so entwined by the digital age that it is hard to imagine our lives before. New devices utilizing digital technology are emerging that can handle every kind of information from data-text, numbers, voice, photos and videos. However, it is the Internet that has heralded the most significant shift as people at work and home increasingly log on. The Internet is a technology born in the early 1970s. It was originally devised as a communication tool for the U.S. Department of Defense. Its first nonmilitary use was as a network between academics and techies. In its early days, few people could have imagined that it would blossom into the force it is today, but the vast amount of information it made available and the easy communication it provided soon made it a valued product. This growing demand opened up an opportunity for entrepreneurs to tap by providing content. As the amount of content on the Internet increased, this made it even more attractive for consumers, and demand continued to grow. In this way, changes in supply and demand fuelled each other, creating a spiraling market. By 1997, 22 million Americans were using the web regularly. The following year, use had climbed to 60 million.[9] Today, there are an estimated 360 million users worldwide, representing 22% of the world's population.[10]

Content providers who create websites are creating new products and adding value to the Internet in the same way that other forward-linking entrepreneurs have done in the past. Entrepreneurial openings have not been restricted to content providers. They include ancillary entrepreneurs who provide infrastructure and professional services. Search engines and portals provide access to the content sites. Hardware and software producers provide the mechanisms on which they run. It has also led to the creation of completely new markets. The web's unique ability to bring people together has enabled it to create markets that did not previously exist. Market-making entrepreneurial ventures like eBay brought together buyers and sellers as never before. Because the Internet makes it easy for a buyer to get information on comparable products and prices and to see how the products have been rated by consumer organizations, it can help to increase demand.

The Internet has revolutionized existing commercial practices. Websites provide information on products, services and specifications; enable customers to make simple orders; and solicit feedback that allows companies to improve their services. Computerized ordering systems provide companies with faster links to customers and reduce the need for large inventories. The Net also reduces the need for physical retail facilities. The effect is a reduction in transportation and distribution costs. For example, in 1998, the U.S. Department of Commerce revealed that airline ticket processing costs $8 through a travel agent with a computer reservation system but only $1 through the Internet.[11] Insurance fees cost $400 to $700 through a traditional agent but only $200 to $350 on the Internet, while banking transactions cost $1.07 through a branch compared with one cent on the Internet.

Direct buying on the Internet has revolutionized distribution with implications for entrepreneurs in the same way that the movie industry has experienced episodes of change that opened and closed opportunities. The Internet is reshaping the relationships of companies with their customers and buyer behavior. Geographic boundaries are disappearing as foreign markets can easily be accessed by entrepreneurs in different countries. Industrial boundaries are also being reshaped, as online retailers integrate to exploit their new market power. We see this in the way Amazon, which originally started with books, has moved into CDs and other products. Also using their assets and reputations as traders to move into other areas are portals like Yahoo, which has started selling products and services. New competition is coming from different directions.

Mistakes and Opportunity

In many of the previous industrial revolutions, economies experience periods of uncertainty, overinvestment and speculation. For example, when the Dutch succeeded in mastering the trade routes to the Spice Islands, a number of entrepreneurs jumped on the bandwagon and imitated the success of the pioneer. The inevitable result was that the market was flooded, and the companies eventually had to consolidate their activities and formed the Dutch East India Company. Similarly, the Dutch had their own speculative bubbles, in particular a speculative bout based on the price of tulip bulbs.

In the late 1990s, the Internet wave endured its own speculative bubble. An investment frenzy took hold as investors speculated on Internet-related companies listed on the Nasdaq Stock exchange. The bubble reached its peak in the first quarter of 2000, but, like all bubbles before them, this one too burst. This has led to a radical realignment in the dot-com sector. While it has been difficult to obtain reliable numbers, webmasters.com estimated from industry sources that near the beginning of the decade there were between 7,000 and 10,000 substantial companies in the sector that had received formal funding.[12] Within three years, nearly 5,000 of these had been acquired or shut down.

In the first two years of decline, 69% of the business that were shut down were in the business/general category, compared with 32% that served the consumer market. This is consistent with the theory that capital providers suffer the most during an economic downturn. As in previous downturns, a common defensive strategy has been amalgamation, and $200 billion has been spent in the acquisition of 3,892 Internet properties.[13]

During the same period, at least 962 substantial Internet companies were shut down or declared bankrupt. Philip J. Kaplan has written a lighthearted account of many of the failures from this period.[14] His book lacks the level of analysis that we would expect from a business book, but nevertheless it reveals some interesting information on why so many companies collapsed. They failed for the same reasons that other companies have failed in the past. Many companies were launched by people who lacked experience in the industry they were entering. For example, Impresse was a company launched with $90 million in funding to act as a middleman between printers and print buyers. In return for a 1% commission, Impresse would provide a website that enabled printers and print buyers to shop around. However, those in the industry already knew they could shop around without their services. Impresse offered very little value to the industry.

In some instances, even people with industry experience invested in businesses they should have known better—a testament to the euphoria of the time. Movie director Spike Lee was a board member of Iam.com, a company that created a database on which models and actors could place their portfolios. With $48 million in funding, this company gave casting directors the opportunity to do away with talent agents and use their website to peruse available talent. However, the idea ignores basic consumer behavior patterns in the industry. Casting directors don't like going through thousands of portfolios. Talent agents perform a useful service because they help to filter suitable talent from the hordes of wannabes. The new company provided less value than the established competition.

A number of companies seized the market-making potential of the Internet, hoping to bring together buyers and sellers who previously might not interact. Among these were group-buying enterprises like OnlineChoice.com, Mercata.com and Zoho.com. These companies worked on the idea that you bring together a number of buyers who want similar products and services, then use their combined buying power to buy in bulk at a cheaper price. These companies received significant backing and support. Ernst and Young picked OnlineChoice.com as its entrepreneur of the year. Paul Allen, cofounder of Microsoft, invested in Mercata.com. However, the new companies did not live up to expectations. Although they did away with retailers, these new companies took their position in the distribution chain and expected their cut of the action. The savings for buyers and sellers often were not that great. Furthermore, waiting for enough buyers to join the group took time and delayed the purchase process compared with conventional buying channels.

Many failures stemmed from the entrepreneurial learning process involved when new technologies are born. In particular, how do you utilize the technology in a manner that complements what people value? In some cases, entrepreneurs hoped to change consumer behavior patterns but learned they would not be changed or, if they did, not at a rate that would support their business. Zoza.com was started by the founders of Banana Republic, so they should have known the garment trade. Their idea was to get people buying clothes over the Net, which they complemented with a network of mini-stores that did not carry stock but only samples of every size and color of their products. Customers were expected to enter the store, try on the sample, and then order from a computer terminal either in the store or at home. This business competed with conventional clothes stores in which customers could try on the precise item they intended to buy.

Some ideas stemming from this period involved a learning process in which entrepreneurs had to learn how consumer behavior could be accommodated within the new technology. Other failings can be linked to the concept of market and technological thresholds. For example, in recent years an English company, Intellifit, has devised a scheme whereby people's body shapes are accurately measured with a machine that assesses their body's water content. The statistics are then entered into a computer, and this enables customers to buy clothes online knowing sizes will be accurate.

Many e-commerce companies thought they could start up and seize the market on the basis of their Internet presence but forgot the realities of competition. Retail shops do offer significant services, and going to the shopping mall to buy a number of products can be a very economical way of buying goods. Competition for the new dot-coms was not just from old businesses but also from the numerous new websites. As on previous occasions when a new technology arrives, the birth of many new Internet companies created a situation of over-supply, a situation made possible because of the ease in making websites and entering the market.

The biggest company to fall during this period was Webvan.com, a company that buried the $1 billion invested in it. Webvan was created so that people could order their groceries on the Internet and then have them delivered. This put them in direct competition with supermarkets, which operate on very narrow margins. Businesses that operate on such small margins need massive turnover in order to be profitable. Webvan didn't have that turnover and could not compete. Today this business exists in a number of locations recognizing the importance of thresholds. However, the current business model for groceries often has the Internet site linked to a major supermarket, which provides economies of distribution and purchasing power.

The difficulties of earning money from a content site were illustrated by Rivals.com. This Seattle-based business was built around a website devoted to sport. It is hard to make money from a website that can be accessed free of charge, and a number of ideas were tried to make the site pay. One idea was to give people the opportunity to buy things like T-shirts from the site. Another involved having a premium-content section that customers would have to pay to access, and, of course, there was advertising. However, the company never found a way to make enough money. This company, which started with $75 million in funding, closed up shop in 2001.

Another proposed strength of Internet shopping was its ability to let customers place their own orders, giving them immediate access to the producers. Even hairdressers and restaurants could take orders over the Internet. However, this involved extra costs, including computer facilities, software, Internet access and backup staff. For many small companies, the extra costs were not justified by the extra revenue (if there was extra revenue). Many companies failed because they did not do an adequate assessment of their costs or their pricing.

Another common mistake was overestimating the size of the market. For example, eToys.com failed after gaining only half the customers they expected. Many mistakes may have resulted from companies driven by "techies" with little understanding of the market realities. Some of these inflated figures also came from scam artists wanting to become rich from the euphoria that pervaded the stock market at the time. Such individuals would create a company, sell shares to the public, take the money and run. And there were enough foolish investors waiting to be milked once the speculative bubble kicked in. Many people saw the upward spiral in Internet share prices and wanted their share of the action, even though they knew little about how these companies would pay.

As we stated at the beginning of this book, it is sometimes hard to predict market size. When a new technology is introduced, no one knows how many people will shift to the new technology and, if they do shift, how long it will take to reach a demand threshold. Some companies had good ideas, but the technology was not yet good enough to carry it. Internet-television failed in the early days, largely due to the poor quality of the transmission. With broader bandwidth, it is becoming a reality. These companies fall into the category of acting too early. The technological threshold needed to make these businesses a reality had not yet been reached.

Many of the ideas that failed will become a reality, and some have already re-established themselves. They rely on environmental shifts, in particular the reaching of technological and demand thresholds. As the twenty-first century evolves, the Internet is a growing tool, and the market will continue to grow. Not only will this mean that some old ideas will be revived, but new opportunities may appear as entrepreneurs find specialized niches in the larger market.

We are still very early in the Internet-driven economic wave. Other techno-economic waves have lasted for approximately 60 years. The ocean-going steamship was not a reality until a century after the steam engine was developed. Although technology moves at a faster pace today, we still have time for opportunities to appear as demand grows, and because of the rate of change, we will see many more mini-revolutions laying the pioneers to bed.

In the Good Times, the Basics Still Apply

Recent history has provided some clear lessons. To be successful, future entrepreneurs of the Internet must confront several issues. First, for those businesses seeking to create new markets, a key question to ask is "Am I making new markets or just a new form of middleman?" If you are just an alternative form of distribution competing with old-style distributors, you better have a competitive edge. If you are indeed creating a new market that hasn't existed before, you might like to ask why it hasn't existed before. It might be because it is not valued. If you are providing a totally new option that consumers are not familiar with, don't assume it will be popular. Even if it's a very useful commodity, it may require time before customers acknowledge its benefits.

Second, does your business add value or reduce costs compared with your competitors? Many of the unsuccessful businesses were driven by techies hoping to find an idea to use the technology. They were so hungry to launch an idea that they downplayed the most important issue: whether this business provides something that customers will value, and, if so, how much will they be prepared to pay for it? These businesses must change from their production focus to a customer focus.

Many of the Internet businesses were based on a market-development strategy, but developing markets is far more effective if it is done in conjunction with cost reduction or value-added strategies. The Internet can reach new markets, but if there is no advantage in your pricing or the quality of your product, you may find your results disappointing.

The importance of industry experience is confirmed. You must have a full understanding of consumer behavior and how the industry operates. You must understand how customers make their purchases and why they like to do it that way. Many businesses fell over due to the ignorance and inexperience of their founders.

Many firms suffered because their prices were not competitive and their costs, particularly for distribution, were unrealistic. Before launching your business, you must do a thorough assessment of the costs involved and the price at which you can sell your product or service.

You must avoid the trap of optimistic perceptions of market size. We live in an information age. There is now a huge amount of information available on market size for most industries. From these figures and information on Internet commerce, we can make rough estimates of potential markets. These figures must be tempered with realistic assessments of growth. It is also unrealistic to think that you will reap all that market. Because of the ease in establishing a website, the Internet produces more competition among vendors. If you come up with a good idea, you can guarantee that imitators will soon follow in your wake.

These high levels of competition and the dangers of dealing with a supplier that cannot necessarily be physically accessed will place greater competitive emphasis on reputation as a competitive weapon. Early movers, like Amazon in the book market, have quickly acquired competitive advantage from building an early reputation and moving down the learning curve.

Finally, you must not underestimate the competitive strength of old-style businesses. They have particular values that consumers appreciate and have helped shape consumption patterns that are not going to change just because you have a new toy. You must evaluate the competitive strengths of all your competition.

*   *   *

It is common to say that it takes a special type of person to become an entrepreneur, and this has been linked to racial and ethnic characteristics. However, we have to be careful how far we take this. The case study of Sri Lanka revealed that poorer incomes compared with the West were not a result of lack of entrepreneurial ability. Nevertheless, some traits were very important, and these are also important to the West. They included a miserly attitude to money, a focus on accumulating capital, recognition of the value of time, and avoiding gambling and alcohol. They were also relationship builders. Luck was also important. Despite their success, their incomes were substantially lower than those in the West, a consequence of a poorer environment. Yet even in the West, opportunities vary over time. Drawing on Einstein, we could argue that opportunity is dependent on the time-space that people inhabit. But it is still important to undergo a process of learning when new technologies open opportunities, and this chapter revealed a number of follies and lessons uncovered in the recent dot-com bubble.

Chapter 9

It's Not Always Fair Out There

Entrepreneurs frequently experience intense levels of stress; they work long hours, face intense competition, operate in highly dynamic environments, and often lack sufficient resources to implement their plans and strategies.

(Robert Baron)[1]

Having identified an opportunity, the next creative phase is the construction of the business, unless you intend to buy an existing business. Much of the business creation phase involves mobilizing resources and contracting with suppliers and developers, a process that leaves you vulnerable if your contractual partner lets you down. This chapter begins with a case study on Tim Nicholls, who identified an emerging niche in boutique hotels but nearly lost it all. The second section of this chapter explores some of the dangers of contractual relationships and identifies some ways you can act to minimize risk.

Case Study: Zen and the Art of Hotel Development

Tim Nicholls was my geography teacher in high school. The movement from school teacher to hotel developer did not happen overnight. It involved a process of learning and capability building, which helped prepare him for his new career. In 1987, while working as a teacher, Tim began investing in property. He gained a franchise in a kit-set construction business. After some time, one client came back to him and asked him if he could redesign the client's building. Tim had always held an interest in design but felt he didn't have the necessary skills to study art or design at school. Nevertheless, he relished the opportunity to do some construction design. His success led to being subsequently asked to design a small art gallery and a lodge. The architectural design skills he developed during this period would play a major role in the development of his hotel.

His teaching career also helped him to develop managerial skills. Promoted to positions as head of departments, he went through an apprenticeship on staff management and organization. When he left to set up his own school, he gained experience in starting a business from scratch, including building a market from scratch. That school was the NZ International School, a network providing American students with an overseas experience in New Zealand. The program was eventually expanded to provide students time in other places such as Italy and Turkey. This meant a great deal of travel, and he spent a large amount of time in hotels, to the point where he could be defined as a "sophisticated consumer" in the hospitality industry. He knew what hotel guests needed and wanted when staying in hotels. He became attuned to the nuances between hotels.

When Tim speaks about this process of development, he is keen to stress another aspect that is important to his life and business philosophy. He stresses how his travels contributed to his spiritual development and how, on gaining a Fulbright scholarship to the United States in 1994, he met people with strong spiritual beliefs, something that had an enduring effect.

It was on a trip to Turkey that Tim got the idea of running his own hotel. Staying in boutique hotels, he felt that he could do the same in New Zealand. On his return, he developed the idea further and eventually settled on the idea of a bohemian chic theme for his hotel, inspired by Ian Shrager and Phillipe Starke, the designers of the famed Studio 54 disco in New York, who went on to design boutique hotels. In many ways, the bohemian chic niche reflects his personal values and motives. The business became a canvas for Tim's creativity.

Chance events had a huge influence on Tim's business career. In New Zealand, Tim continued to develop the hotel idea while still running the NZ International School, but the terrorism activities of 9/11 undermined his business. Americans were no longer keen to send their children overseas. "Every student group was cancelled," he says. This pushed him further into his hotel business. "History is a huge determinant of where you're placed."

Back in his home town Christchurch, he ran into a businessman working on a property development in the central city. It was an area directly on the tram route. This location offered great possibilities as the trams linked many of the cities' main tourist destinations. Tim signed a contract with the developer. It was agreed that the developer would build and own the building, which Tim would lease and operate as a hotel. Tim's business was financed mostly by his own savings (55%) and by a bank loan (45%). With no other partners, Tim was the sole owner and manager of the hotel. Although the bank loan was approved early on, he spent his own contribution first before drawing on the bank loan and incurring interest charges.

The developer hired the builders and was responsible for constructing the building. He also employed the architects who were responsible for the structural work and the project managers who oversaw the project. The interior was all Tim's design. Tim spent the following year developing the internal design of the hotel. This included designing towels, cushions and furniture, and he also managed the marketing. Tim estimates that if he had contracted out the design work, it would have cost him three times as much.

The bohemian chic design was intended to appeal to a target niche consisting of free independent travelers (FITs) who book through the web and make their own plans, corporate or business travelers, and those at the upper end of the market. The hotel was designed with these markets in mind and included an artistic, up-market look. He was not interested in the tour-group market, which is a lower-paying market. He had initially intended to offer five classes of rooms, but he was advised that it would be too hard to market and he needed to be more selective about what niche he was in, so he confined his offering to two classes of room: standard economy and superior.

Tim did quite a lot of research. He went to the United States and Europe talking to travel wholesalers and asking them if they would send people to his hotel. He spoke to the local regional tourism office for Christchurch and visited the New Zealand tourism office in Frankfurt, as well as talking to local hotel managers.

He also did a business plan. He needed it to get finance. But with little experience, he found it very hard to estimate business costs. He had no idea about some items such as the electricity bill, so he just guessed. For revenue projections, he went to a friend who was a travel wholesaler. The friend gave him some figures to work on. He was told if someone in the United Kingdom books a room for $180, the UK wholesaler will take 20% and the New Zealand inbound-operator will take another 10%. He also had to deduct tax, and that is before he deducted internal expenses like wages. Suddenly, the $180 didn't look so good.

One thing he did not anticipate in his business plan was the losses he made in the first two years. These years were "bloody hard work." Tim's business launch sounds like a nightmare but is typical of many new ventures. First, his mother died the day he was to get the keys to the building. Second, the developer was way behind schedule with the building. Tim first realized something was wrong when he returned from his European market research trip to find that the builders had not yet started the building. As the building commenced, another problem popped up. The building site was previously used as a mechanics garage. The mechanics had dumped oil into a hole in the ground. This made the ground unstable for the building foundations. A dispute arose between the builder and the developer over who should pay for the strengthening costs. With no certainty about payment, the builders walked off the job, and for 12 weeks no building work was done, bringing the project further behind schedule. Although Tim was not part of this contract, he suffered.

The building was meant to be completed in June 2002 but was not opened until April the following year. And even when it was finally opened, Tim got saddled with another problem. The hotel was meant to have an emergency fire stairwell. The stairwell was meant to serve as the fire escape for two buildings, but the other was not yet complete. Tim ended up in dispute with the developer who refused to give the stairwell priority; however, without the fire escape, the City Council would not give Tim permission to fill the hotel with guests. In fact the council only gave him permission for five rooms. For three months, he was paying wages for staff to run a 36-room hotel but only had five rooms available. He was operating at huge loss. Finally, by October 2003, the stairwell was built and the hotel was opened with all rooms.

Coupled with this was the problem that all new businesses have in getting the market aware of them. There were some nights in which they had no guests at all, but they still had to pay wages and stay open in case some arrived.

All in all, the hotel's launch was more than a year late, and Tim incurred more than $100,000 in legal fees. This had implications for the financial operation of his business. He quickly reached the end of his bank overdraft. Before long, the bank came to him and suggested he refinance (i.e., get another financier). Tim pointed out that his business was picking up and all the rooms were booked for February, but the bank didn't care. One of the problems in this industry is the time between the customer arriving and actually paying; a customer may stay on the 1st of the month, but the money won't come from the booking agent until the 15th of the following month.

Tim was now pressured by the developer on one side and the bank on the other. The bank would extend no more credit and pressured him to get another banker. To make matters worse, on two occasions he did not have enough money to pay his staff. He was squeezed from all sides.

The wage problem was overcome when friends lent him money, enabling him to pay the wages. Tim did not ask his friends. They unexpectedly came to him. This for Tim illustrates the importance of a philosophical basis of business and the need to think beyond money. If Tim was the sort of man who was merely out for money, he would not have the sort of friends who came to the rescue. "When you put yourself on the line, the energy is there."

Nevertheless, he still had to refinance, and changing financial backers cost another $30,000 as well as having to pay a higher interest rate with the new company. Squeezed on all sides, Tim says the first two years were "very scary." In those years, he didn't sleep well and lost a lot of weight. "You never know if it's going to close out on you and you lose the whole lot. Would I do it again? No, I wouldn't want to do it again."

He says he got through on persistence. He believes that "90% of businesses fail because the owner gets tired." The other reason they fail is they are "not operating in an emerging market," a reflection of the need to align your personal goals with market development. The bohemian chic look reflects an emerging niche. "No other hotel is like this in New Zealand."

He discovered his business plan had been overly optimistic. The costs came in $450,000 more than he budgeted. I asked him if he has made the money back that he lost in those two years, and he replied that as "cash in hand" he has not made the money back, but the value of the business has increased substantially and, in that way, he has. After a nightmare start, Tim has succeeded in establishing a lucrative business. It took two years before the company made a profit, but he says most hotels take three to seven years to mature. They achieve their optimum in the five- to seven-year period, after which they try to maintain their place against the new hotels entering the market.

He has successfully tapped his target market. Customers come from the UK, Europe, Australia, North America and New Zealand. The hotel is marketed through a number of means. First is through ACCOR, a hotel network that provides world-wide marketing, booking systems, booklets, and information and systems for revenue streaming. Second is the hotel's own website. The hotel also utilizes a number of third-party websites, such as wotif.com and hotdeals.com. They also use the local regional marketing office (Christchurch and Canterbury Tourism); however, he stresses the limitations of their work: "No one comes for things like busker festivals" that they organize.

Since the early days when Tim first put together his marketing plan, the nature of tourism wholesaling has changed dramatically. While he still uses Kuoni, a wholesaler he contacted on his research trip to Europe, the industry is based more on web-based sales. With these websites, he practices "revenue streaming" to maximize revenue. Prices are massaged every day in a process that can be seen in websites like wotif.com, in which cheap rates are posted in an attempt to fill unused capacity. In the early days, it was necessary to change the price on each website, one at a time, but with new software, it is possible to change prices on eight or nine websites at the same time.

Recognizing the limits of his skill base, Tim employed a manager from India with experience in the hotel industry. Together, they employed the necessary staff, which includes 27 full- and part-time employees. The manager is responsible for introducing many of the systems he now uses, such as the daily flash report, which records occupancy rates, income per room, and things of that nature. The manager provides a number of daily reports such as these flash reports and bank statements, which assist in control and decision making.

Tim continues to develop the bohemian chic concept. For example, hotels traditionally have a Gideon's Bible in every room, but Tim decided to have a broader, more original approach. He has made a range of devotional books available in the lounge, ranging from the Koran to Ronald Reagan's memoirs. He also has artwork for sale on display in the foyer and hallway.

Tim Nicholls's business is intrinsically linked to his philosophical beliefs. He dispels the popular belief that business and spiritualism don't go together. Spiritualism can mean time in his garden, on his surfboard, or in the way birds come close in an expression of trust, but it also means business. "Spiritualism and business are not contra forces. . . . I still do the nuts and bolts," he says, but he balances this with a spiritual approach to business. He quotes the example of how Internet businesses have brought communities together. Faith in his inner feelings can be linked to notions of intuitive learning and entrepreneurship as a process of learning. The spiritual and rational can be bound together.

In his own business, the influence of his philosophy can be seen in his approach to decision making. When making a decision, Tim draws strongly on his subconscious. He is guided from his spiritual being, which he sees as a much more powerful force. And he takes pride in the accuracy of his decisions. "Intuition is so powerful, and you can work on it in the business world too," he says. But it is important to define the problem carefully and what you need to know. He is also careful not to appear arrogant: "It's not coming from me, I just pass it on. . . . Some people have it as children. I didn't develop awareness of it until I was 50."

Sometimes Tim places his decisions completely in the hands of fate. If stuck with a hard decision, he may on occasion place the alternative solutions in separate envelopes and blindly choose one of them, adopting the decision in it. On first sight, this may seem reckless, but it is not without logic. Often managers choosing between equal alternatives end up either not making a decision or procrastinating. This approach stops Tim from procrastinating. The decision is made, and he can quickly move to implement it. However, such an approach relies on only putting good alternatives in the envelopes. There must be some selection of alternatives beforehand.

Consistent with his spirituality is his contribution to charities. At the end of every day, he takes the money out of his pocket and places it in a bag. He then doubles it with money from the company. Any money that the staff contributes is also doubled by the company. The money is then given to charities such as the earthquake in Pakistan or disadvantaged children in Laos.

Although his teaching background provided limited assistance to this new career, it also provided some useful skills. "I teach all the time; I'm a mentor," particularly when dealing with staff. In explaining his success, Tim cites Richard Branson, who stressed the importance of passion: "If you don't have it, you're not going anywhere." It is a reminder of the motivating power that comes from loving your business. The second factor that Richard Branson stressed is persistence, because your business is not going to happen overnight.

Tim believes a third vital factor is reciprocity: "You are not going to get anything done unless you have a long-term relationship that benefits both parties." Unfortunately, not all business people operate under the notion of reciprocity, as Tim discovered when dealing with the developer. At a time when business schools place an emphasis on ethics and social responsibility, Tim's experience reveals that the business world can be cutthroat. He refers to one developer who said to him, "I don't like to see other people make a dollar." Tim isn't impressed with such attitudes. "Most developers . . . try to use other people's money."

Some of the problems Tim faces stem from the problem of incomplete contracts: "You lose control when you contract people. . . . Lots of links could sink the project." If he was to do it again today, he would be more cautious and demanding, and he would put those demands into the contract.

One of his problems occurred as a result of what economists call contractual hold up, in which the other party uses its position in a contract to exploit further gain. On this occasion, Tim organized a tiling job, which he determined would cost $49 per square meter. By the time the bill came through the developer, it had been raised to $120 per square meter, adding another $30,000 to his costs. On this occasion Tim paid or else he would not get the keys to the hotel.

He has twice been to the disputes tribunal over contractual obligations with the building owner. He won the first case and lost the second. But he draws on his Zen philosophy and takes the loss on the chin. He sees losses such as this as preparation for the good times, an outlook that is compatible with a view of entrepreneurship as a learning process. With the strength of his philosophy, he has no fear in losing such cases.

Since then, Tim has been approached by major developers in Thailand to act as a consultant for hotels being built there. Tim is excited by the role and enjoys his current life. He clearly enjoys the diversity of guests he meets and the ability to run a business consistent with his value system. His business gives him the opportunity to express his creativity and enjoy the independence of self-employment. The hotel is now profitable with high income per rooms and occupancy ratios, and his relationship with the banks is now excellent as they now see him as a secure credit risk. He has even managed to repay a significant part of his original debts. After only four years, he has seen a significant gain in the value of his business and if he were to sell his business now, Tim would live a very comfortable life.

Contracts, Traps and Entrepreneurs

In writing this case study, we could have focused on Tim's success and the position he now enjoys, but this would be a false portrayal of the entrepreneurial process. He was very close to losing it all. What got him through were friendships and a philosophy that helped him endure the hard times. Business is not all about money. For Tim, the creative process is very important, and he clearly takes pride in the artistic layout of the hotel that he designed.

Tim succeeded after a period of capability building and research, and then tapped into an emerging niche in the market. If he had not chosen this niche, the outcome may have been very different, a strong reminder of the need to match your personal capabilities with favorable trends in the business environment. The difference between success and failure can be pencil thin, and many capable businesspeople have ended up on the wrong side of that line. Tim was pushed close to that line through the contractual relationship with the developer. Contracts define relationships with those on whom your success relies. They provide the ground rules of the relationships with suppliers or, alternatively, licensors whom you contract to make your product.

Another reason we should concern ourselves with contracts is they can reduce the amount of capital needed to start a business. Instead of investing large amounts of money in plant and distribution, you can hire others to manufacture, distribute and market on a contract basis. The amount of work you contract will depend on the nature of your business. In some cases you may only contract with a supplier to provide materials. On other occasions, you might want to build your whole business around contracts.

A business structure based on contractual relationships is known as a "network structure," and it contains significant advantages for an entrepreneur. In reducing the amount of capital, it can allow you to start your business more quickly and help save you money. It allows you to hire specialized people who have skills that you don't have while you focus on your core competencies. It is an attractive option, for example, if you have marketing and design skills and want to start your own clothes label but lack production capabilities. Similarly, if you have production skills but not marketing and design skills, you could act as a subcontractor for other labels. Subcontracting is also advantageous when the business experiences an economic downturn, as you can quickly reduce these costs, which you might not be able to do if you had invested in significant plant and staff. In effect, you are turning a fixed cost into a variable cost.[2]

Network structures are most suitable in times of rapid change and uncertainty. You can contract with different people as you need them. The result is a flexible business that can respond quickly to the changes in the market. However, network structures change the nature of management. No longer do you tell staff what to do. You must now coordinate relations with people over whom you have little control. This has the potential for many conflicts, as other companies might not be so committed to your goals and might have different ideas of what is required. Issues of responsibility and quality control can easily occur.

A contract defines your relationship. It sets out what you expect from each other, the obligations of the parties and the working principles under which each will operate. The contract, if properly constructed, will become the framework for your ongoing relationship. However, there are several limits to the coverage of contracts.

The first limitation is referred to as "incomplete contracts." When we sign a contract, we anticipate future problems and how they will be dealt with, but no one can possibly imagine every eventuality that might occur in the future. For that reason, they are incomplete. When a dispute pops up that had not been anticipated, these holes leave both parties exposed. A second reason why contracts are incomplete is because, even when you can imagine future problems, they are so intricate that describing them in full would take a lawyer months, and your legal bill would negate the benefits of contracting. The incomplete nature of contracts leaves you vulnerable to "post-contract opportunism." This is where someone attempts to gain advantage by exploiting the loopholes in the contract.

Another common contractual problem is "hold up," where you are forced to accept disadvantageous terms after the contract is signed. This occurred to Tim Nicholls when the developer made him pay an inflated price for the tiles or else he wouldn't get the key. Tim had so much invested in opening that he was better off to pay. He could have gone to the courts, but it would have been expensive and the time delays would have deprived him of significant revenue. He needed to open the hotel. Hold up occurs when your investment makes you vulnerable to a threat by other parties seeking better terms than agreed to in the contract.

The size of your commitment can also leave you vulnerable if, at some time in the future, you need to renegotiate your contract. When you start your business, you will be unsure about its long-term position, so you may wisely negotiate limited-term contracts. Things can change substantially in that time, altering the power to renegotiate. A good example of unequal power in renegotiating can be seen in Wal-Mart's relationship with its suppliers. Some businesses were initially excited to gain a contract with such a large retailer, but in subsequent renegotiations, Wal-Mart's pressure to reduce prices has left many struggling. However, the suppliers cannot quickly replace a customer who takes so much of their output. This places them in a position of weakness when renegotiating.

Some problems occur because of information asymmetries. This is where parties to a contract have different information that could affect the future relationship. The one with the most information is at an advantage (and reinforces the need to stick to industries you know). Information advantages can make a big difference when determining future responsibilities and evaluating performance.

One problem with contracts is that you will not always be able to monitor the behavior of the other party. This leaves open the possibility that one party may pursue its own interests at your expense. The insurance industry came up with a term for this: moral hazard. The insurance industry found people with insurance contracts often reduced the care they took to avoid losses to their property. This could occur because the insurance companies were not in a position to monitor their behavior. Today the term is applied to other contracts in which people's actions that are required under the contract are not observable, so they take the opportunity to pursue their private interests at others' expense.

We would like to think that most people act fairly. If they want to be in business a long time, their desire for a good reputation may temper their behavior, but conflicts are not always a result of skullduggery. They can occur because people have different expectations or simply because some people are not up to the job. However, knowing that they didn't mean to hurt you will provide no comfort if you lose your business. You need to protect yourself from all possibilities. Each contract type has its own traps, whether it be for supply of goods, production of manufacture or development of a building or software, and it is your responsibility to familiarize yourself with each. It is impossible to predict all future problems, but it is possible to reduce your exposure by heeding the following precautions.

Selection and Assessment

You can dramatically reduce your future problems by taking care in choosing your contractual partner. Do not accept the first or cheapest offer that becomes available. It is wise to take solicitations from at least three different sources. Second, verify the background of the other party. This includes finding out about its reputation, previous contracts, and the adequacy of its service standard and quality control. Also look at its strategies to see if its goals are compatible with yours. Is it in the market for the long term (in which case its reputation will be important)?

Integrity is important, but it is not the only factor. You should also consider how much experience the other party has in the type of work you want done. Could you suffer because this company is still learning? You are about to enter a relationship that could destroy your life, so take time out. Select someone who best serves your interests.

Risk Assessment

Your contract is an attempt to deal with future outcomes, so you need to invest significant time trying to envision what could go wrong in the future. Your ability to do this will be dramatically enhanced if you have experience in the industry (another reminder of why you should stick to what you know). If the contract covers a number of technical areas, you may want people with different backgrounds to look at the contract. You may even consider using a multidisciplinary team, drawing on people with experience in such contracts. Do not think that your lawyer will identify all the problems, as the contract may go into technical or commercial aspects of which your lawyer has little understanding.

If you feel there is a possibility that "hold up" might occur in the future, you might choose not to contract out that work but keep it in-house. You are most exposed to hold up when you have made an investment directly linked to that contractor, what economists call "asset specificity." The greater the degree of asset specificity, the more likely that transactions will be carried out in-house.

Another factor to consider is what will you do if the contractor goes bankrupt.[3] If you are waiting for an order from the contractor, it could affect your income for that period and your own relationship with customers who may have to switch to an alternative supply. What are the costs of switching to a new supplier if the contractor doesn't deliver? Do you have an exit strategy? The exit strategy of one property developer involved having alternative uses for his projects, in case the first one failed. For example, if he purchases a building to convert to rental apartments, he will always bear in mind other possible uses if that market goes into decline. Exit strategies are important to get you out of awkward situations. You may need to accept a small loss in order to avoid a much bigger one at a later stage.

Content of the Contract

When Tim Nicholls was asked what he would do differently if he started a hotel today, he replied that he would be more cautious and demanding, and put those demands into the contract. With this in mind, you should not rush into a contract but go through it point by point.

Your contract will define the obligations of each party. The more completely you define your demands, the better prepared you will be. The description of the work to be done is often referred to as a statement of work, but do not settle merely for a description of the task. To avoid delays, include completion dates or, in the case of supply contracts, delivery dates. To avoid the situation where the contractor uses poor-quality materials, specify the inputs to be used. You can refer to a brand name "or equal" if it isn't available.

In some more complicated types of work, such as research or product design, it is impossible to detail all tasks, so you may write a statement of objectives. Instead of detailing the tasks, a statement of objectives defines the general parameters of the requirements. It is much looser than a statement of work, so the contractor has more freedom to propose solutions and methodologies.[4]

To ensure performance, contracts can include incentives for good outcomes. In some industries, contractors are required to post a monetary bond to guarantee performance. If the contractor does not perform, it loses the money in the bond. In such instances, it is necessary to fully describe what constitutes satisfactory performance, using criteria that can be measured. Other items to consider when making a contract include:

- Protection of your intellectual property rights and ownership of any property rights created.
- How to monitor quality. Specify standards of performance that can be measured.
- Areas you may have to supplement the supplier with another.
- Who is responsible for loss or damage of property.
- The ability to terminate the contract and method of termination (as part of your exit strategy).
- Methods of conflict resolution.

Monitoring

Once the contract is signed and the relationship begins, you need to ensure the other party performs as required. This involves a process of monitoring, which can be done in a number of ways and will be determined by the nature of the contract. It could include approval of designs or other output, progress meetings, evaluation of subcontractors and onsite quality checks. Any paperwork should be double-checked. This includes checking receipts and invoices to ensure they match what is delivered and what was ordered. Monitoring should be done on a regular basis so that any delays or other problems are identified quickly and addressed before they become major problems.

When monitoring, you must always remember the human element; everyone makes mistakes. On the other hand, you have a business to run, and the contractor made a commitment to you. And its failure to keep that commitment has implications for the jobs you create and the clients expecting your output. It would be unwise not to expect problems, but that doesn't mean you run to the lawyer each time a discrepancy occurs. If the relationship is ongoing, it is wise to develop a method of working through problems. One project manager explained that "everyone is entitled to one mistake as long as it's not significant."

Those who find themselves in the right place at the right time must act quickly before the window of opportunity closes. Contractual relationships enable you to act quickly without investing in the huge capital outlay required to build a factory or hire a workforce. With this in mind, understanding contractual traps is pivotal to entrepreneurship in the twenty-first century.

Chapter 10

Leaping, Failing, Learning—Success!

If you see a bandwagon, it's too late

(Sir James Goldsmith)

In the second chapter, it was revealed that the value of having an idea should not be overstated. It is merely the first part of a process that also involves evaluating the idea and pulling the capital and resources together. It is highly possible that when you get to this stage you may suffer from apprehension; after all, you are about to put your life savings at risk. Self-doubt is rational when you could lose everything. On the other end of the spectrum, you don't want to be a perpetual dreamer. At some stage you either have to take the leap or say "this idea is not as good as I thought."

Many people do not follow up on their ideas. This chapter considers what it is that stops people from taking the leap. It stresses the importance of continually acting to bring your idea to fruition. Entrepreneurship is action based. Sadly, equal courage is often needed to bring a project to an end. In a world of closing market niches and products that become obsolete, knowing when to cut your losses is a vital skill that can stop a bad situation from turning into disaster.

Leaping, Dumping or More Analysis?

Robert Ronstadt surveyed 102 people who seriously considered starting a business.[1] They spent anywhere between one month and one year researching the idea, including gathering market information; looking at sites; preparing a business plan; consulting bankers, attorneys and accountants; investigating; and developing prototypes. However, for some reason, they did not make the final leap. There were a number of reasons for this. Some discovered their idea was not as good as they thought, in which case they were wise not to proceed. Others had family pressures they had to consider. However, the most common reason was financial considerations. Of course some people may simply have not had the gumption to make the leap, but they are unlikely to admit that in a survey.

It is interesting that, when compared with entrepreneurs who did make the commitment, those who decided not to pursue their ideas had different goals. They

Table 10.1 Reasons for Not Starting a Venture (Source: Ronstadt, 1983)

Financial considerations	39
Idea not as good as originally thought	14
Family considerations	16
Lack industry experience	7
Time commitment	7
Other	17
	100%

expected higher rates of profit and sales than those who went ahead. Consequently, if their research indicated a lower profit level, they were not prepared to change their career. The entrepreneurs who went ahead did not have such high expectations. In fact, some chose their ventures for lifestyle reasons. There is good reason to believe that those people who have had their careers disrupted through unemployment are more likely to lower their expectations and take the leap.

Another interesting finding is that those who didn't go ahead were less likely to have associations with people who could act as entrepreneurial role models. Being able to observe others who have been successful is good encouragement and provides a model on how to proceed. Not having these models undermines people's confidence. Another motivating factor can simply be the passion that you feel for your idea. Novice entrepreneurs frequently "fall in love" with their ideas, and this fills them with enthusiasm and commitment.[2] However, falling in love can be a double-edged sword. It can blind you to the project's deficits and make it very hard to end a project.

A significant barrier to starting a business is the opportunity cost of leaving your job. When you are working for someone else, you have the security of employment, a continual wage, and the support of skilled workers who contribute to job security. It is only when people become dissatisfied with working for someone else that they finally do something. One entrepreneur describes the feeling:

> I'd had an idea to set up in business for years and years and years. I'd always had an ambition to set up in business. I just didn't know quite how to do it. Also I was concerned about other risks and the issues of having family responsibilities and what to do. But I suppose as I got older I got more and more and more dissatisfied with my lot working for other people and I got to a stage where I turned 40 and I thought, if I don't do something pretty damn soon, it will be too late.[3]

In a U.S. study that looked at the difference between people who started a business and those who didn't, the key difference was the level of activity undertaken to make the businesses happen.[4] Starters were more aggressive in making their businesses real and undertook more activities that made their businesses tangible. They looked for facilities and equipment, sought and got financial support, formed a legal entity, organized a team, bought facilities and equipment, and made the jump to working full time on the business. Individuals who started a business seemed to act with a greater level of intensity and put themselves into the day-to-day process of running an ongoing business as quickly as they could. It was these activities that resulted in generating sales. Entrepreneurship is action based. It involves getting off your butt and working to put your ideas into process.

Of course just because a business has been launched does not mean it is going to be successful. The same research revealed that 50% of the firms that started had not obtained a positive cash flow at the time the study was done. It is highly possible that some of the starters were foolhardy and rushed into a business that was not sustainable. Certainly a number of people surveyed gave up their idea because their research indicated it would not be successful. Those in this group were just as aggressive and undertook similar activities to those who started firms, but, as the business unfolded and they gained more knowledge, they decreased and then ceased their activities. These people could be regarded in two lights. First, it might be that they were wise in that they tested their ideas before jumping and stopped when they realized that they might lead to failure. Alternatively, it might be that they lacked the flexibility and creativity to overcome the problems that stopped their ideas from being successful.

Those in the third group in this study were those who had not started, nor had they given up. They were still trying. A key characteristic of members in this group was they did not appear to be putting enough effort into the start-up process in order to find out whether they should start a business or give up. They had been much less active and were still doing things like saving money and preparing a plan. They were not doing activities that would make the business real. In fact a key difference between this group and those who gave up was those who gave up had developed a model or prototype and had tested their ideas out, and found they did not work as expected. The still-trying group had not gotten this far. Perhaps those in this group were all talk and little action, or maybe they were being wise and patient, taking time to ensure their businesses were a success. Only time will tell.

If you are thinking of setting up a business, you will probably relate to all of these groups. It is such a big decision to commit your life to an idea. If it fails, the repercussions could have a disastrous effect on your life and loved ones. This leads to uncertainty and procrastination. It is easy to let an opportunity slip by. The key lesson from this study is that, if you are considering starting a business, you should act aggressively toward evaluating and establishing your business. You will have a far better idea through these activities whether the business is worthy of a start-up or a poor choice that should be abandoned. What you do on a day-to-day basis matters. The kinds of activities you do, the number of activities you do, and the order that you do them all affect whether you will create a new venture. Individuals who do not put the time and effort into undertaking these activities may find themselves perennially "still trying," rather than succeeding or learning.

Should I Make a Business Plan?

A great way of making those first steps is to make a business plan. Business plans are a great way of constructing your business model in your head, and they help you come to terms with the tasks ahead. There are a number of advantages from planning. First, it provides a basis for budgeting decisions. Second, it provides a business framework around which strategic decisions can be made. Business plans need not be rigid. Contingencies can be built into them. In fact by clearly identifying factors that are important for success, they may in fact make it easier to be flexible in decision making. Another advantage of business planning is that they are often required by banks and venture capitalists when seeking to raise finance.

Finally, business plans help you to identify the steps you need to bring your dream to fruition. Unless a business is broken down into bite-size chunks, it can seem a bit too much to take on. Often we don't proceed because we feel we don't have enough information. Business plans can help you identify the information you need and make you feel more comfortable about making a leap.

Plans can also increase clarity of vision about your project and explore many of the important issues before you commit your life and savings. Before you can feel comfortable that the market will provide income that will cover your expenses, some form of evaluation is needed. An assessment of market size is needed, and this involves looking at the market for similar products and services and an evaluation of competitors. Costs must also be assessed. These include not just fixed and operational costs but also costs of introducing your business to the market. The resources you have available to launch your business could have a major impact on the rate of market growth and the length of time it takes to reach break-even point. Many good businesses have fallen over simply because it took a long time for the market to wake up to the product, and the company did not have the resources to survive a long establishment period.

Many financiers and banks complain that the business plans they receive show that the entrepreneurs have no idea of the expenses involved. It is often hard to identify the costs of a new business. It is much easier with mature industries, especially if you have experience in those businesses. With experience, you know the equipment you will need, its cost, and its operating expenses. Entrepreneurs without such knowledge often find they are paying unexpected costs, which drag their profit below expectations.

The limitations of business plans must be recognized as they are not a cure-all. There are so many unexpected variables at the start-up phase that the business plan rapidly becomes obsolete. It is impossible to cover every contingency. When their business starts, entrepreneurs will need to improvise, especially in ambiguous environments where new features are constantly emerging. It seems likely that, in newer and faster growing industries and those experiencing technological volatility, a higher level of improvisation is needed for survival.[5] You cannot be overly committed to your business plan. In the face of customer feedback, changes should be expected.

Perhaps the biggest advantage of doing a business plan is that it forces you to analyze the business before you invest your time and energy. You explore the processes and problems you will encounter in situations that are not stressful. If you start a business and encounter these problems without giving them any thought, you may find yourself under heavy stress. Finally, in forcing you to confront these issues, the plan sets you on your way. You have already started to confront the management problems and lay out the steps for success. Instead of being trapped by thinking you don't know where to start, the business plan propels you forward and lays out your future steps.

Clarity of Vision

It was once believed that, for some reason, the people who started businesses have a smaller adversity to risk, and in many instances that may in fact be the case. For example, people with a family dependent on them are likely to be more cautious than someone without any dependents. However, recent research tends to suggest that entrepreneurs are not more open to risk. They merely perceive the level of risk differently.[6] Entrepreneurs tend to view business situations more positively than do non-entrepreneurs. They perceive strengths and opportunities where others see weaknesses and threats. But is this always a good thing?

Related to this is the high level of optimism that entrepreneurs are found to possess. Those who make the leap are often overly optimistic in their assessment of business opportunities.[7] One study links this optimism to the way people process information.[8] It appears that entrepreneurs put together information in their minds differently than other people do. They are prone to making what psychologists call "cognitive biases." These biases lead them to make optimistic assumptions about risk. Cognitive biases are common mental shortcuts that people use to make judgments.

Three cognitive biases have been reported in entrepreneurs. The first is a failure to know the limits of their knowledge. This can lead to overconfidence. Such entrepreneurs think they have sufficient knowledge to proceed, when, in reality, they are well short. The lesson is simple: review all information even if the information suggests your business will fail. That information may save you from bankruptcy.

The second bias is an illusion of control. This occurs when individuals overemphasize the extent to which they have control of a situation. They believe that with the right skills, they can overcome problems when confronted with them. However, often factors are beyond their control. This book has stressed the importance of environmental factors. It frequently comes down to chance, and skill is not necessarily the deciding factor.

The third bias is their belief in the "law of small numbers." This occurs when a small amount of information is used to make judgments. For example, you might be encouraged by feedback from a small group of potential customers who state they would buy a new product. However, this group may not represent the population as a whole and the market might be much smaller than expected. Another example of the law of small numbers is the disproportionate number of success stories we hear in the media. People are far more likely to trumpet their successes than their failures, and successes are also more likely to be publicized. These stories of successful entrepreneurs provide a distorted view of entrepreneurial activity, which lowers our perception of venture risk.

The effect of these biases is that some individuals start ventures because they do not accurately perceive the risks involved. Because of this distorted view of reality, there is a clear danger that entrepreneurs are setting themselves up for failure, and, given the high failure rate of new businesses, this may in fact be the case. However, overconfidence is not always a bad thing. It enables entrepreneurs to proceed quickly with an idea before all the necessary information is in. This can allow them to seize an opportunity when it appears and gain a head start over potential competition. Second, if overconfident people are lucky, they can build a successful business. Third, just because people underestimated the size of the tasks they have taken on does not mean they won't stick to it and endure the hardship. An inflated sense of self-belief might be unrealistic, but it helps to keep people motivated, and this can lead to success.

Nevertheless, entrepreneurs can benefit from more accurate perceptions of their businesses. Recognizing that you may be biased is a start. The next step is working to minimize these biases and creating more accurate assessments of your future business. This can be done by seeking and listening to the advice of outsiders, conducting thorough research and utilizing group decision-making techniques. More use can be made of various qualitative and quantitative market research approaches and analytical risk analysis. These have the added advantage of providing a strong foundation on which to build a business plan, and this in turn increases the likelihood of obtaining funding. Most importantly, by reducing the level of uncertainty, these techniques will make it more likely that entrepreneurs decide to pursue the venture, if the information is favorable.

Unfortunately, sometimes we simply don't have access to all the information we need. Entrepreneurs operate in a world of greater uncertainty than that faced by a manager working in a corporation. We often have to make decisions where there are no historical trends, no previous levels of performance, and little if any specific market information. If we delay our decision to start up until all the facts are in, we run the danger of seeing someone else jump the gun, and the window of opportunity closes. Consequently, many entrepreneurs tend to rely on simple rules of thumb (heuristics) to guide their decision-making processes. This speeds up the decision-making process during the period of uncertainty, which typify start-up situations. Although there is an obvious danger with simplification, it does allow an entrepreneur to proceed before all the necessary information is known (and available to others). One entrepreneur surveyed went as far as saying:

> People who are engaged in business such as mine are rarely influenced by surveys because they don't place any stock in them. Survey reports, in general, are most highly prized by those individuals who lack sufficient knowledge of a matter in which they are required to make a decision. It is my considered

opinion that those individuals are not going to be found successfully engaging in entrepreneurial business.[9]

Of course, this statement could also illustrate the importance of intuitive knowledge and experience over statistics. A person in an industry can seize an opportunity before the statistics come out. Nevertheless, formal market and technological information can help to re-evaluate our biases, and with modern research techniques, we can greatly improve our prior assessment of outcomes.

The Entrepreneurial Process

In 1994, Mahesh Bhave interviewed a number of successful entrepreneurs from New York State to reveal the processes they went through in establishing ventures.[10] The feedback he received suggested that there were common processes involved. This process began with the formation of the idea and culminated when the products and services were sold in the market.

In 41% of the cases examined, the idea came first. The entrepreneur perceived an idea and then decided to start a business. The opportunity was revealed to them in ways similar to those mentioned earlier. Commonly, they encountered a problem, solved it and that solution formed the basis of a business idea.

In contrast to those businesses where the idea came first, 59% of entrepreneurs decided they wanted to start a business before they had any idea of what that business would be. Their decision to start a business was often derived from personal and environmental circumstances in their lives. For example, if their employer relocated, some decided they did not want to move, so they started their own businesses. Some felt their existing career path was blocked, while others had simply had enough of working for other people and believed it was time to go out on their own. Once these people had decided to start a business, they went searching for a suitable business idea. Most had no trouble finding ideas. The problem was finding one that was suitable. It is important to find one that matches your skill base, as one entrepreneur explains:

> There are so many opportunities out there, oh so many. . . . Every time an opportunity comes along, I think I am supposed to take advantage of it. So, I get lost, who knows where until it becomes apparent I have no experience to know how to make it happen, no base of knowledge. So I see lots of opportunities every time I turn around, but I (tell myself) that's not where you belong.[11]

A major part of searching for an idea was filtering out those opportunities that required knowledge, experience, skills and other resources that the entrepreneur did not possess. The danger of entering a business of which they have little knowledge was widely recognized. The business ideas chosen were those that they felt they personally had the capabilities to make work.

Once an idea was chosen, there was a process of refinement whereby the idea was developed into a business concept. For most, this involved following what others had done before them. Only a small fraction of the ventures could be described as novel. Most ventures were based on familiar business concepts, although most had some feature about them that gave them a unique advantage, for example location.

The task was a lot harder for those developing new ideas, for they had no precedents to guide them. They had to go through a learning process, which involved introducing the product, receiving customer feedback and developing the idea further until they had a business concept that matched the need in the marketplace. In some cases, they also had to educate potential customers about the advantages of the product, as one entrepreneur found to his chagrin:

> I thought these companies will be happy . . . that they would need this kind of service. But the fact of the matter was that they weren't ready for it and didn't understand what it was. From my point of view, if I had gotten in the pizza business, it would have been easier. . . . What I was doing was missionary work—educating for the client.[12]

Not all new products required an education process. One woman introduced a product for which there was a well-recognized need. Consequently, there was no need to educate the customer.

Through this process of feedback and education, the entrepreneurs developed a business concept in which the product or service is aligned with the market. The next step is the critical stage of physically creating a business. The entrepreneur must make the decision to commit time and resources to create a business. The actual start-up only occurred when there was a customer or a fairly guaranteed potential customer. In fact, most had their initial customers lined up before production started.

The next step is to set up an organization and technology to produce the product or service. There was a great deal of variety in this task, depending on the nature of the business. Businesses in service industries had the most modest requirements, requiring not much more than office facilities and equipment. For these people, the productive technology was mostly in the head of the entrepreneurs: their knowledge and expertise. Other businesses required more facilities. For example, those businesses with high production technology novelty developed their technologies in laboratories.

The differences in equipment meant that some firms needed more finance than others. Sources of funding varied from personal savings, venture capitalist backing and at least one had funding from a parent company. In complete contradiction to most texts on the subject, which highlight the role of financial and resource acquisition, the entrepreneurs surveyed did not see it as a strategic issue. It was merely viewed as something to be taken care of along the way.

The entrepreneurial process did not finish with the business launch. Once the product hits the market, it unleashes a raft of feedback ideas that can affect the success of the business. Customer feedback and sensitivity to market changes are vital when entering a market with a new product or service. Some feedback might call for making changes to product features or product quality. These operational changes can normally be incorporated without too much difficulty. On the other hand, some may call for a complete change in the way things are done. Such changes require more resources. However, failure to act on them could leave a window of opportunity open for another entrepreneur to take up on the improvements and steal the market.

* * *

One of the biggest fears that people have that stops them form starting a business is fear of failure and bankruptcy. This is a rational fear. The statistics on the survival rate of new businesses are not very encouraging. Most evidence shows that a high proportion of new businesses fail within a short time. In 1983, the U.S. Small Business Administration estimated that three out of every four new businesses fail.[13] At Harvard, Jeffrey Timmons studied a number of studies on survival rates and found that 23.5% fell in their first two years, 51.7% in their first four years, and 62.7% in the first six.[14] This is not just an American phenomenon. For example, a German study also reported a high rate of failure, albeit lower than in the United States.[15] The German study found 27% failed in their first two years and 37% after five. In the United Kingdom, the failure rate for small firms is 10 to 15% per annum. This suggests that, over a three- to five-year period, 50% of the firms will fail.[16]

There are many reasons why companies fail. They vary from pure stupidity to overly optimistic expectations of market size, underestimation of costs, or an unfavorable environment. There are a number of features that consistently have an impact on business success, and the German study mentioned previously has highlighted some of these. This study was based on interviews with 1,849 businesspeople who founded new businesses in Munich and Upper Bavaria. The interviews were conducted five years after the businesses were founded, giving insight into who had failed and why. The findings are summarized in Table 10.2, which shows that 23.7% of businesses failed after two years and 37.1% after five years.

The research links failure rates to characteristics in the business. Standing out as a driver of success are the individual qualities of the entrepreneur. There seems to be a strong linkage between success and education. A founder with less than 12 years of schooling was substantially more likely to go out of business than one with more than 15 years of education. Other key factors were whether the founder had previous experience being self-employed and supervising staff. Someone with these experiences will be more familiar with the requirements of their businesses. Consequently, those who had previously been self-employed and supervised staff were most likely to make a success of their new venture.

The most important qualities that an entrepreneur can bring to his or her business appears to be previous experience in the same industry. This suggests that being an "expert" or being "knowledgeable" is not only useful in finding an idea. It also helps with implementing it. Those who leapt into a new industry were more than twice as likely to fail than those who stuck to what they knew. If you do not have the necessary

Table 10.2 Factors Related to Business Survival (Adapted from Bruderl, Preisendorfer and Ziegler)

Percent gone out of business	After 2 yrs	5 yrs	Percent gone out of business	After 2 yrs	5 yrs
All Businesses	23.7	37.1	**Human Capital**		
			Years of schooling of founder		
Organizational Characteristics			Less than 12 yrs	29.1	44.7
Newcomer v. follower business			12 to 15 yrs	22.9	35.9
Newcomer	26.3	41.7	15 or more	17.2	28
Follower	15.7	23.3			
			Years of work experience of founder		
Independent v. affiliated			Less than 10 years	33.4	48.9
Independent	22.8	35.5	10–20	21.0	33.7
Affiliated	31.3	51.9	20–30	15.0	26.6
			30 or more	16.7	28.9
Amount of capital invested					
Less than 20,000DM	36.6	55.4	*Industry-specific experience of founder*		
20–50,000DM	25.7	38.0	No	36.9	54.5
50,000DM	8.3	16.1	Yes	14.9	25.5
No. of employees at time of founding			*Self-employment experience of founder*		
1 or fewer	35.9	54.2	No	27.9	42.0
1–2	15.4	27.6	Yes	15.1	27.0
2–3	16.2	23.3			
More than 3	7.5	13.1	*Leadership experience of founder*		
			No	30.4	45.5
Legal form			Yes	17.8	29.7
Small tradesman	32.0	49.1			
Registered firm	5.6	11.4	*Self-employed father of founder*		
			No	25.6	40.1
Generalist v. specialist			Yes	19.5	30.7
Generalist	28.7	43.5			
Specialist	18.7	31.1	**Environmental Conditions**		
			Branch of industry		
Traditional v. innovative			Manufacturing	11.2	19.2
Traditional	27.3	42.7	Construction	15.7	24.1
Innovative	17.8	27.3	Wholesale/retail trade	28.1	42.5
			Transportation	37.8	55.6
Local v. national market-scope business			Restaurants	29.4	43.6
Local market scope	30.7	47.1	Computer services	14.2	28.4
National market scope	14.9	24.5	Other services	24.1	38.6
			Intensity of competition in industry		
			Low	20.9	33.9
			High	26.7	40.5

knowledge and skills when you start your business, you will have to learn them as you go, and this increases workload and stress levels. It also increases the chance that bad decisions will be made during the learning phase. Starting a new business is stressful enough without these dangers.

Founders who started a business by buying an existing business had a better chance of survival than firms that were started from scratch. There is far less work to do when taking over an existing firm. Many of the connections to customers have already been established. Much of the equipment and procedures are in place and many of the teething problems solved. The new business owner can build on where the old owner left off.

This last fact must be tempered with the fact that those companies who innovated by offering new products and services were more likely to survive than those who imitated existing businesses. Only 27% of innovative businesses had failed after five years compared with 43% of traditional enterprises who offered conventional products. Another successful strategy was to develop a small niche. Those who focused on a specialized niche were more likely to survive than those providing products or services aimed at a broad range of customers.

One surprising result from this study was that independent businesses had significantly better survival rates than those affiliated with other businesses. The researchers were at a loss to explain why this was so, but it seems that getting a franchise is not always a guarantee of success, even though many of the set-up problems have already been solved. It appears that some companies in the franchise sector had been giving licenses with difficult or even fraudulent conditions. The new franchise owner was being set up for failure. It emphasizes the need to thoroughly research and question everything.

In a world of market evolution, we must expect companies to fail. As market niches close and products become obsolete, there is no shame in shutting the doors on what may have been an exciting adventure. The closing of niches is as natural as their opening, and anyone running a business must recognize that, at some stage, market forces may act against them. Whole industries have virtually disappeared as a result of evolving technologies and consumer demands. These include whaling, mechanical typewriters, telegraphy, gas lighting, shoe repair, mechanical watches, television receivers, and transistors.[17] And it is not just small firms that fail. One-third of the Fortune 500 companies listed in 1970 had disappeared by 1983. So high is the failure rate that it has been suggested that long-term survival might be best regarded as a purely random result.

Not surprising, some industries produced higher failure rates than others, but this is not just a case of evolution. For example, in the United States, service and retail industries account for a significant number of failures. One particular problem with retail and restaurants is they are not difficult businesses to set up, so they are often highly competitive. Industries with higher barriers to entry will have fewer aspiring competitors to threaten new businesses.

Although even the biggest companies yield to the Grim Reaper, there is a definite liability of smallness in that smaller firms find it tougher going than bigger firms. Bigger firms have larger financial resources, which helps them weather the critical start-up period and random shocks from the environment. They may also have advantages raising capital, may face better tax conditions and may be in a better position to recruit qualified labor. However, in some circumstances, small enterprises also have advantages. They have lower overheads and require minimal resources for sustenance. Nevertheless, the evidence is clear—size does matter.

There are a number of management failings that occur repeatedly in failing companies. They include not enough emphasis on marketing or financial control. Strategic failings include a tendency to compete on price rather than more profitable options, and they spread their product range too wide when a more focused approach is likely to produce better results. Finally, many entrepreneurs simply fail from poor organization.[18]

Studies repeatedly confirm the importance of what economists call "human capital." The personal qualities of the entrepreneur have a big impact on the success of a new business. This includes education, work experience, leadership and self-employment experience, but most important was prior experience in an industry before starting a business in that industry. If entrepreneurs have industry-specific experience, not only are they more likely to identify promising opportunities, they are also significantly less likely to fail when they put those opportunities into action.

So what if you want to start a business in a new area? Perhaps the best way to do this is to gain employment in the industry, possibly in a small company where all the operations can be seen. Second, you can research. By this I don't mean reading a book. I mean significant research on all features of the industry, reading every piece of information available, talking to those in the know, and continually learning. Entrepreneurship is a learning process.

* * *

> Sir Angus Tait (founder of Tait Electronics) said after his first company crashed that his banker asked if he was going to make the same mistakes a second time.
> "I told him certainly not—this time I am going to make different ones."
> The experience gained was extremely valuable, he said.
> "Too valuable to be wasted by not going for it again."

Many entrepreneurs pull out along the path and with good reason. It involves evaluating and rejecting ideas before settling on one that is worth developing. Deciding not to pursue an idea does not mean that your time has been wasted, for the experience you gain doing that evaluation will help you to evaluate other ideas in the future. Entrepreneurial evaluation is a skill in itself that requires cultivating over time. Knowing when to pull out is part of the process on the way to success. It is a learning process.

Business failure is also part of that process, but the pain of business failure can be great. Few books on entrepreneurship talk about the pain of business failure. Most books tend to be motivational and try to excite people with what can be done, but these books paint a false picture. The truth is many businesses fail, and the cost of that failure can be great. One academic who was brave enough to do research in this area is Dean Shepherd at the University of Colorado.[19] Shepherd's father had a family business that eventually went under. He saw personally the pain that comes with a business loss, and the lessons he learned are essential for all entrepreneurs.

Shepherd realized that many entrepreneurs are emotionally attached to their businesses. The businesses are their "babies," and they link their identity to the success or failure of that business. It is therefore no surprise that if the business fails, it can lead to much grief. Shepherd describes his father's emotions at the time:

> There was a numbness and disbelief that this business he had created twenty years ago was no longer alive. There was some anger towards the economy, competitors and debtors. A stronger emotion than anger was that of guilt and self-blame. He felt guilty that he had caused the failure of his business, that it could no longer be passed on to my brother, and that as a result, he had failed not only as a businessman, but also as a father. These feelings caused him distress and anxiety. He felt the situation was hopeless, became withdrawn, and at times depressed.[20]

Given his closeness to the business, it is no surprise that Shepherd's father continued to plough the family's personal wealth into the business right up until the day that it ceased operations. He did what he could to keep it afloat, but the result was that he lost the family's wealth. If he had cut his losses earlier, he would have lost his business but still kept the family home and other wealth. Why did he persist with the poorly performing business? Perhaps he thought the decline was temporary and he just had to get through the bad patch. Perhaps he was going through denial, brought about by the shame of failure, or perhaps it just reflected how much the business meant to him.

These feelings are common among those who have experienced failure; the consequences can boil over into the family life. The resulting stress can undermine marriages and affect health. Shepherd quotes another entrepreneur:

> [The business is] a child. . . . [Losing my business] was devastating. . . . The things that were going on in my life—I'd lost my company, lost my home, lost everything. I couldn't handle it. . . . There was a time . . . when I sat in my office and cried, and then put a gun to my head. . . . When I finally got over all that [pain and anger associated with the loss of the business] was when I quit blaming other people. . . . It was my fault because I didn't plan far enough ahead. It was stupid as hell of me to sit there exposed like that. . . . Listen, this lesson was extremely expensive. I paid dearly, my family paid dearly. . . . Yeah, I learned a lot.[21]

It is common for failed entrepreneurs to experience debilitating grief. If you find yourself in this position, it is important to know that the feelings and reactions you experience are normal. There are psychological and physiological symptoms associated with grief. If you recognize that these responses are normal, you will be less inclined to feel shame and embarassment and more inclined to discuss your emotions. There is also a process of recovery from grief. The negative feelings will diminish in intensity over time, but recovery will not be an even process. Your thoughts and emotions will oscilate between a sense of loss and a sense of rebuilding. But once you have recovered, you have the opportunity to use your knowledge gained from your failure to start a new business. It is a chance to turn your experience into a learning process.

It is very easy to say you should learn from your mistakes, but when you have lost everything, it can be very hard to override your emotions. There are many barriers that stop people from learning from their failures. First is simply the extent of the grief. The failure is simply too painful to think about. You don't want to analyse the lessons. The loss is something you want to move on from. The second is the shame and embarassment—you simply don't want to go there.

Another reason we fail to learn is we choose to blame other people or the environment. We will blame the market, the bank or creditors. Like the second entrepreneur quoted above, his initial response was to blame other people, and he did not recover until he accepted responsibility for what happened. But once he admitted his mistakes and learned from them, he recovered and eventually founded eight companies.

The experiences we learn from business failure can provide us with the skills to have great success but often we don't exploit these lessons. We become scared of failing again and lose confidence. We may simply be emotionally exhausted and lack the energy to try again. The sad thing is, after experiencing business decline, we are often in the best situation to recognize what is happening and stop it from happening again. You are now ready to succeed! People who fail in their first business and don't get up to start a second may be wasting all the experience they gained in the process.

Chapter 11

Government Policy and New Business Development

Entrepreneurship is most likely to flourish in business environments that are conducive to the emergence and growth of young businesses. When opportunities are available, more businesses are likely to be born. And when the environment provides entrepreneurs with the knowledge and skills required to start and manage a business, people will be encouraged to take advantage of the opportunities available. The need for a conducive environment is particularly relevant for young, small companies because, unlike large companies, they are likely to have little control over the environment in which they operate.[1] In this chapter, we look at what the government can do to improve that environment. Once again, we will begin to illustrate the importance of government policy by focusing on an extreme example, then narrow in on key points.

One of the most hostile environments in the world for entrepreneurs can be found in parts of Africa. This is a turbulent environment with very high risks. Even those African nations that are not at war suffer from great instability, with economies based on fluctuating commodity prices and high susceptibility to crop failure. These fluctuations mean supplies are not always reliable and business customers frequently default. The problem of defaulting business partners is not helped by the inadequacy of African legal systems. There are long delays, and the courts cannot be relied on to solve legal disputes.[2] This increases the chance that businesses intentionally default.

The infrastructure in most African nations is deplorable.[3] The density of the road network is only one-fifteenth of that in India. Africa possesses only one-tenth the telephones of Asia, with triple the number of technical problems. This can present a huge problem for business communication. One exporter in Zimbabwe reported having to travel 30 kilometers to make a telephone call. One might think that the cheap cost of land and labor would compensate for these disadvantages, but this is far from the case. For example, port charges for a container in Abidjan, Côte d'Ivoire, are $200 compared with $120 in the European port of Antwerp. Would you want to risk all you own to launch a business in this environment? Africans certainly don't feel comfortable investing in this environment, and the region has the highest level of capital flight in the world.

It is no surprise that there are few manufacturing and service businesses in Africa, and these countries are confined to exporting resources to the world's developed nations. In the past, Africans could blame their colonial legacy for this situation, but conditions have only got worse since independence. The old white minority has been replaced by small groups of privileged blacks. These governments have introduced policies that distort market activity to their benefit.

Of course, some African governments are more enlightened than others, and in the 1990s the region underwent substantial liberalization. However, even in the most advanced African nations, entrepreneurs face huge difficulties. Burundi is considered one of the most liberal trading regimes south of the Sahara, yet even here, the growth of firms is hampered by institutional and environmental conditions, in particular the absence of well-functioning resource and product markets. Entrepreneurs complain that financial markets do not provide access to the necessary credit. At the same time, markets for their products are characterized by insufficient demand, a function of the nation's poverty. There is no lack of competition, which many economists stress as a vital factor in developing industrial success. In fact, firms in the metal-working and textile sector complain about the toughness of the competition in light of the small market. Some firms also suggested they were over-regulated by government.[4]

In contrast to Africa, the United States seems like entrepreneurial heaven. However, in the early days, the United States actually showed some similarities to a country like Rwanda. It was resource-rich and exported raw materials to more modernized nations. Like some African nations, the United States also had its own civil war. However, the U.S. Civil War had a definite end and was followed by a period of peace that made it possible to perform economic transactions in safety.

Even in the early days, the United States had significant advantages compared to Africa. The United States benefited from immigrants coming from the most advanced commercial nation on earth, Britain. They brought with them skills, commercial practices and an understanding of how to operate in a market. The U.S. government also performed some small but important roles in the economy. The government made market activity easier through the coining of money and provided an efficient infrastructure for the day, which included postal and road services. A system of patents and copyrights was created, which encouraged innovation. The legal system was effective in dealing with commercial disputes and, in contrast to the African situation, law courts made decisions that showed a strong sensitivity to commercial interests.

After the Civil War, U.S. government activity stepped up another gear. It granted land for the building of colleges to teach agriculture and mechanical engineering. It created a national banking system and introduced a federal income tax. Several bills were introduced that gave grants for rail expansion and further developed the transportation network, a key plank in building a national market. A number of new federal bureaucracies were created, and the military became an important customer for industrial producers. Tariffs were introduced to protect American producers from foreign competition, and this played an important role in developing the nation's industrial capabilities. The most rapidly expanding industries between 1870 and 1914 were those protected by tariffs.[5]

After the second World War, when the United States entered a period of industrial leadership based on new technologies, the government again played a pivotal role. It financed half the nation's R&D spending, an amount similar to the total public and private expenditure in the UK, Germany, France and Japan combined. From this, a number of new technologies were born that led to many future entrepreneurial openings. The computer was a result of military expenditure and incorporated the research interests of MIT, IBM and AT&T. The semiconductor was developed privately by Bell Telephone Laboratories in anticipation of the government market. NASA and the U.S. Army were major early purchasers and provided significant funding for the semiconductor's early development.[6] Many of today's businesses are based on these technologies.

*　　*　　*

Governments can play a key role assisting young businesses, both directly and indirectly, in the way they shape the environment. We saw in Chapter 3 how the government can have a direct effect creating business opportunities. The government also has an effect through the policies it introduces. However, policies can have different effects depending on the country. For example, the levels and types of government assistance needed in many African nations are very different from that required in Western nations like the United States. To be effective, government policy should be shaped depending on the nature of the environment and the problems it contains.

The idea that different countries require different policies is common sense, yet it sometimes runs against our basic political instincts. When asked how the government can help, a common reply is "reduce taxes and then get out of the way." For many people, their attitude to government intervention is intrinsically linked with previously held political convictions. Many do not believe in any level of government assistance (unless, of course, they are the recipients).

The call for small government has much validity. Taxation deprives businesses of revenue, while many procedural and regulatory requirements create compliance costs. Many small companies feel weighed down by the time and effort they must devote to officialdom. It is not surprising that many prefer the government to take a small role in the economy. Research has shown that entrepreneurs may be discouraged if they have to follow too many rules and procedural requirements. Countries that keep rules and regulations at a minimum are likely to see more start-ups. However the same research also shows that a government that is proactive, offering tax and other incentives, and providing training and counseling services increases the likelihood of new venture start-ups.[7]

Despite this, the government is often held responsible for economic performance. We witness this every election time. Governments that have the misfortune to be in power when economies turn down are often removed from office even though they were not responsible for the decline. Similarly, presidents and prime ministers in office during a period of economic prosperity are frequently associated with the good times. Given that voters make a connection between prosperity and government, most elected officials try to secure economic prosperity through industrial policies. If governments can improve environmental conditions, it can increase the birth and survival rate of new ventures. Table 11.1 identifies environmental factors and policies that can be used to target deficiencies.[8]

One of the most important features of the environment is demand, and here the government can pursue a number of policies. Central to maintaining high levels of demand are government policies geared toward growth. This normally means low inflation, few restrictions on business activity and low taxation. Other methods of promoting demand include policies whereby governments give local businesses preference when buying goods and services. However, there are problems with this. When local producers do not need to compete with international suppliers, they frequently become complacent about their standards. To overcome this, governments should demand high standards for their purchases.[9]

Many infant industry programs include trade barriers that preserve the domestic market for local producers. However, this policy has the same problem of removing pressure that forces firms to be competitive. It can also raise the cost of imported supplies needed by local producers. It is possible to have a discriminating tariff structure, whereby resources and machinery needed by local businesses are tariff-free, but such policies often need to be changed as local business needs evolve. The policy can be expensive to continually review and upgrade. Another option to enhance demand is to introduce policies that help access foreign markets. This includes export assistance and providing a quality infrastructure, including transportation and communication facilities.

The social environment plays an important part in directing and motivating potential entrepreneurs.[10] Government policies that promote entrepreneurship as a desirable career can help encourage people to set up business. Official recognition of successful entrepreneurs can play an important part, sending a message to potential entrepreneurs that business is an attractive career option. In Japan, during the Meiji Restoration, the government had to change social values that were anti-materialist and anti-commerce. The government promoted entrepreneurs and corporate men as the samurai of the new era.

Sources of finance are essential for the birth and survival of a new enterprise, yet capital markets vary from country to country. Encouraging competition among finance companies is an important policy plank to ensure entrepreneurs are provided with sufficient service. Other policy options that ease financial pressure on young enterprises include the provision of venture capital funds, subsidies, grants and tax-based incentives. Financial pressure can also be relieved if facilities are provided free or at a reduced cost. Facilities are often provided by governments in the form of business incubators that provide start-up services including office space, shared office facilities, counseling and advisory services at a reduced cost. Incubators can also perform important social and informational functions. Close proximity to other entrepreneurs provides the opportunity to build networks, garner support and motivation, learn from others, and gain access to opportunities, resources and information.

Table 11.1 Policies Aimed at Improving Environment for New Businesses (Adapted from Gnyawali and Fogel)

Environmental Factor	*Government Policy*
Demand	Restrictions on competing imports Policies devoted to economic growth Government procurement programs for small business Export assistance for foreign markets
Skills	Provision of technical and vocational education Provision of business and entrepreneurial training Temporary and permanent immigration visas
Social Values	Promote positive public attitude toward entrepreneurship Recognizing successful role models
Financial Capital	Provision of venture capital Low-cost loans Credit guarantee program for start-up enterprises Promoting competition among financial institutions Tax incentives and exemptions Direct grants and subsidies Promoting competition in finance sector
Technology	Government support for research and development Protection of property rights for advanced nations Ignoring foreign property rights for developing nations
Information/Knowledge	Provision of information Promoting entrepreneurial networks Counseling and support services Incubator facilities
Existing producers	Policies to attract foreign investment Policies that assist particular industries
Resources & Infrastructure	No restrictions on imports of supplies Local and international information networks Modern transport and communication facilities
Government Policies and Procedures	Provision of bankruptcy laws Entry barriers Procedural requirements for registration and licensing Minimize number of institutions for entrepreneurs to report to Minimize regulations governing entrepreneurial activities

Technology has become increasingly important as firms are more likely to grow if they are in highly innovative industries. Governments can play an important role in advancing and diffusing technology. Copyright and patent laws that protect new ideas encourage innovation while government funding of education and research increases the pool of technology that entrepreneurs have to draw on. Government provision of business and technological education can target other deficiencies in the environment. Without the necessary technical and business skills, entrepreneurs may find they are ill-equipped for the task they have chosen. Education is also important in providing businesses with a pool of skilled labor.

Finally governments can look at themselves and how they actually implement policies. This involves maintaining legal and institutional frameworks that facilitate the efficient functioning of private enterprise. Government agencies should consciously support entrepreneurs in their day-to-day operations, thereby reducing the barriers and problems they face. Rules, regulations and requirements should be kept to a minimum. All in all, research has found that entrepreneurial opportunities tend to be higher in economies that are deregulated, where market mechanisms operate freely and where entrepreneurs have to face few barriers to entry.[11]

While there are a large number of policy options, when governments intervene to assist entrepreneurs, they frequently do a bad job. In fact, they can increase the failure rates of new businesses by encouraging marginal entrepreneurs. Financial incentives that reduce the need for banks to screen loan applicants lead to higher failure rates. Similarly, tax breaks increase the incentive for investment in businesses that otherwise would not receive it. Government policies can result in excessive market entry and over-investment, made worse by the ever-present over-optimism that entrepreneurs display. When these new businesses fall, it is not just the entrepreneur that fails. Their exit leaves a trail of destruction to customers, employees and suppliers. In fact, Simon Parker suggests governments should act to discourage entrepreneurs; otherwise, too much investment is channeled into unproductive activities.[12] When combined with the tendency of bureaucrats and politicians to stamp their personal biases on the process, we have grave cause for concern. Scott Shane at Case Western Reserve University also thinks governments do a poor job:

> They stimulate people to start new companies disproportionately in competitive industries with lower barriers to entry and high rates of failure. Nor do businesses formed in response to government intervention generate much employment or substantially enhance productivity. . . .[13]

The problem is, although some companies contribute significantly to economic growth and job creation, the typical start-up company does not. We end up with more construction firms, hair salons and taxi services, companies that generate little innovation. These businesses may even hinder economic growth because new businesses are on average less productive than existing ones. We need to move away from the naïve idea that all entrepreneurship is good and recognize that only a few entrepreneurs move the economy forward. A policy that revolves around blindly increasing the number of new businesses is based on a flawed perception of economic growth. Shane suggests that policy makers need to think more like venture capitalists and concentrate time and money identifying the select few entrepreneurs who are most likely to succeed. The emphasis should be on quality not quantity, finding the businesses that innovate, create jobs and enhance economic growth. As for the others, Shane suggests we should actually reduce incentives so that marginal entrepreneurs do not start businesses.

Shane's emphasis is on selecting entrepreneurs who are most likely to be successful. In raising the issue of selecting entrepreneurs, we are led to another more controversial concept: selecting industries. Sometimes governments prefer to target assistance to those industries with the highest growth potential, but such programs are not without controversy. First, to tax one industry in order to pay for assistance to another hints at "robbing Peter to pay Paul." A good manager in a declining industry is punished while a mediocre entrepreneur in a growing industry is rewarded.

Second is the issue of which industry to support. A government that chooses certain industries to assist is "picking winners," and many doubt the ability of governments to do this. After all, we have learned that one of the key components in identifying opportunities is expert knowledge and industry experience. How can a bunch of bureaucrats in the capital city, far from the workings of the market, have any idea on market shifts? Of course, we have also learned that entrepreneurs can identify opportunities through extensive searching, and there is no reason why government officials cannot do this. However, their success might be hampered if they haven't gone through some process of entrepreneurial learning, and their rigorousness can be undermined if they don't bear the cost of failure. One solution to this problem is to seek industry advice, but this exposes governments to the danger of "political capture," where government policy is directed by professionals who direct taxpayer funds into their own industry. For these reasons, many economists warn against picking winners.

Targeting industries has been a common pillar of economic growth in Japan, Taiwan, Singapore and South Korea. Governments in these countries have actively searched for entrepreneurial opportunities. Their officials have consistently monitored world markets in search of export opportunities and new types of demand. With knowledge of these trends and opportunities, they have then channeled the limited available capital into those industries.[14]

Often industrial assistance is targeted at not just specific industries but at individual firms. The government presents a proposal to a selected private firm and, through credit and financial guarantees, encourages the firm to take on the project. The company may also be given monopoly rights, which removes vulnerability over demand, and in return the government maintains the right to monitor the company. In other cases, the government actually became the entrepreneur, using or creating a public enterprise to develop the project. In this way, Asian governments have successfully created industrial sectors from scratch, such as steel, shipbuilding, transportation, petrochemicals and semiconductors.

Companies born in this way include Hyundai Heavy Industries, Samsung and Goldstar: household names that illustrate such policies can work. These companies grew under state guidance and a number of forms of assistance including subsidized credit. Technical assistance included the identification of foreign technologies and funding to help acquire it. The companies also received heavily subsidized R&D and technical advice.

Recognizing the importance of demand, these Asian governments have protected their young manufacturers with trade barriers that shielded them from foreign competition. However, they were well aware of the limitations of protection, so they coupled protection with competition. A number of local firms were encouraged to grow in each industry. This provided a level of competition while protecting them from foreign producers. In this way, the lethargy-inducing effect of protection did not sink in. However, the level of competition is monitored to keep investment levels stable and aid investment decisions. This means there are fewer occasions of speculative investment leading to economic downturns caused by over-supply.

The governments also encouraged these industries to export very quickly. Not only did this provide access to greater levels of demand than that provided in the local economy, but it increased the level of competition they faced. In these foreign markets, the Asian firms were faced with competitors who used best-practice production techniques. This forced them to improve their product offering. In this way, these nations have avoided the trap of Latin America and sub-Saharan African countries, where substandard producers were protected and tolerated for very long periods.

These countries were not unaware of the dangers of government intervention and realized that government bureaucrats may not be as familiar with an industry and that this could affect their ability to identify opportunities. They were also aware that the incentives for bureaucrats to find opportunities are nowhere near as strong as those for private entrepreneurs who benefit from their ideas. So policy networks were established with contacts operating in particular industries. This of course opens up the potential for bribes, political capture and pressure from interest groups. However, in these countries, there is a tradition of interaction between business and government where all parties know what is expected of them. They are certainly not immune to corruption, but there is a general tendency for national interests to be placed ahead of those of particular interest groups. Nevertheless, we should not understate these dangers as, in the economic downturn of the 1990s, many Asian nations found their economies riddled with cronyism that had led to substantial inefficiency and corruption.

These governments have also been aware of the rigidity of bureaucracy in implementing policy and have strived to be pragmatic and flexible. If results indicate that decisions and policies have been incorrect or undermined by changing circumstances, they act like private entrepreneurs and quickly discontinue or reverse their decisions. These governments have also concerned themselves with creating a broader environment that is conducive to the viability of new industries. They provide essential items of infrastructure such as highways, telecommunications, transport, dams and colleges with a particular emphasis on vocational and technical education. Most importantly, government agencies and policies place great importance on encouraging entrepreneurs to exploit their talents. So, although the government plays a leading role, entrepreneurs find the environment supportive. The businesses are still privately owned and they still make the vast bulk of the decisions affecting their industry. And, of course, they retain the profit.

Capability Building

We have repeatedly seen how existing companies are a very important source of new business ideas. Many market shifts and new ideas are discovered at work. Established organizations also serve as incubators for entrepreneurs, providing them with the skills, knowledge and contacts they need when they start their own businesses.[15] With this in mind, countries with a strong productive base have an advantage for new venture creation. They have more firms from which entrepreneurs can spin off. On the other hand, a nation with limited productive capabilities is at a serious disadvantage when it comes to producing entrepreneurs.

We in the West have much faith in the market mechanism. We believe if a sunset industry goes into decline, the market will soon create a sunrise industry to take its place. However, this does not always happen. At times, the most flexible business people have had to watch as their domestic economy deteriorates and drags them down with it. Although markets are highly flexible, there are limits. To illustrate this, consider one of the key points in this book: that entrepreneurs succeed when they build on what they know. This implies that the future potential of entrepreneurs is determined by their past investment in knowledge and skills. If their industry goes into decline and they want to enter a new industry, they may have to go through the process of learning to gather the necessary skills and capabilities. This need to acquire capabilities in new industries can also occur at a national level, if the country's industries have limited growth potential.

An example of this can be seen in China in the nineteenth century. At that time, China had one of the most flexible market economies in the world. In 1800, China was still producing 33% of the world's manufactured goods. Its products were among the world's most sophisticated, and its ceramics were exported as far away as Europe. However by 1900, its share of manufacturing output had reduced to only 6.2%,[16] and the resulting political-economic turmoil led to a number of revolutions and the rise of the communists. We in the West frequently see communism as the cause of China's economic woes in the twentieth century, but the communists only came to power after a century of economic decline under a market economy.

Chinese entrepreneurs were extremely capable, and as late as 1850 the richest man in the world lived in Canton Harbor, China. However, traditional Chinese industries were not providing the returns that the new ones in the West were creating, and Chinese entrepreneurs did not invest outside these industries. They realized the folly of investing in industries they knew little about, so very few foreign technologies were acquired. The Chinese economy became entrapped on low-growth trajectories. This stands in contrast to Japan, which in the mid-nineteenth century was in a similar industrial position to China but entered on a government program of capability building that created the second-largest economy in the world.

When a nation's industries have reached their growth limit, the government may need to act as a circuit-breaker and promote the development of new industrial capabilities. Otherwise, the whole nation runs the risk of economic decline. To some extent the U.S. government unintentionally acted as a circuit breaker when it financed research into computers and semiconductors, funded for purposes of defense. The result has been new technological capabilities that have created new pathways for American industry.

Of course, government intervention is not always necessary to broaden a country's productive capabilities. One country to succeed in developing a large number of companies from a small production base was Hong Kong, and it did so with little involvement from the government. In the 1960s and 1970s, Hong Kong had few important producers, and those that existed had to contend with a small domestic market, limited natural resources and low technological skill.[17] These unfavorable conditions affected the options for their entrepreneurs. With a poor environment for pioneering, Hong Kong entrepreneurs engaged in imitation and arbitrage. The arbitrage option was helped by the one resource advantage Hong Kong possessed: location. Hong Kong served as an entrepot with imported goods redistributed throughout East Asia.

The other option followed in Hong Kong was imitation. To be successful at imitating, firms need some competitive advantage, but most countries with limited technology have problems adding value. Their main advantage is cheap labor, which might not be enough to compete with foreign giants who can achieve significant economies of scale. Small Hong Kong firms managed to compete not just on cheap labor but also through a strategy of product differentiation. They did not compete in the mass-market styles where economies of scale favored large firms. Instead, they chose to compete in smaller niche markets where long production lines could not be exploited by the foreign giants. The Hong Kong entrepreneurs varied their output and provided a small number of each product. In these markets, the foreign giants had no cost advantages. In fact, Hong Kong producers with their cheap labor held the advantage.

On occasions where the larger market was targeted, Hong Kong companies competed by accepting lower margins. In large markets, even if margins are thin, the large volumes can contribute to substantial total earnings. Another successful strategy in Hong Kong is subcontracting, where firms produced products for foreign labels and, in the process, gained knowledge of international markets and quality requirements.

The environment advantages in Hong Kong that made imitation possible were location and cheap labor. Another advantage was the inflow of migrants with business skills and capital after 1949, when the communists came to power in China and Hong Kong. Consequently, the government played a small role. The process was driven at all times by private enterprise.

Innovation

For countries at the edge of the technological frontier, it is hard to copy the industries that exist in other nations, unless they have something that makes their industries highly competitive. However due to their higher wages, they are normally at a cost disadvantage, so they must look to innovation as a way of building industrial capabilities. This places the country's education and technological research institutions in the limelight. A country is more likely to produce spin-off companies if it is endowed with quality universities and research laboratories. However, a country's education and technological facilities are normally aligned to meet the needs of its industries. Therefore, these institutions are just as capable of being trapped on a trajectory as the industries they serve. Nevertheless, if a country is going to innovate, these institutions can serve as the bedrock of change.

Many countries are experiencing low-growth despite having very high levels of private R&D, levels of education, university research and public research. For many years, Sweden had the highest ratio of GDP invested in R&D, yet it failed to achieve payoff in terms of employment creation and economic growth.[18] Disappointing results have also been felt in Japan and other parts of Europe. They discovered it is not enough to merely create new knowledge and that knowledge must be commercialized.

A significant government policy in the United States that helped mobilize the nation's research potential was the Bayh-Dole Act of 1980. Until this time, new technologies were being created but not commercialized. The federal government had accumulated 30,000 patents, but only 5% had been licensed and even fewer resulted in commercial products. The Bayh-Dole Act gave academic institutions property rights for the results of federally funded research. With the new law, 200 universities became engaged in technology transfer, creating an additional $21 billion worth of economic activity each year.[19]

With universities now owning and managing the intellectual property they create, they have a tool with which they can increase their own funding and an incentive to commercialize their output. Many research universities established technology transfer offices to manage and protect their intellectual property, including the distribution of licenses to industry wanting to use their intellectual property.[20] Of course, the act by itself is not sufficient and the universities' own organizations must be conducive to the task. Universities must have an organizational culture, incentive structures and staff with the capabilities to produce and mobilize new technologies.

The transfer of new ideas from university research to industry occurs through various channels. First are the research publications and journals in which academics publish their findings. Second is through the employment of graduate students and research staff. A third method is through the selling of licenses and patents to companies, which give them the right to use the new technology. The fourth method is through the creation of spin-off companies that exploit the idea. However, only the last of these ensure that the idea is developed locally. Foreign companies can read the journals, buy the patents and employ the graduates, which means the benefits of the research goes offshore.

One way of ensuring that the technology is exploited in the place it originated is to make structures that help to commercialize the technology. This means that universities and research centers do not just produce technologies. They also give birth to companies that commercialize them. This normally occurs in two ways. First are the planned spin-offs when the university creates a new business and provides it with the technology. The second type is spontaneous spin-offs, when employees of the university take the technology and find a new company with little encouragement from their old employer.

One popular policy of local governments is to create science parks where firms and educational institutions are located in close proximity to each other. This should hopefully lead to increased communication and cross-fertilization of ideas. However, the jury is still out on their effectiveness. Research to date has found little evidence of higher growth or survival rates for businesses that locate in science parks.[21]

A recent survey of firms that had located their businesses in a science park to be close to a higher education institute (HEI) found that commercial links with higher educational institutions were valuable.[22] High-technology businesses with links to a HEI were significantly more likely to survive, a reflection of science-driven product development as described in Chapter 4. Small firms with limited R&D and staff budgets can greatly benefit by tapping into local educational resource networks.

However, an important finding of this research was that linkages with higher education institutions were valuable regardless of whether the firm was in a science park or not. Location was not a factor. In fact, the firms that had shifted to the science park were disappointed with the outcome. Firms in the science park were no more likely to have received a visit from a representative from a higher education institution than off-park firms. A danger in developing science parks is that they become exercises in real estate. Companies are attracted as tenants, but the effect on innovation is not forthcoming.

Spin-offs from universities and research centers have been a major contributor to new business formation. They have led to the creation of technopolises (technology cities), such as Austin, Texas; Boston's Route 128; Silicon Valley; and Cambridge, England. Each of these technopolises is centered around a research university. However, we have to be careful not to think that these regions can easily be copied. Governments have been criticized for producing policies that "resemble recipes or magic potions such as combine liberal amounts of technology, entrepreneurs, capital and sunshine; add one university; stir vigorously."[23]

Often these regions have had something in their environment that has favored growth. Silicon Valley benefited from the proximity of Stanford University, but it also enjoyed significant defense sector investment, which helped create a critical mass of scientific talent. In France, the government believed many high-tech companies would be attracted by the sun and sea of the French Riviera. It invested in significant infrastructure to create the Sophia-Antipolis research center, which attracted firms like IBM and Texas Instruments. In Aberdeen Scotland, many engineers and chemists arrived in the region to work in the oil industry but eventually spun off to form their own companies. A common theme of many of the success stories is the existence of high-quality public and private institutions that attract businesses and skilled workers who eventually form their own companies.[24]

Although we associate university-centered growth with large centers, recent research suggests that even smaller locations can benefit from this type of entrepreneurial activity.[25] Albuquerque is not a booming high-tech area, but here, the University of New Mexico has established organizational mechanisms to encourage spin-offs and other types of technological transfer with some success. An example of a spin-off company from the university is Khoral Research Inc. (KRI), formed in 1992 by the creators of Khoros technology, a software product for computer image processing. The company sells licenses, technical support, and educational services related to the Khoros technology, which has 20,000 users worldwide. By 1997, KRI employed 32 individuals.

The company's origins can be traced to 1987, when the Khoros software program was created by a research group in the university's Department of Electrical Engineering and Computer Engineering (EECE). The success of new start-up companies is partly dependent on the level of support it receives from the parent organization during the start-up process. In the case of Khoros, the university's EECE department served as an incubator organization. In the early 1990s, the company was located in the department, and most employees worked part time for both KRI and the department. It was not until 1994—when KRI received a four-year R&D contract from the U.S. Air Force—that KRI separated from the department and rented its own premises.

Such a relationship leaves open possible areas of conflict, as staff and facilities are devoted to two masters, the university and the new company. Potential problems include the fact that the university was not paid an overhead, conflicts of interest for staff on both payrolls, and questions as to ownership of intellectual property rights. Although such conflicts can occur, the authors of this study found few deep conflicts between the university and the spin-off company. Lengthy negotiations were required for the new company to acquire the intellectual property rights for its core technology. This negotiation process was laborious but constructive, and it resulted in a situation in which both the university and the department of EECE are paid royalties from company sales and both own equity in the company.

To assist the commercialization of technologies stemming from university research, the university founded the Science and Technology Corporation in 1995. The STC oversees all aspects of intellectual property management, promotes UNM research capabilities, develops relationships with private industry, assists research-based innovations, identifies potential licensees of UNM intellectual property, and negotiates technology licenses or other commercialization agreements. It is also responsible for the UNM Science and Technology Park.

Spin-offs have benefits for both the parent organization and the new company. The university gains a share in the ownership of the new company and a source of revenue. It also gains experience as an entrepreneur and developing commercial technologies, and it is no surprise that the number of patent disclosures from the University of New Mexico rose from 200 to 475 between 1986 and 1996. Spin-offs such as these also provide role models for other potential entrepreneurs. They also ensure that technology transfer remains a local process, creating jobs and new wealth. Graduates from the university can gain jobs without having to leave the region.

*   *   *

If a government is going to expand a nation's industrial base, it runs into many of the issues that entrepreneurs face in choosing between an imitative or innovative strategy. Should it promote new industries or those that already exist in other nations? A common strategy for developing an industrial base involves providing incentives to encourage foreign companies to invest locally. The company arrives with all its previously developed expertise and becomes an instant employer. They are a far more reliable source of jobs than entrepreneurial ventures that can take time to grow. They can also serve as an incubator in which local workers gain skills that will later help them launch their own companies.

However, it is important not to overemphasize the benefits of foreign investment. Much foreign investment involves building manufacturing facilities with little R&D capability. This means there is little development of the expertise useful in the creation of spin-offs, and even when R&D facilities are included the results are often not applied locally. The new technologies may be put to work in other nations where the parent company has other subsidiaries. Most importantly, many decisions on the company's activities are made in the country where the HQ is based and reflect concerns that are not necessarily the same as the host country's concerns.

Another problem with foreign investment is the size of the carrot needed to attract the company. If financial incentives are offered, they can mitigate the benefits of the company's arrival. Instead of offering financial incentives, it is far preferable to offer an environment that, in itself, reduces costs for the company. This can include good transportation infrastructure, quality educational institutions that provide suitable skilled staff, and research organizations that can provide assistance evaluating new technologies and in technical standards issues. Stable and open macroeconomic policies are also important. These benefits are not restricted to the multinational company but can be enjoyed by any firm in the area, and they help to contribute to the development of an industry cluster.

A common imitation option is where a local business enters industries that are no longer economically viable in the nations that pioneered them. This is the strategy that saw production of televisions and many forms of apparel shift sites to Asia. It is the process described in Vernon's International Product Life Cycle model.[26] This model said that innovations are most likely to be born in modernized nations, where demand will support the introduction of new products, and high wages will encourage the search for cost-reducing innovations. However, once a product technology has developed to a point of standardization where it can easily be imitated, producers transfer their operations to low-wage nations that become the new centers of production.

There are several advantages in an industrial policy based on imitation, and they are similar to those mentioned for entrepreneurs. Imitators do not have to invent the product nor go through the tiresome process of trial and error that the pioneer had to go through. The imitator can study the past performances of the developed nations along with the most recent projections for the industry's future. With the benefit of hindsight, the newcomer can avoid the mistakes made by pioneers, deciding whether to do things in the same way as the pioneer or develop new, improved ways. Late-comers also have the advantage of not having to create or educate the market for a new product.

However, an imitating nation faces huge catch-up costs. It faces higher investment costs than the first mover who built up its assets gradually. It must acquire experience and the technical knowledge to run the necessary productive equipment while at the same time competing with established producers. It is a big task.

The imitating nation also misses out on a lot of economic activity that occurs when an industry is first created. In Chapter 7, we saw how the founding of a new industry stimulates economic activity in a number of areas, including experimentation with technologies and searching for industrial supplies. This creates opportunities for forward-linking and backward-linking entrepreneurs. The founding of a new industry is full of excitement and brings with it new development opportunities. However, when the same industry is set up 20 years later, there will be fewer satellite industries created, since the technological problems are by then largely solved and the industry is past its phase of fastest progress. Many of the inputs can be acquired, not through new industries but through imports from experienced producers who can create products far superior to anything a local newcomer could produce.

Missing out on those linkages can have major implications, for satellite firms are important for long-term competitiveness. They help to form the "industrial clusters" that help to contribute to a nation's economic success. When firms in related industries are situated close together, the costs of doing business between them are reduced. They can also share collective assets including shared information, specialized institutions and a regional reputation. This regional expertise also helps innovation and speed productivity growth. Firms without a cluster lack these benefits.

A final problem with imitating is that it runs the risk of trapping the nation in mature cost-competitive industries in which low wages are paid to compete. This means the people in these nations will remain low-wage earners. One option to escape this low-income trap is to view imitation not as end in itself but as a step toward greater levels of commercial success. Hong Kong entrepreneurs used the imitation process to develop production skills and experience, and then, once established in the market, they built other sources of competitiveness. Through the introduction of better machinery and managerial techniques, they enhanced productivity and quality. They also moved into markets that were less cost-sensitive, creating niche brands. In some cases, they moved into totally new industries, leaving the labor-intensive ones behind them, moving toward technology-intensive industries. In other words, they began by imitating, and then later they innovated. In this way, a poor country caught up with advanced nations.

Some observers warn against a policy of being imitators.[27] If a nation wants to provide high wages for its people, they suggest entering an industry in the early stages of major transition. When an industry goes through a major transition, everyone is learning, so old and new producers are at the same level. It is a window of opportunity where everyone starts again, so no one has advantages from experience. In fact new producers may be in a better position as they are not restricted by their past investments and old performance requirements. Newcomers can adopt new methods that old firms have trouble switching to.

Windows of opportunity are at their greatest during periods of rapid technological change or paradigm shifts. It is not just established firms that must divest their now-superseded technologies in such periods. Whole economies face an overhaul. All parts of the economy related to the technology must endure the cost of change. This includes regulatory bodies, education institutions and suppliers, which must delete the "old" and acquire the "new." These are the times that a government should be most prepared to help the establishment of a new industry.

Many governments hoping to innovate finance R&D institutions and provide high-level technical education, but, without a strong link to commercial capabilities, these policies may fail. Students leave the education institutions and are unable to find jobs because there are no employers to utilize their skills. This means they do not gain the "incubating" experience that employment gives to entrepreneurs. In such instances, students frequently have to leave the country to get a job in their chosen field. Innovations stemming from the research institutions are picked up not by local entrepreneurs but by foreign firms with expertise in commercializing technologies. In such cases, technologies are learned but not commercialized. With these problems in mind, we can see the wisdom of Japanese policy for its shipping industry. The Japanese government first focused on establishing a shipping organization and then tied its assistance to expanding capabilities.

To be commercially exploited, technological capabilities must be coupled with the right business capabilities. This suggests policies should combine technological and commercial-capability development.[28] To achieve this, Linsu Kim suggests evaluating such policies from a "technological flow perspective." This perspective has three components:

1.   **Transfer of Technology from Abroad**. The first part of the process is when a nation acquires the technologies to produce a good or service. Countries can acquire foreign technologies through a number of mechanisms, including foreign direct investment, the purchase of turnkey plant and machinery, foreign licenses, and technical services. In Japan's early days, a key method of obtaining foreign technologies was through the use of foreign workers who were brought into Japan and required to pass on their skills to the Japanese they worked with. The Japanese also sent a number of missions overseas to study foreign production techniques and a number of students

to study at foreign colleges. Another method used by Japan was reverse engineering combined with the importation of capital equipment from abroad. Reverse engineering involves taking apart a product to see how it was made, while the capital goods provide the machinery and equipment to make those products.

One policy for introducing new industrial technologies is immigration. What better way to place your nation on new economic trajectories than to bring in entrepreneurs with the necessary skills? However, this policy has had mixed outcomes at best. New Zealand and Canada introduced policies to attract business migrants with entrepreneurial experience; however, few new businesses materialized, and those that did often ended in failure. The new migrants had to learn all over again how to do business in the new environment. They had to go through a process of knowledge building, learning how markets and industries work in their new environment. They also learned that some businesses that worked in their home countries, like manufacturing, would not work in a country like Canada, where wages were high and the necessary supporting industries did not exist. It is a clear illustration of how complex the entrepreneurship process is. It is not just a case of finding enterprising people and throwing them into a new environment. There must be a good fit between the capabilities of entrepreneurs and opportunities that appear. These migrants had skills more suited to their home countries and, when they immigrated, they found they were in the wrong place at the wrong time.[29]

A policy much disliked in the West but undeniably helpful in the imitation process is loose enforcement of patents. Patent law is good for encouraging imitation but can be a barrier to imitation. If a country doesn't recognize patent law, there are few legal barriers stopping its entrepreneurs from copying foreign products. This is an issue very central to current trade relations between nations like the United States and China. The irony is that when the international convention on copyrights was drawn up at Berne in the 1880s, the United States refused to join saying that, as a newly industrialized nation, it needed access to foreign works.[30] Now that the United States is the leading supplier of intellectual property, its position has changed. There is some degree of double standard here.

2. Diffusion of Imported Technology. To maximize its benefits, imported technology has to be diffused throughout its economy. If technology is only transferred to one local firm, it may give the firm monopoly power for a period of time, but the broader economic effects may be considerably limited. Other domestic producers must gain access to the technology. The Japanese used a number of methods to do this, including cooperative development and information sharing between producers. For example, when the American Daniel Ludwig transferred his shipbuilding plant to Hiroshima, the contract from the Japanese government specified that the yard would grant access to Japanese shipbuilders and engineers so they could examine all aspects of their building processes. This played an important role in bringing Japanese yards up to the world's best practice in shipbuilding techniques.

In Korea, the most important diffusion agents were government enterprises established in the 1950s and 1960s. The government plants performed a role we normally associate with private enterprise. Engineers who accumulated production experience in state-owned fertilizer and machinery plants later spun off to head engineering and production departments of private enterprises, taking their technological knowledge with them. Another important factor was the Engineering Services Promotion Law of 1973. This stipulated that, if possible, all engineering projects should be given to local firms as major contractors with foreign partners as minor participants. Initially, the law had limited success, but over time it was important in stimulating the growth of local engineering firms and providing those firms with opportunities to learn from experienced foreigners.

3.   **Indigenous R&D**. The final stage in the technological flow is where local firms begin to assimilate and improve imported technologies and develop their own indigenous technologies. In the case of Korea, true development of indigenous technology did not begin until the 1980s, after a period of 20 years of imitating foreign technologies. The earlier period provided business and technical capabilities on which the Koreans built. This situation was aided by policies that promoted R&D at universities, and the establishment of government-funded research centers associated with particular industries. While it is true that research centers had existed since the 1960s, in particular the Korean Institute of Science and Technology, their impact was minimal. It was not until other skills and capabilities had spread throughout the economy that the research centers could truly be exploited.

This technological flow process is one way of viewing the succesful development of countries like Japan and Korea. In their earlier stages of industrialization, these nations had limited ability to innovate. Initial advance was more easily achieved through imitation. But through imitation, diffusion and incremental improvement, these nations acquired the capabilities with which they then became innovators. However, the success of such policies is still open to debate.

Case Study: Industrial Policy in Shannon, Ireland

One region to introduce a sophisticated combination of policies is Shannon in the west of Ireland.[31] Here, a number of foreign multinationals were invited to set up operations, tempted through financial grants and low tax rates. It was hoped the foreign companies would serve as a "growth pole" from which spin-off companies would be formed. Other policies included the establishment of a free-trade zone in the region and the development of the University of Limerick as a technology-driven university with strong links to the business community. A number of technical colleges were also created with a similarly applied bent. The university became the core component of a science technology park designed to meet the needs of technology- and knowledge-based companies. It incorporated an Innovation Center, which provides incubation facilities and support services for start-up firms.

This is a capability-building process that gave the Irish experience and skills in manufacturing and managing in high-tech companies, and some indigenous electronics and mechanical research-driven firms have appeared. But by 2000, the feeling was that the policies had not succeeded in closing the technological gap with other European nations. The skill levels in the companies were still low, a common criticism of foreign direct investment. The jobs that multinationals relocate are often at the lowest level of the skill range. Second, the Irish discovered that the multinational companies have a low propensity to build up ties with local firms. In many ways, this should not be surprising. Multinationals are, by definition, global companies, sourcing their inputs from all parts of the world. The situation also reminds us that latecomers to an industry often miss out on forward and backward linkages that occur when new industries are created for the first time. By the time a latecomer arrives, many of these suppliers and other satellites are already in existence elsewhere in the world.

The third concern is associated with feeble absorptive capacity and weak indigenous technological capabilities. Absorptive capacity refers to the ability of domestic firms to understand, apply and upgrade technology introduced from abroad. Ninety-five percent of R&D is performed within formal R&D departments, with few external links. Some blame for the low absorptive capacity has been placed at the feet of the government. There has never been an active science and technology policy in Ireland. Another barrier to innovation in Ireland is the financial sector. The Irish banking system has been criticized for not being adequately involved in financing technological upgrades and innovation in small- and medium-sized enterprises.

In terms of entrepreneurship policy, the results may be disappointing; however, in terms of economic growth and job creation, the policies have been very successful. By 2007, the Shannon Free Zone employed 7,200 people in 110 companies with annual sales of 3.3 billion euros.[32] Some indigenous companies have been created as well, but the majority are subsidiaries of multinationals. As this book goes to press, one final concern with relying on multinationals has come to the fore: multinational corporation Dell computers is axing 1,900 jobs in Limerick and relocating them to Poland.

* * *

This chapter began with an extreme example where governments have little impact in creating a positive environment for entrepreneurs, and then it moved on to the situation in the West. A number of policy options were considered but were tempered by the fact that governments have a poor record when assisting entrepreneurs. The times when government action is most justified are those periods in which the country's industries do not appear to have the potential for further growth, and new industries must be acquired. In such instances, the country needs to acquire new capabilities, either through innovation or imitation of industries already in existence.

In many Western nations, the opportunity for imitation is limited by their high wages, and, even if they do commence this option, they often miss many of the entrepreneurial opportunities that normally occur when a new industry is started. That is because suppliers, forward linkages and backward linkages already exist.

However, a foreign-owned company can act as an incubator, providing the skills for future entrepreneurial activities. This is most likely to happen if the company invests in R&D facilities, not just production. Governments can increase the likelihood of this happening by the province of quality research institutions in the vicinity. When R&D facilities are based around a quality research institution or industry, it increases the chance that technological advance will give birth to new firms. On the other hand, when investment is based solely around production, the nation is in danger of becoming a low-wage competitor.

The potential exists for governments to create a positive environment for growth. The key, in all cases, is to adequately define the problem and tie the solution to that problem with minimal political interference.

Chapter 12

What Type of Entrepreneur Should I Be?

Never hesitate to steal a good idea.

(Al Neuharth, founder of *USA Today*)

Many people want to start their own business but have trouble working out where they fit in. They ask themselves, "What type of entrepreneur should I be?" Their answer should be a combination of their own personal characteristics and the opportunities available. This chapter draws on previous chapters to create a framework whereby you can think about how you can enter a market and become self-employed.

Up until the 1930s, economists showed little interest in entrepreneurs. Economists focused on how markets operated in response to the forces of supply and demand, and, in their eyes, entrepreneurs were people who responded to those forces. If the market experienced an increase in demand, this would create an opportunity for someone to mobilize resources, set up a business and enter the market. Entrepreneurs examined the price of inputs needed to set up business, compared it with the price at which they could sell their goods, and, if a profit could be made, they would enter the market.

No one would deny that entrepreneurs do these things, but this early view had some major limitations. In particular, entrepreneurs don't just *react* to market forces. They are often proactive and creative. It was Joseph Schumpeter who first identified this in his book *The Theory of Economic Development*.[1] Schumpeter pointed out that entrepreneurs are prime movers of economic change. They are innovators, introducing new goods and new production methods. They open new markets and new sources of materials, and create new types of industrial organization. The sort of entrepreneur that Schumpeter speaks of is an innovator, a pioneer who introduces new goods and new ways of doing things.

This innovative entrepreneur is an economic hero whose creativity invigorates the economy with new ideas that lead to economic growth. But less imaginative people can also play an important role. They can copy the business ideas of pioneers. In so doing, they spread new business techniques and raise productivity throughout an economy.[2] In fact, it has been suggested that, on average, some 5% of the technical progress can be linked to the work of innovative entrepreneurs, while the remaining 95% involved the entrepreneurial imitators. This suggests that the vast majority of entrepreneurs are not creative geniuses but copycats. To put it another way, entrepreneurship is not brain surgery.

Of course imitators need not restrict themselves to copying. Even copycats have potential for creativity. They can improve on what is being done by those they are copying and in so doing improve the efficiency of economies. Such opportunities exist because existing companies operate within their potential.[3] We have already discussed some of the reasons for this.

On the surface, there appears to be a contradiction in this book. On the one hand, it says you don't have to be a genius, but on the other it says you have to be an expert. Isn't this a contradiction? The answer is no. You don't have to be a genius, but you do need expertise in the industry you want to enter. That means understanding the market and production technologies. Work hard and keep your eyes open.

While this book downplays the intellectual requirements needed to succeed, some level of alertness is needed. In fact, according to Israel Kirzner, alertness to opportunities is the distinguishing characteristic of the entrepreneur.[4] Entrepreneurs recognize things in the market that others do not, and this provides them the opportunity to exploit. This alertness is enhanced in those who have expertise in the relevant area[5] and in those who are actively searching for opportunities.[6]

The market is a world of continuous change and with each change comes an opportunity to discover new opportunities.[7] These include new technologies and new knowledge of people's consumption patterns. Mostly, it involves increased awareness of what people want at different times and different places. However, not everyone is aware of these discoveries, because they are localized. People living in different places at different times have access to different information. People with this information can act on their discoveries in the market.

The importance of information advantages can be seen in the career of Aristotle Onassis, who at one time wore the mantle of the world's richest man. In his early years, Onassis worked as a telephone operator in Argentina, where he listened to other people's telephone conversations. On one occasion, he overheard that the Argentine military was about to order a substantial amount of leather. With this privileged information in hand, he bought a large amount of leather, which he later sold at a much higher price when the military entered the market. Onassis advised, "The secret of business is to know something that nobody else knows."[8]

Opportunities for entrepreneurship are provided by the availability of new information, through discoveries and updates. Consequently, greater opportunities exist in times of change. However, when change occurs, there is a level of uncertainty as to what the final outcome will be. This uncertainty stops some people from seizing the opportunity. The successful entrepreneur is someone who has better or more relevant information than others and is therefore in a better position to act. They are in the right place at the right time.

*   *   *

When economists now talk of entrepreneurs, they normally divide them into the creative type identified by Schumpeter or those who are alert and react to market forces, as identified by Kirzner.[9] The Kirzner-type entrepreneur can be involved in arbitrage, speculation, imitation, or adaptive imitation. They are *alert* while Schumpeter's entrepreneurs *create*. But these divisions are too broad to be of practical use. Another typology divides entrepreneurs into Craftsmen and Opportunists.[10] Craftsmen usually come from blue-collar backgrounds and have narrow educational and managerial experience. They prefer technical work and are generally motivated by a desire to earn a comfortable living. By contrast, opportunists have a higher education and welcome managerial challenges.

These typologies are of little use to someone thinking about starting a business. Consequently, a typology is presented below to provide a framework for those thinking about how to enter the market based on the opportunities discussed in this book.

The Pioneer

Pioneers are entrepreneurs who release new products and services into the economy. As a pioneer, your job requires a number of skills, including the creation of the new product and making a market where none existed before. This may involve overcoming barriers to trade. You may have to make contact with potential customers and discover the specifications required for the new product or service to succeed. There will be negotiations with customers and distributors, and, through this process, you will gain information with which you can make intelligent pricing and quality decisions. In effect, you are learning to balance supply with demand. You will also need to organize transport, insurance and administration. As a pioneer, you will have to overcome the lack of an established reputation in order to give the customer confidence that the product and doing business with this new company is safe. This will require quality controls and standards and some method of ensuring that contracts will be met and enforced.[11]

When pioneering, a new business model is created, often through experiment and trial and error. The pioneer is often multi-skilled in order to handle the diversity of technical and commercial requirements. However, a pioneer who is not mutli-skilled can open up opportunities for people to come in as partners. For example, a technical innovator can pair up with someone who has commercial skills. In this case we are dealing not with an entrepreneur but with an entrepreneurial team.

The Imitator

This form of entrepreneur starts a business that has nothing new about it. You copy a pre-existing business model, perhaps directly from a pioneer. Many imitators are ex-employees who use their knowledge learned in their previous job to spin off and create their own company. There are many advantages to being an imitator. Most of all, you are saved the cost, time and uncertainty involved in developing the business idea. It has all been done for you. You merely imitate what has been done before. If the pioneer has educated the market to accept the product or service, an imitator can also benefit from the growing wave of demand as more consumers start buying the product. They have effectively created a wave for you to ride.

The major problem with imitation is recognizing the carrying capacity of the market. Too many imitators jumping on the bandwagon can overcrowd the market. You are struggling for a piece of the action against other businesses that are doing exactly the same as you. Whether you are thinking of setting yourself up as a painter, a restaurateur or a computer-repair service, all these industries already have established providers with whom you must compete. Studies show that entrepreneurs who enter traditional industries have the highest failure rate.[12] To avoid this situation, you need to assess the growth rate of the demand versus the growth of supply. If you are thinking of entering a market with an established product or service, you should consider its future growth and the ease with which others can enter the market in the future.

The imitator who spots a market shift, caused perhaps by an increase in demand, can do quite well. This imitator becomes a wave rider. Although it is the least innovative strategy, it can be highly successful if you time your entry with periods of growth. If there is no growth, you may struggle against existing competition.

Imitation works well for products and industries that are in the early growth stages of their life cycle. During these periods, demand is growing rapidly, and there is room for new suppliers to enter the market and capture that demand. Of course, the earlier the entry, the less information there is available, so there may be some areas of uncertainty that make financial and market planning difficult.

There are some advantages in entering a market when it is mature. One of the biggest advantages is that information is now easy to obtain. This makes planning much easier. Entrepreneurs are less likely to have unexpected costs pop up, especially if they have done their research or are experienced in the industry and its cost structure. During the maturity stage, production techniques are well known. It is relatively easy to find out what machines are needed, how much they cost to buy and operate, and how many staff are needed and their associated costs. Such certainty makes forecasting easier and reduces the chance of failure. However, these advantages are more than offset by the disadvantages of a mature market; in particular, competitors that are firmly established and experienced. A mature market is stable, and, with no market growth, entrepreneurs find they are competing for market share with very competent rivals. Unsurprisingly, failure rates at the mature stage of the life cycle are very high.

Imitating a mature product can work if the market is going through a period of growth. This increases the carrying capacity of the market, thereby reducing the intensity of competition. More customers are available to capture. The question is how to identify this increase in demand. It requires knowledge of the market. Sometimes, salespeople are well placed to pick up on these trends. One budding entrepreneur got his idea to open a restaurant in an established area for restaurants when he could not get a seat on peak nights. After this happened a number of times, he realized he was obviously not the only one being rejected and that current supply was not sufficient for demand. So he opened up a new restaurant in the area.

A common successful imitating strategy involves taking an established idea into a new market or region that has no established provider. This is what happened with the spread of movie theaters. Once the first pioneers created theaters, imitators built theaters in different cities and countries that the pioneer hadn't touched. More recently, the same thing occurred in video and DVD rental stores.

Franchising is a common form of imitation. If a franchisee is given a particular region, the crowing-out effect can be avoided, but the problem with this is your future growth is limited to the size of the territory that you have been given. However, without that territorial protection, you may find yourself struggling with other franchisees. A territory is a geographically defined niche, and, as with other niches, you have to ensure the niche you have been given has sufficient carrying capacity for your business to prosper.

The Adaptive Imitator

Imitation of other people's business activities can be effective if you have some source of competitive advantage, for example, if you have distribution or competitive strengths that the pioneer lacks. This is particularly important if the market is not growing, as you will need a competitive edge to survive. In this case, you will need to change the business model, introducing a strategy that either helps develop new markets, reduces costs, or adds value through additional product attributes or raising quality.

Richard Branson's entrepreneurial approach has been one of adaptive imitator. The airline industry was well established when he created Virgin Airlines, but he strove to provide better service. Similarly, when he entered the recording industry, the industry was well established, but he competed on a cost-reduction strategy. Similarly, the ongoing business success of the Japanese company Matsushita is based upon this strategy. It lets its competitors launch new products, and, when consumers' acceptance is proven, it begins producing large volumes of an improved product at lower prices.

An adaptive imitator takes an existing business model and changes it slightly, perhaps adding new technologies, modified production processes or modified products. In the case of the disgruntled ex-worker, the modification may be something their old boss didn't want to introduce, thereby providing an opportunity to spin off and start a new business.

The Niche Developer

One common strategy for the adaptive entrepreneur is developing niches, whereby you discover a proportion of the population that demands product specifications that others in the market don't want. So the original idea is combined with some product adaptations to cater for the new niche. In this way, a new niche can be created for an established product or service. This can be a lucrative strategy if the niche is big enough to support the business (i.e., there are enough potential customers who will want this type of product).

The opportunity to pursue this strategy occurs more often as the market grows and new niches open up. But they can also occur when the market is mature but is undergoing internal change, driven perhaps by changes in tastes and new knowledge on what customers want from their products. Changes in technology can also affect the internal evolution of niches.

You can wait until a niche appears, as in the hotel example in Chapter 5. Alternatively, you can act to create a niche. This may involve looking for a gap in the market where existing customer values are not being met or alternatively creating a new combination of product values and an entirely new market combination.

The Follower or Purchaser

There is a common adage in golf development that 'new courses are developed by individuals with a passion who end up bankrupt before completion.' The project is then bought by an enthusiast who finishes it but cannot get a return on the investment and subsequently sells out to mainstream operators at a realistic price who can then make a handsome profit.[13]

A follower is like an imitator in that he or she enters an industry that has already been developed. However, while an imitator sets up a business in imitation of the pioneer, the follower buys an existing company. In buying an existing company, a follower avoids all the hassles of setting up a business. Much of the machinery, equipment, procedures and contacts will all be in place.

Many successful businesses are established by followers. But this requires a solid assessment of why the business is being sold. Sometimes a pioneer does a good job of establishing a product but suffers from burnout due to the sheer weight of the task. So the business is sold. Alternatively, pioneers might have exhausted their funds during the customer-education process. In these instances, a follower can benefit from all the work done by the previous owner but without the hassles. On the other hand, these advantages might be reflected in the cost of the business, and it may require more money to purchase a going concern rather than build up your own business over time.

A study of entrepreneurs in Germany revealed that those who buy an existing business have a much lower failure rate than businesses started from scratch. After five years, 41.7% of the new businesses had fallen over compared with only 23.3% of the followers. Nevertheless, there are many dangers with buying a business. It may be that the owner is selling because he has gained gloomy knowledge on the market and wants out. In which case, you are buying a lemon. Alternatively, there may be flaws in the business setup. Once again, you could end up buying someone else's mess. You need to conduct substantial research before buying a business.

Adaptive Follower

Often, a new owner can be successful simply because he or she invigorates the business with new blood, is less stressed out or catches a wave of rising demand. But sometimes this is not enough. An adaptive follower will adapt the existing business by introducing new strategies.

One of the most simple but common advantages that some owners bring is less debt. Often the original owner, in dealing with the complexities of launching a new product, has to continually increase his or her debt. If you can buy the business with a smaller debt load, your costs will instantly be lower because you will have to spend less on interest and debt repayment. Other adaptive strategies include developing markets, adding value and other forms of cost reduction.

As with the adaptive imitator, people taking this route need to ask themselves what tangible difference they can make to this business. Many entrepreneurs with high levels of self-confidence feel that their energy and intelligence will get them through. But this is insufficient. You need a tangible new approach that adds value, reduces costs or develops markets. Optimism is not enough.

* * *

Earlier in this chapter, we described how entrepreneurs can operate as speculators, producers or traders (arbitrage). For each of these entrepreneurial types, it is possible to innovate or be a copycat. It is possible to create niches or buy out someone else's business. In Table 12.1, we have listed the entrepreneurial types, the methods of entering the market and the growth strategies. Your new venture will be a combination of things from these lists.

We could also identify other categories of entrepreneurs by the environmental opportunity they seized. These categories include the entrepreneur who rode the wave of changing demand and supply; the forward linker, who adds value, develops markets and in some cases makes new markets; and the backward linker, who creates products for the new industry. There are also opportunities for ancillary linkers, who provide products and services that complement the new industry, for example, a magazine to cater to people in the new industry.

This book has shown that markets are awash with opportunities for you to seize. It is one of the things that makes the market economy so exciting. Frequently, entrepreneurial success is a case of being in the right place at the right time and linking your skills and abilities with changes in the market. With greater knowledge and sensitivity, you may be able to place yourself, so that the opportunity opens for you. There are consistent patterns to new business creation. Understanding these patterns will make it easier for you to embark on your road to wealth.

Table 12.1 Entrepreneurial Opportunity Throughout Product Life Cycle

Entrepreneurial Type	Strategy	Stage of Cycle
Pioneer	New value creation	Opens market (a pioneer can open another market at any stage of the cycle)
Imitator	Pure imitation	Best in growth phase as growing demand accommodates new suppliers. Has danger of over-supplying the market if crowded, especially in mature stage.
Niche developer	Focus	Best in growth phase as niches reach sufficient size and information on consumers is revealed. Also possible in mature markets with shifting tastes and technologies.
Follower	Imitation	Suitable for all stages if market has sufficient carrying capacity and acquired company has healthy potential.
Adaptive follower and adaptive imitator	Cost reduction, adding value, or reducing costs	Suitable for all stages.

The Right Place at the Right Time

Being quite good academically, I was encouraged to stay in school and then go on to college. My friend Stephen was not an academic achiever, so he left school early to learn a trade as a carpet layer. While I received a theoretical education on such issues as organizational structure and commercial law, Stephen spent his days learning about his industry and how to work in it. He learned how to lay carpet and what different customers expected from their flooring. He also learned how to buy carpet, the distribution network, and complexities of delivering, storing and ordering.

After a number of years in the industry, Stephen decided to set up his own shop selling carpet with a partner whose skills complemented his. This was a small step for Stephen who, by now, knew the industry well. This company was an imitator in a mature industry, so they did not become rich. The company grew slowly but not spectacularly. In his first 10 years, he went through periods where he struggled to survive while at other times he did quite well. His fortunes would fluctuate, driven in a large extent by the state of the construction market, which drove demand for products like carpet.

Things changed for the company in its second decade, at which time the government changed its policy on immigration. More people were allowed to enter the country, especially those with a lot of money. Wealthy immigrants arrived, buying land and building new houses. This lead to a building boom, and Stephen rode the wave. His business expanded, and the boom lasted so long he was able to reduce his debt. He is now asset rich, and his life is very comfortable. With his debt reduced, so too have his loan repayments been reduced. He now keeps the income that previously went to the bank. Stephen's story is a common one. He took small steps, stuck to what he knew and caught a wave.

Chris was another entrepreneur who left school early. At the age of 16, he left to work for an airline. Working in the travel industry in the early 1970s gave Chris knowledge of his industry in much the same way as Stephen gained knowledge in his. After nine years in the industry, Chris started his own travel warehouse in partnership with a friend. Their entry strategy was as a follower; they bought another travel warehouse. Their business involved negotiating with hotels, airlines, rental car companies and other suppliers for favored rates on their products and services, which they would combine as travel packages. They would then sell these packages to retailers who would sell them to customers.

In 1986, Chris launched his own travel warehouse. This time Chris didn't just follow; he was an adaptive imitator. At the time, two organizational forms characterized the market. On one hand, there were small local travel agents who had little input into the products available and, on the other, were large companies driven by head office–type people who had little incentive or investment in the retail side. Chris believed a closer association between the two was needed. He set up a new travel brand for retailers to operate under. New retail travel shops were opened with funding from both his warehouse and the local owner and operator. Joint funding meant that both had a strong incentive to succeed. They operated as business partners with a joint interest in making sure they had the right products at the right price and everything else they need to drive their business.

Like Stephen, Chris took small steps and stuck to what he knew. He also rode a wave as declining airfares meant air travel became in reach of people who could previously only dream of it. The market for air travel and international holidays soared. The company expanded dramatically, opening a new outlet on average every nine and a half weeks. The business is now hugely successful, and Chris is doing very nicely.

* * *

Luck is what happens when preparation meets opportunity.
—Seneca, Roman philosopher

Psychologists often talk about self-serving bias. That is, we have a tendency to interpret things in a way that makes us look good in comparison to those around us. For example, when things go badly, we say we have been unlucky and blame the environment, the market or the weather. But when things go wrong for someone else, it seems to "serve them right" for being so greedy, stupid or ambitious. Conversely, if things go right for other people, we say they were lucky (or were in the right place at the right time).

Successful people are often lucky. They are often in the right place at the right time, and it is easy to get jealous watching from the sidelines. But what is luck? A common saying is "luck is where opportunity and preparation coincide." There are two features of that description. "Opportunity" is driven by forces in the environment, the sort of forces talked about in this book—forces that we cannot always control. The other part of the description, "preparation," comes down to you. In the examples above, both Chris and Stephen rode waves, but they were prepared for that wave. They had spent many years in their industries building up the expertise needed to succeed, so when the opportunity came, they caught the wave and rode it to prosperity. They were in the right place at the right time, but if they were not prepared, that opportunity would have passed them by.

This brings us back to another common saying: "The harder I work, the luckier I become." Generally speaking, the harder you work, the better prepared you will be. You will be in a better position to spot an opportunity, and you will be in a better position to exploit it. But some people who work hard fail or achieve little. They are trapped in industries with low growth and little dynamics. Life can be frustrating for these people who work hard for little reward while others, who are no more deserving than them, enjoy the benefits of a growing market.

We are very selective when we attribute success, but our biases can lead us into a huge trap. First, it may blind us to opportunities to be an imitator or follower. But more important is the way we respond to our own success. When things go right, our success serves as evidence of our hard work and talent. And while this might be true, it would be foolish to deny the market shifts that helped to shape your prosperity.

It is sad to see a once-successful entrepreneur fail in a second venture because he or she failed to acknowledge the importance of the environment. The person who was at the forefront of infomercials can fail when she dives into tourism. The person who masters radio can bomb when he enters construction. They weren't prepared for those industries. They may have been in the right place at the right time, but they were the wrong person. However, some people who have built enough wealth can straddle a number of industries by employing industry experts to help them in their later ventures. This helps overcome their own deficiencies.

So what if you are in a stagnant industry? There is a danger that if you move into a new industry, you have to start learning all over again, so it is best to move into one that has some compatibility with your own. Many of the skills you have learned in one industry can be applied to others, particularly supervision and small business management. But it is wise to take small steps. Business people who leap into something totally new may find themselves out of their depths.

Another possibility for someone in a stagnant industry is to become a searcher. Spend time investigating and examining industries. Develop hobby industries that you study in your spare time and slowly gain expertise in. Learn how they produce and market their products. Study what drives demand and the cost structure of the industry. In other words, prepare yourself for that wave. At the same time, read as much as you can on the changing business environment, so you can see the wave coming.

Finally, if your industry is stagnant, there may a reason. Question the assumptions behind the industry's products and processes. Discover ways of doing things better, and become an adaptive entrepreneur. If you discover totally new ways of doing things, you may give your industry the boost it needs.

Many books stress the importance of overcoming your internal barriers to success, but motivational books often understate the importance of the environment. These books run the risk of setting people up to fail. Your hard work does not occur in a vacuum. You operate in a market of numerous forces whose fluctuations can lift you up or drive you under. It requires the ability to read markets, industries, technology and consumers; for it is in these environmental factors that opportunities lie. It is up to you to understand those forces for your particular industry, for success will favor the person who catches the wave.

Those who mistake their good luck for merit are inevitably bound for disaster.
J. Christopher Herold

References

1 If You're Such a Genius, Why Aren't You Rich?

1. Sandberg, L. G. 1981. The Entrepreneur and technological change. In *The economic history of Britain since 1770* Vol. 2, eds. R. Floud and D. McClosky. Cambridge: Cambridge University Press, 99–120.
2. Chiasson, M., and C. Saunders. 2005. Reconciling diverse approaches to opportunity research using the structuration theory. *Journal of Business Venturing* 20: 747–767.
3. Chiles, T., A. Bluedorn, and V. Gupta. 2007. Beyond creative destruction and entrepreneurial discovery: A radical Austrian approach to entrepreneurship. *Organization Studies* 28(4): 467–493.
4. Sarason, Y., T. Dean and J. F. Dillard. 2006. Entrepreneurship as the nexus of individual and opportunity: A structuration view. *Journal of Business Venturing* 21(3): 286–305.
5. Timmons, J. 1999. *New venture creation: Entrepreneurship for the 21st Century*. New York: Irwin McGraw Hill.
6. Schumpeter, J. 1934. *The theory of economic development*. Cambridge, MA: Harvard University Press.
7. Hooton, A. 2003. Why didn't I think of that? *Good Weekend: The Age Magazine*, April 26: 30–32.
8. Galbraith, J. K. 1967. *The new industrial state*. London: Andre Deutsch, 58.
9. Chiles, T. H., A. D. Meyer and T. J. Hench. 2004. Organizational emergence: The origin and transformation of Branson, Missouri's musical theatres. *Organization Science* 15(5): 499–519.

2 Creativity and Opportunity Recognition

1. Hooton, 2003, 32.
2. Kirzner, I. M. 1973. *Competition and entrepreneurship*. Chicago: University of Chicago Press.
3. Simon, H. A. 1988. Understanding creativity and creative management. In *Handbook for creative and innovative managers*, ed. R. L. Kuhn. New York: McGraw Hill, 11–24.
4. Woods, C. R. 2002. *Entrepreneurial action: Casting the entrepreneur in a market process*, unpublished PhD thesis, Auckland University.

5. Earl, P. 2003. The entrepreneur as a constructor of connections. *Advances in Austrian Economics* 6: 117–134.

6. Koestler, A. 1975. *The act of creation*. London: Picador. See also Shackle, G. L. S. 1979. *Imagination and the nature of choice*. Edinburgh: Edinburgh University Press.

7. Casson, M. 1982. *The entrepreneur: An economic theory*. Oxford: Martin Robertson & Co, 51.

8. Earl, 2003.

9. Lamont, L. M. 1972. The role of marketing in technical entrepreneurship. In *Technical entrepreneurship: A symposium,* eds. A. C. Cooper and J. L. Komines, Milwaukee Center for Venture Management.

10. Susbauer, J. C. 1972. The technical entrepreneurship process in Austin, Texas. In *Technical entrepreneurship: A symposium,* eds. A. C. Cooper and J. L. Komines, Milwaukee Center for Venture Management.

11. Kuhn, T. 1963. The function of dogma in scientific research. In *Scientific change: Historical studies in the intellectual, social and technical conditions for scientific discovery and technical invention from antiquity to the present,* ed. A. C. Crombie. London: Heinemann, 347–369.

12. Earl, P. 1984. *The corporate imagination: How big companies make mistakes*. Brighton: Wheatsheaf, 102–103.

13. Simon, 1988.

14. Kaish, S., and B. Gilad. 1991. Characteristics of opportunity search of entrepreneurs v executives: Sources, interest and general alertness. *Journal of Business Venturing* 6: 45–61. See also Bailey, J. 1986. Learning styles of successful entrepreneurs. In *Frontiers of entrepreneurship research,* ed. R. Ronstadt, J. Hornaday, J. R. Peterson and K. Vesper. Wellesley, MA: Babson College, 199–210.

15. Craig, J., and N. Lindsay. 2001. Quantifying "gut feeling" in the opportunity recognition process. In *Frontiers of entrepreneurship research,* eds. W. D. Bygrave, E. Autio, C. G. Brush, P. Davidsson, P. G. Greene, P. D. Reynolds and H. J. Sapienza. Wellesley, MA: Babson College, 124–137.

16. Hills, G. E., and R. C. Shrader. 1998. Successful entrepreneurs' insights into opportunity recognition. *Frontiers of entrepreneurship research,* 30–41.

17. Hashemi, S., and B. Hashemi. 2002. *Anyone can do it: Building Coffee Republic from our kitchen table,* Chichester: Capstone Publishing, 15–16.

18. Hashami et al., 2002, 1.

19. Buffett, W. 2007. MBA talk, part 5. http://www.youtube.com/watch?v=sYx-Cr_RVzE& feature=related (accessed June 30, 2008).

20. Shane, S., 2000. Prior knowledge and the discovery of entrepreneurial opportunities. *Organizational Science* 11(4): 448–469.

21. Hsieh, C., J. Nickerson, and T. R. Zenger. 2007. Opportunity discovery, problem solving and a theory of the entrepreneurial firm. *Journal of Management Studies* 44(7): 1255–1277.

22. Schumpeter, J. A. 1934. *The theory of economic development,* Cambridge, MA: Harvard University Press, 214.

23. Stinchcombe, A. L. 1965. Social Structure and Organizations. In *Handbook of organizations,* ed. J. G. March, 142–193. Chicago: Rand McNally, 154.

24. Feinstein, J. S. 2006. *The nature of creative development*. Stanford, CA: Stanford University Press.

25. Porter, M. E. 1990. *The competitive advantage of nations*. London and Basingstoke: MacMillan.
26. Gnyawali, D. R., and D. S. Fogel. 1994. Environments for entrepreneurship development: Key dimensions and research implications. *Entrepreneurship Theory and Practice* 18: 43–62.
27. Ibid.
28. Ibid.
29. Bruderl, J., P. Preisendorfer, and R. Ziegler. 1992. Survival chances of newly founded business organizations. *American Sociological Review* 57(2): 227–242.
30. Case, J. 1989. The origins of entrepreneurship. *Inc,* June: 54. See also Hills and Shrader, 1998; and Cooper, A. C., W. C. Dunkelberg, C. Y. Woo, and W. J. Dennis. 1990. *New business in America*. Washington, DC: NFIB Foundation.
31. Timmons, 1999, 226.
32. Bhave, M. P. 1994. A process model of entrepreneurial venture creation. *Journal of Business Venturing* 9: 223–242.
33. Ibid.
34. Case, 1989, 54.
35. Hills and Shrader, 1998.
36. Ibid.
37. Ibid.
38. Earl, P., and T. Wakeley. 2005. *Business economics: A contemporary approach*. Maidenhead: McGraw-Hill.
39. Hargadon, A. B., and D. Yellowlees. 2001. When innovations meet institutions: Edison and the decision of the electric light. *Administrative Science Quarterly* 46(3): 476–501.
40. Timmons, 1999, 76.

3 Environmental Change and Windows of Opportunity

1. Jackson, T. 1994. *Virgin king: Inside Richard Branson's business empire*. London: Harper Collins.
2. Dean, T. J., and D. G. Meyer. 1996. Industry environments and new venture formations in U.S manufacturing: A conceptual and empirical analysis of demand determinants. *Journal of Business Venturing* 11(2): 107–132.
3. Hayek, F. 1949. *Individualism and economic order*. London: Routledge. See also Kirzner, I. M. 1973. *Competition and entrepreneurship*. Chicago: University of Chicago Press. See also Knight, F. H. 1921. *Risk, uncertainty and profit*. Boston: Houghton Mifflin.
4. Bolton, B., and J. Thompson. 2000. *Entrepreneurs: Talent, temperament, technique*. Oxford: Reed Educational and Professional Publishing Ltd.
5. Dean and Meyer, 1996.
6. Bolton and Thompson, 2000.
7. Dean and Meyer, 1996.
8. Freeman, C., and C. Perez. 1988. Structural crises of adjustment: Business cycles and investment behavior. In *Technical change and economic theory*, ed. G. Dosi, C. Freeman, R. Nelson, G. Silverberg and L. Soete. London: Pinter Publishers, 38–66.
9. Richardson, I. 1960. *Information and investment*. Oxford: Oxford University Press.
10. Bolton and Thompson, 2000, 109.

11. Bruderl, Preisendorfer and Ziegler, 1992.
12. Jackson, 1994, 154–159.
13. Johnson, C. 1982. *MITI and the Japanese miracle*. Stanford, CA: Stanford University Press, 218.
14. Misa, T. J. 1995. *A nation of steel: The making of modern America 1865–1925*. Baltimore: John Hopkins University Press, 279.
15. Misa, 1995, 170.
16. Kawahito, K. 1981. Japanese steel in the American market: Conflict and causes. *The World Economy* 4(3): 229–250.
17. Department of Foreign Affairs and Trade. 1995. *Overseas Chinese business networks in Asia*. Canberra: Commonwealth of Australia, 314–315.
18. Weidenbaum, M. 1980. Public policy: No longer a spectator sport for business. *Journal of Business Strategy* 3(4): 46–53.
19. Yoffie, D. B., and Sigrid Bergenstein. 1985. Creating political advantage: The rise of the corporate political entrepreneur. *California Management Review, 28*(1): 124–139.
20. Hillman, A. J., and M. A. Hitt. 1999. Corporate political strategy formulation: A model of approach, participation and strategy decision. *Academy Of Management Review 24*(4): 825–842.
21. Fleisher, C. S. 2002. Managing business political activities in the USA: Bridging between theory and practice—another look. *Journal of Public Affairs 2*(1): 376–381.
22. Vining, A. R., D. M. Shapiro, and B. Borges. 2005. Building the firm's political (lobbying) strategy. *Journal of Public Affairs 5*(2): 150–175.
23. Bouwen, P. and M. McCown. 2007. Lobbying versus litigation: political and legal strategies of interest representation in the European Union. *Journal Of European Public Policy, 14*(3): 422–443.
24. Vining, Shapiro and Borges, 2005.
25. Yoffie and Bergenstein, 1985.
26. Ibid.
27. Fu-Lai Yu, T. 1997. *Entrepreneurship and economic development in Hong Kong,* London: Routledge, 105.
28. Ibid.

4 Technology, New Products and Pioneers

1. Utterback, J. M. 1994. *Mastering the dynamics of innovation: How companies can seize opportunities in the face of technological change*. Boston: Harvard Business School Press, 58.
2. Tushman, M. L., and P. Anderson. 1986. Technological discontinuities and organizational environments. *Administrative Science Quarterly* 31(3): 439–465, 460.
3. Gibbons, M., and R. Johnston. 1974. The roles of science in technological innovation. *Research Policy* 3: 220–242.
4. Klevorick, A. K., R. C. Levin, R. R. Nelson, and S. G. Winter. 1995. On the sources and significance of inter-industry differences in technological opportunities. *Research Policy* 24(2): 185–205.
5. Shane, S. 2000. Prior knowledge and the discovery of entrepreneurial opportunities. *Organizational Science* 11(4): 448–469.

6. Ibid.
7. Hills, G. E., and R. C. Shrader. 1998. Successful entrepreneurs' insights into opportunity recognition. *Frontiers of Entrepreneurship Research,* Wellesley, MA: Babson College.
8. Fellman, M. W. 1998. Forecast: New products storm subsidies. *Marketing News.* March 30: 1.
9. Timmons, 1999, 81.
10. Iyer, G., P. J. La Placa and A. Sharma. 2006. Innovation and new product introductions in emerging markets: Strategic recommendations for the Indian market. *Industrial Marketing Management 35*(3), 373–382.
11. Hargadon and Yellowlees, 2001.
12. Ibid, 498.
13. Ibid.
14. Legge, J., and K. Hindle. 1997. *Entrepreneurship: How innovators create the future.* South Melbourne: MacMillan Education.
15. Lambkin, M., and G. S. Day. 1989. Evolutionary processes in competitive markets: Beyond the product life cycle. *Journal of Marketing 53*(3): 4–20.
16. Golder, P. N., and G. J. Tellis. 1993. Pioneer advantage: Marketing logic or marketing legend? *Journal of Marketing Research* XXX, May: 158–170.
17. Chandler, A. D. 1990. *Scale and scope: The dynamics of industrial capitalism.* Cambridge, MA: Belknap Press.
18. Kay, J. 1995. *Why firms succeed: Choosing markets and challenging competitors to add value.* New York: Oxford University Press, 100–101.
19. Polanyi, M. 1967. *The tacit dimension.* New York: Anchor Books.
20. Simon, M., B. Elango, S. M. Houghton, and S. Savelli. 2002. The successful product pioneer: Maintaining commitment while adapting to change. *Journal of Small Business Management 40*(3): 187–203.
21. Tellis, G. J., and P. N. Golder. 1996. First to market, first to fail? Real causes of enduring market leadership. *Sloan Management Review 37*(2): 65–75.
22. De Liosa, P. 1994. What business am I in? *Fortune,* November 14: 24.
23. Labich, K., and P. De Liosa. 1994. Why companies fail. *Fortune,* November 14: 22–28.

5 Market Evolution: Niches and Opportunities

1. Low, M. B., and E. Abrahamson. 1997. Movements, bandwagons and clones: Industry evolution and the entrepreneurial process. *Journal of Business Venturing* 12(6): 435–457.
2. Langlois, R., and P. Robertson. 1995. *Firms, markets, and economic change: A dynamic theory of business institutions.* London: Routledge.
3. Case, 1989: 54.
4. Klepper, S. 1997. Industry life cycles. *Industrial and Corporate Change 6*(1) 145–181.
5. Klepper, S., and K. L. Simons. 1996. Innovation and industry shakeouts, paper presented at the Business History Conference, Columbus, OH. See also Klepper, S. 1996b. Evolution, market concentration, and firm survival, mimeo.
6. Hannan, M. T., and J. Freeman. 1984. Structural inertia and organizational change. *American Sociological Review* 49: 149–164.

7. Boone, C., A. van Witteloostuijn and G. R. Carrol. 2002. Resource distributions and market partitioning: Dutch daily newspapers, 1968 to 1994. *American Sociological Review* 67(3): 408–431.

8. Abernathy, W., and K. B. Clark. 1985. Innovation: Mapping the winds of creative destruction. *Research Policy* 14(1): 3–22.

9. Swaminathan, Anand. 2001. Partitioning and the Evolution of Specialist Organizations: The Role of Location and Identity in the U.S. Wine Industry. *The Academy of Management Journal* 44(6): 1169–1185.

10. Swaminathan, Anand. 1998. Entry into new market segments in mature industries: Endogenous and exogenous segmentation. *Strategic Management Journal* 19(4): 389–404.

11. Mitchell, M. F., 2000. The scope and organization of production: Firm dynamics over the learning curve. *RAND Journal of Economics* 31(1): 180–205.

12. Barrett, R., and A. Rainnie. 2005. Small firms and new technology. *New Technology, Work & Employment* 20(3): 184–189.

13. Klepper, S., and P. Thompson. 2006. Submarkets and the evolution of market structure. *RAND Journal of Economics* 37(4): 861–886.

14. Ibid, 861.

15. Ibid, 871.

6 Trajectories and Emerging Niches

1. Carter, C. F. 1963. Economic incentives and consequences of technical invention. In *Scientific change: Historical studies in the intellectual, social and technical conditions for scientific discovery and technical invention from antiquity to the present,* ed. A. C. Crombie, 678–690. London: Heinemann, 687.

2. Rosenberg, N. 1969. The direction of technological change: Inducement mechanisms and focusing devices. *Journal of Economic Development and Cultural Change* 18(5): 1–24.

3. Nelson, R. R., and S. G. Winter. 1982. *An evolutionary theory of economic change.* Cambridge: Harvard University Press.

4. Dosi, G. 1982. Technological paradigms and technological trajectories. *Research Policy* 11: 147–162.

5. Dosi, G. 1988. Institutions and markets in a dynamic world. In *The economics of institutions,* ed. G Hodgson, 389–416. Aldershot: Edward Elgar.

6. Dean and Meyer, 1996.

7. Sinha, R. K., and C. H. Noble. 2005. A model of market entry in an emerging technology market. *IEEE Transactions on Engineering Management* 52(2): 186–198.

8. Moore, G., and K. Davis. 2001. *Learning the silicon way.* Working paper 00–45, Stanford Institute of Economic Policy Research, 23–24.

9. Bower, J. L., and C. M. Christensen. 1995. Disruptive technologies: Catching the wave. *Harvard Business Review* 73: 43–53.

10. Ulwick, A. 2005. *What Customers Want.* New York: McGraw Hill.

11. Ibid, xviii.

12. Buffett, W. 2007. MBA talk, part 3, http://www.youtube.com/watch?v=r7m7ifUz7r0& feature=related (accessed June 30, 2008).

13. Kim, W. C., and R. Mauborgne. 2005. *Blue ocean strategy.* Cambridge, MA: Harvard Business School Press.

7 Industrial Development: Linkages and Opportunities

1. Hirschman, A. O. 1958. *The strategy of economic development*. New Haven: Yale University Press.
2. Mezias, S. J., and J. C. Kuperman. 2000. The community dynamics of entrepreneurship: The birth of the American film industry, 1895–1929. *Journal of Business Venturing* 16(3): 209–233.
3. Wyver, J. 1989. *The moving image: An international history of film, television and video*. Oxford: Basil Blackwell Ltd, 7.
4. Ibid, 12.
5. Timmons, 1999.
6. Wyver, 1989, 15.
7. Ibid.
8. Brown 1995, 6–7.
9. Anderson and Tushman, 1990; Dosi, 1984; Utterback and Abernathy, 1975.
10. Brown, G. 1995. *Movie time: A chronology of Hollywood and the movie industry from its beginnings to the present*. New York: MacMillan, 6.
11. Wyver, 1989, 21.
12. Brown, 1995, 6.
13. Mezias and Kuperman, 2000, 216.
14. Wyver, 1989, 22.
15. Ibid, 23.
16. Brown, 1995, 4.
17. Ibid, 7–8.
18. Ibid, 9.
19. Musser, C. 1990. *The emergence of cinema: The American screen to 1907, from the series history of the American cinema Vol. 1*. New York: Charles Scribner and Sons, 450–451.
20. Wallace, H. S. 1998. *Competition and the legal environment: Intellectual property rights in the early American film industry*. University of Connecticut Department of Economics Working Papers Series.
21. Aldrich, H. E., and C. M. Fiol. 1994. Fools rush in? The institutional context of industry creation. *Academy of Management Review* 19: 645–670.
22. Brown, 1995, 5.
23. Mezias and Kuperman, 2000, 216.
24. Brown, 1995, 4.
25. Ibid, 8.
26. Mezias and Kuperman, 2000, 216.
27. Ibid, 217.
28. Widen, L. 2000. *John Frueler and Harry Aitken: Local Boys Make Good*. www.widen online.com/oldmilw/articles/frueler.htm (accessed Feb. 2, 2003).
29. Time Life Books. 1999. *100 years of Hollywood*, Alexandria, VA: Time Life Books, 31.
30. Bowser, E. 1990. *The transformation of cinema: 1907–1915*. New York, Charles Scribner's Sons.
31. Mezias and Kuperman, 2000, 222.
32. Brown, 1995, 8.
33. Mezias and Kuperman, 2000, 216.
34. Widen, 2000.

35. Wyver, 1989, 32.
36. Brown, 1995, 18, 26 and 30.
37. Koszarski, R. 1990. *An evening's entertainment: The age of the silent feature picture 1915–1928.* New York: Charles Scribner's Sons.
38. Mezias and Kuperman, 2000, 220.
39. Smith, A. E. 1952. *Two reels and a crank.* New York: Doubleday, 254.
40. Mezias and Kuperman, 2000, 218.
41. Ibid.
42. Brown, 1995, 27.
43. Widen, 2000.
44. Mezias and Kuperman, 2000, 218–222.
45. Brown, 1995, 26 and 30.
46. Blockbuster.com. 2003. *Artist biography: Edwin S. Porter,* www.blockbuster.com/bb/person/details/0,7621,Bio-P106883,00.html (accessed February 2, 2003).
47. von Harleman, G. P. 1917. Motion picture studios of California. *Moving Picture World.* March 10 1917. http://employee.oxy.edu/jerry/mpstud02.htm (accessed February 2, 2003).
48. Brown, 1995, 18.
49. Mezias and Kuperman, 2000, 222.
50. Mezias and Kuperman, 2000, 220.
51. Wyver, 1989, 68.
52. *Artist Biography: Edwin S. Porter.*
53. Wyver, 1989, 22.

8 Environments of Constraint and Abundance

1. Pfeffer, J., and G. R. Salancik. 1978. *The external control of organizations.* New York: Harper and Row.
2. El-Namaki, M. S. S. 1988. Encouraging entrepreneurs in developing countries. *Long Range Planning* 21(4): 98–106.
3. Kodithuwakku, S. S., and P. Rosa. 2002. The entrepreneurial process and economic success in a constrained environment. *Journal of Business Venturing* 17(5): 431–465.
4. Reynolds, P., and S. White. 1997. *The entrepreneurial process: Economic growth, men, women and minorities.* Westport Conn: Greenwood.
5. Hamilton, B. H. 2000. Does entrepreneurship pay? An empirical analysis of the returns to self-employment. *Journal of Political Economy* 108(3): 604–631.
6. Reynolds and White, 1997.
7. Shane, S. A. 2008. *The illusions of entrepreneurship: The costly myths that entrepreneurs, investors and policy makers live.* London and New Haven: Yale University Press.
8. Freeman and Perez, 1988.
9. Gates, B. 1999. *Business @ the speed of thought,* Ringwood, Victoria: Viking, 116.
10. Internet World Stats. 2008. http://www.internetworldstats.com/stats.htm (accessed December 18, 2008).
11. Margherio, L. 1998. *The Emerging Digital Economy.* Washington, DC: The U.S. Department of Commerce.
12. Webmergers 2003. http://www.webmergers.com/data/article.php?id=67 (accessed February 2, 2003).

13. Data in this report does not reflect the $157 billion merger of AOL and Time Warner.
14. Kaplan, P. J. 2002. *F'd Companies: Spectacular dot.com flameouts*. New York: Simon and Schuster.

9 It's Not Always Fair Out There

1. Baron, R. A. 2008. The role of effect in the entrepreneurial process. *Academy of Management Review* 33(2): 328–340.
2. Pai, A. K., and S. Basu. 2007. Offshore technology outsourcing: Overview of management and legal issues. *Business Process Management* 13(1): 21–46.
3. Ibid.
4. Strasina, P. R. 2005. Contracting for supplies and services in the federal government. *Contract Management* December: 26–30.

10 Leaping, Failing, Learning—Success!

1. Ronstadt, R. 1983. The decision not to become an entrepreneur. In *Frontiers of Entrepreneurship Research*, eds. J. Hornaday, J. A. Timmons and K. Vesper. Wellesley, MA: Babson College, 192–208.
2. Estrada, C. A., A. M. Isen, M. J. Young. 1997. Positive affect facilitates integration of information and decreases anchoring in reasoning among physicians. *Organizational Behaviour. Human Decision Processes* 72(1): 117–135.
3. Cooper, S. Y., and J. S. Park. 2008. The impact of "incubator" organizations on opportunity recognition and technology innovation in new, entrepreneurial high-technology ventures. *International Small Business Journal* 26(1): 27–56.
4. Carter, N. M., W. B. Gartner, and P. D. Reynolds. 1996. Exploring start-up event sequences, *Journal of Business Venturing* 11(3): 151–166.
5. Baker, T., A. S. Miner, and D. T. Eesley. 2001. Fake it unto you make it: Improvisation and new ventures. In *Frontiers of Entrepreneurship Research*, eds. W. D. Bygrave, E. Autio, C. G. Brush, P. Davidsson, P. G. Greene, P. D. Reynolds, and H. J. Sapienza. 153–163. Wellesley, MA: Babson College.
6. Palich, L. E., and D. R. Bagby. 1995. Using cognitive theory to explain entrepreneurial risk-taking: Challenging conventional wisdom. *Journal of Business Venturing* 10(6): 425–438.
7. Cooper, A. C., C. Y. Woo, and W. C. Dunkelberg. 1988. Entrepreneurs perceived chances of success. *Journal of Small Venturing* 3(2): 97–108.
8. Simon, M., S. M. Houghton, and K. Aquino. 2000. Cognitive biases, risk perception and venture formation: How individuals decide to start companies. *Journal of Business Venturing*, 15(2): 113–134.
9. Busenitz, L. W., and J. B. Barney. 1997. Differences between entrepreneurs and managers in large organizations: Biases and heuristics in strategic decision making. *Journal of Business Venturing* 12(1): 9–30.
10. Bhave, M. P. 1994. A process model of entrepreneurial venture creation. *Journal of Business Venturing* 9(3): 223–242.
11. Ibid, 229.
12. Ibid, 230.

13. Small Business Administration. 1983. *The state of small business: A report of the president, transmitted to Congress.* Washington, DC: Small Business Administration.

14. Timmons, 1999, 32.

15. Bruderl, Preisendorfer and Ziegler, 1992.

16. Ganguly, P. 1982. Births and deaths in firms in the UK in 1980. *British Business* 29 January: 204–207.

17. Stubbart, C. I, and M. B Knight. 2006. The case of the disappearing firms: Empirical evidence and implications. *Journal of Organizational Behavior* 27(1): 79–100.

18. Shane, S. 2008. *The illusions of entrepreneurship.* New Haven: Yale University.

19. Shepherd, D. 2005. The theoretical basis for my plenary speech about our success and failures at research on business failure. Paper presented at Regional Frontiers of Entrepreneurship Research Conference, Melbourne, Australia.

20. Ibid.

21. Ibid.

11 Government Policy and New Business Development

1. Pfeffer and Salancik, 1978.

2. Collier, P., and J. W. Gunning. 1999. Explaining African economic performance. *Journal of Economic Literature* XXXVII: 64–111.

3. Ibid.

4. Goedhuys, M., and L. Sleuwagon. 1999. Barriers to growth of firms in developing countries: Evidence from Burundi. In *Innovation, Industrial Evolution and Employment,* eds. D Audretsch and R Thurik, 297–314. Cambridge University Press.

5. Ray, E. J. 1991. Changing patterns of protectionism: The fall in tariffs and the rise in non-tariff barriers. In *International political economy: Perspectives on global power and wealth,* eds. J. A. Frieden and D. A. Lake. New York: St. Martin's Press, 343.

6. Clydesdale, G. In press. *The rise and fall of economic empires,* London: Constable and Robinson.

7. Gnyawali, D. R., and D. S. Fogel. 1994. Environments for entrepreneurship development: Key dimensions and research implications. *Entrepreneurship Theory and Practice* (Summer), 43–62.

8. Adapted from Gnyawali and Fogel, D. S., 1994.

9. Lundvall, Bengt-Ake. 1992. *National systems of innovation: Towards a theory of innovation and interactive learning.* London: Pinter Press.

10. McClelland, D. C. 1961. *The achieving society.* Princeton: Van Nostrand Co.

11. El-Namaki, M. S. S. 1988. Encouraging entrepreneurs in developing countries. *Long Range Planning* 21(4): 98–106.

12. Parker, S. 2007. Policy makers beware! In *Handbook of research on entrepreneurship policy,* eds. D. B. Audretsch, I. Grilo and R. Thurik. Cheltenham: Edward Elgar, 54–63.

13. Shane, 2008.

14. Fu-Lai Yu, T. 1997. *Entrepreneurship and economic development in Hong Kong.* London: Routledge, 162–170.

15. Brockhaus, R. H. 1982. The psychology of the entrepreneur. In *Encyclopedia of Entrepreneurship,* eds. C. Kent, D. Sexton, and K. Vesper. Edgewood Cliffs, NJ: Prentice Hall, 50–55.

16. Kennedy, P. 1988. *The rise and fall of the great powers*. London: Unwin and Hyman, 149.
17. Fu-Lai Yu, 1997.
18. Audtretsch, D. B., and I. A. M. Beckmann. 2007. From small business to entrepreneurship policy. In *Handbook of research on entrepreneurship policy*, eds. D. B. Audretsch, I. Grilo and R. Thurik. Cheltenham: Edward Elgar Cheltenham, 36–53.
19. Ibid.
20. Siegel, D. S. 2007. Quantitative and qualitative studies of university technology transfer: Synthesis and policy recommendations. In *Handbook of research on entrepreneurship policy*, eds. D. B. Audretsch, I. Grilo and R. Thurik. Cheltenham: Edward Elgar Cheltenham, 186–199.
21. Ferguson, R., and C. Olofsson. 2001. The role of science parks in the support of NTBF: The entrepreneur's perspective. *Frontiers of Entrepreneurship Research*, 653.
22. Westhead P., and D. J. Storey. Links between higher education institutions and high technology firms. *Omega: The International Journal of Management Science* 23(4): 345–360.
23. Moore and Davis, 2005, 9.
24. Cooper, S. Y., and J. S. Park. 2008. The impact of "incubator" organizations on opportunity recognition and technology innovation in new, entrepreneurial high-technology ventures. *International Small Business Journal* 26(1): 27–56.
25. Steffensen, M., E. M. Rogers and K. Speakman. 1999. Spin-offs from research centers at a research university. *Journal of Business Venturing* 15(1): 93–111.
26. Vernon, 1966.
27. Perez, C., and L. Soete. 1988. Catching up in technology: Entry barriers and windows of opportunity. In Dosi, et al., *Technical change and economic theory*. London: Pinter Publishers, 458–479.
28. Kim, L. 1997. *Imitation to innovation*. New Haven: Harvard Business School Press, 22.
29. Clydesdale, G. 2008. Business immigrants and the entrepreneurial nexus. *Journal of International Entrepreneurship* 6(3): 123–142.
30. Blass, A. 1992. Learning the soft way. *Far Eastern Economic Review* Dec. 3: 5–6.
31. Andreosso-O'Callaghan, B. 2000. Territory, research and technology linkages—is the Shannon region a propitious local system of innovation? *Entrepreneurship and Regional Development* 12(1): 69–87.
32. Shannon Development. 2007. Annual Report 2007, Limerick: Shannon Free Airport development Company Limited.

12 What Type of Entrepreneur Should I Be?

1. Schumpeter, J. 1934. *The theory of economic development*, Cambridge, MA: Harvard University Press.
2. Baumol, W. J. 1988. Is entrepreneurship always productive? In *Entrepreneurship and economic development*, eds. H. Leibenstein and D. Ray. New York: United Nations, 85–94.
3. Leibenstein, H. 1976. *Beyond economic man: A new foundation for microeconomics*. Cambridge, MA: Harvard University Press.
4. Kirzner, I. M. 1973. *Competition and entrepreneurship*. Chicago: University of Chicago Press.
5. Simon, 1988.
6. Kaish and Gilad, 1991.

7. Hayek, F. 1949. *Individualism and economic order*. London: Routledge.
8. Woods, J. 2000. *The quotable executive*. New York: McGraw Hill.
9. Kirzner, 1973.
10. See for example Woo, C. C., A. C. Cooper, and W. C. Dunkelberg. 1991. The development and interpretation of entrepreneurial typologies. *Journal of Business Venturing* 6(2): 93–161.
11. Fu-Lai Yu, 1997, 31.
12. Bruderl, Preisendorfer and Rolf, 1992.
13. Ransley, J. 2004. Design. In *Developing hospitality properties and facilities,* eds. J. Ransley and H. Ingram. Oxford: Elsevier Butterworth Heinemann, 53.

Index